# Scientific Discovery Processes in Humans and Computers

*Theory and Research in Psychology and Artificial Intelligence*

**MORTON WAGMAN**

PRAEGER

Westport, Connecticut
London

**Library of Congress Cataloging-in-Publication Data**

Wagman, Morton.
    Scientific discovery processes in humans and computers : theory
and research in psychology and artificial intelligence / Morton
Wagman.
    p.  cm.
  Includes bibliographical references and indexes.
  ISBN 0–275–96654–2 (alk. paper)
  1. Discoveries in science.  2. Cognitive science.  3. Artificial
intelligence.  I. Title.
  Q180.55.D57W34   2000
  001.4'2—dc21       99–32026

British Library Cataloguing in Publication Data is available.

Library of Congress Catalog Card Number: 99–32026
ISBN: 0–275–96654–2

First published in 2000

Praeger Publishers, 88 Post Road West, Westport, CT 06881
An imprint of Greenwood Publishing Group, Inc.
www.praeger.com

Printed in the United States of America

The paper used in this book complies with the
Permanent Paper Standard issued by the National
Information Standards Organization (Z39.48–1984).

10 9 8 7 6 5 4 3 2 1

**Copyright Acknowledgments**

The author and publisher gratefully acknowledge permission to use extracts from the following materials:

Dunbar, K. (1993). Concept discovery in a scientific domain. *Cognitive Science, 17*, 397–434. Reprinted/adapted with the permission of the Ablex Publishing Corporation.

Klahr, D., Fay, A. L., and Dunbar, K. (1993). Heuristics for scientific experimentation: A developmental study. *Cognitive Psychology, 25*, 111–146. Copyright © 1993 by Academic Press, Inc. Reprinted with the permission of Academic Press.

Langley, P., & Zytkow, J. (1989). Data-driven approaches to empirical discovery. *Artificial Intelligence, 40*, 283–312. Reprinted with the permission of Elsevier Science Publishers.

Shen, W. M. (1990). Functional transformations in AI discovery systems. *Artificial Intelligence, 41*, 257–272. Reprinted with the permission of Elsevier Science Publishers.

Thagard, P. (1989). Explanatory coherence. *Behavioral and Brain Sciences, 12*, 435–467. Reprinted with the permission of Cambridge University Press and Paul Thagard.

Valdés-Pérez, R. E. (1996). A new theorem in particle physics enabled by machine discovery. *Artificial Intelligence, 82*, 331–339. Reprinted with the permission of Elsevier Science Publishers.

Valdés-Pérez, R. E. (1995). Machine discovery in chemistry: New results. *Artificial Intelligence, 74*, 191–201. Reprinted with the permission of Elsevier Science Publishers.

Wagman, M. (1999). *The human mind according to artificial intelligence: Theory, research, and implications.* Westport, CT: Praeger. Copyright © 1999 by Morton Wagman. Reproduced with the permission of Greenwood Publishing Group, Inc., Westport, CT.

Wagman, M. (1997a). *Cognitive science and the symbolic operations of human and artificial intelligence: Theory and research into the intellective processes.* Westport, CT: Praeger. Copyright

# Contents

# Illustrations

**FIGURES**

## TABLES

# Preface

This book presents a critical analysis of current theory and research in the psychological and computational sciences directed toward an elucidation of scientific discovery processes and structures, ranging from the domain of human scientific discovery heuristics to the domain of artificial intelligence scientific discovery systems.

The book is organized in four parts. In part I (chapters 1 and 2), human scientific discovery processes are examined. In part II (chapters 3, 4, 5, 6, and 7), computer scientific discovery processes are analyzed. In part III (chapters 8 and 9), human and computer scientific discovery processes are discussed. In part IV (chapter 10), conclusions are presented.

In the first chapter, the scientific reasoning of the discoverers of the mechanism of gene control (Monod and Jacob, Nobel Prize winners, 1965) is examined in the setting of a university experiment in which students replicated in one hour a discovery that had taken scientists 20 years to accomplish. Given the same knowledge that Monod and Jacob possessed just prior to their discovery, the students, using a computer-based experimental simulation of genetic hypotheses and experiments, follow the same course of scientific reasoning, positing a false activation mechanism of genetic control, obtaining inconsistent experimental results, revising their hypotheses, and concluding with the correct explanation that inhibition is the mechanism of gene control.

In the second chapter, scientific discovery heuristics used at different developmental levels are discussed. Experimental research in the differential use of effective search heuristics in the space of hypotheses and in the space of experiments is presented in detail. Implications for the philosophy of science conclude the chapter.

In the third chapter, artificial intelligence and mathematical discovery are discussed. In the first part of the chapter, the general logic and characteristics of the Automatic Mathematician (AM) system are described in depth. AM made a number of mathematical discoveries, including the concept of prime numbers and Goldbach's conjecture. The constraints and limitations of the AM system are evaluated. In the second part of the chapter, the concepts of functional transformation are introduced, and their embodiment in the ARE mathematical discovery system is described in detail. The chapter concludes with a systematic comparison of the ARE and AM mathematical discovery systems.

In the fourth chapter, the mechanism of explanatory coherence in scientific discovery processes is discussed. In the first part of the chapter, a theory is developed for evaluating the extent of coherence between scientific hypotheses and scientific propositions. In the second part of the chapter, a computational account of explanatory coherence is presented and implemented in the ECHO system. The logic of ECHO transforms the problem of evaluating competing theories and hypotheses into an algorithmic constraint satisfaction problem. In the third part of the chapter, the generality of the ECHO system is demonstrated in an extensive series of applications that range across several domains of biological and physical science. The chapter concludes with a critique of this computational account of the mechanism of explanatory coherence.

In the fifth chapter, the evolution of artificial intelligence approaches to scientific discovery is described. The concepts, methods, and results of several scientific discovery systems including BACON, FARENHEIT, and IDS are described in depth, and their strengths and weaknesses are examined. The discovery systems are discussed from the perspective of the philosophy of science.

In chapter 6, the MECHEM system that contributes new computational and architectural strategies in machine chemistry is described. The MECHEM system has yielded valuable applications within industrial chemistry and has advanced development in the theory of artificial intelligence approaches to scientific discovery in general.

In chapter 7, the PAULI system and discovery in particle physics are discussed. The PAULI system enabled discovery of a novel theorem in particle physics. The theorem specifies a single conservation law and resulted in ensuing complications in particle physics research and theory.

In the eighth chapter, scientific discovery processes in the context of artificial intelligence and human psychology are discussed. The processes by which BACON.3 achieved its scientific discoveries are described. BACON.3's rediscovery of Kepler's Third Law of Planetary Motion is compared with its rediscovery by university students in the setting of a laboratory experiment and with the original discovery by Kepler.

In the ninth chapter, an artificial intelligence system that emulates the cognitive processes in scientific discovery is described, and its implications for human creativity are discussed. In the first part of the chapter, the general logic and specific characteristics of the computer program are presented. KEKADA constitutes a close simulation of the specific pattern of experimental investigation that characterizes an important discovery in biochemistry. The potential usefulness of KEKADA as a general model of scientific discovery processes is critically analyzed in the second part of the chapter.

In the tenth and concluding chapter, the extent to which computational discovery systems can emulate a set of ten types of scientific problems ranging from theory formation to experimentation and data analysis is examined.

*Scientific Discovery Processes in Humans and Computers: Theory and Research in Psychology and Artificial Intelligence* is the latest volume in a series of published and planned volumes that have the consistent theme of developing intellectual grounding for establishing the theoretical and research foundations and the psychological and philosophical implications of a general unified theory of human and artificial intelligence (Wagman, 1991a, 1991b, 1993, 1995, 1996, 1997a, 1997b, 1998a, 1998b, 1998c, 1999). Each volume contributes important aspects of this enterprise, and each reflects new theory, research, and knowledge in both human and artificial intelligence across the domains of problem solving, reasoning, analogical thinking, learning, memory, linguistic processes, and scientific creativity.

All the volumes are mutually supportive and all are directed to the same audience: scholars and professionals in psychology, artificial intelligence, and cognitive science. Graduate and advanced undergraduate students in these and related disciplines will also find the book useful.

# Acknowledgments

I wish to express my thanks to LaDonna Wilson for her assistance in the preparation of all aspects of the manuscript. I am grateful to Steve Wilson for his excellent work in assisting in the preparation of the tables and figures and for his assistance in the production of the final complete manuscript. I am also grateful to Lori Seitz and Kathleen Pritchett for their excellent typing of portions of the manuscript.

# PART I

---

# HUMAN SCIENTIFIC DISCOVERY PROCESSES

# Conceptual Discovery in Molecular Genetics

## *SCIENTIFIC REASONING AND DISCOVERY IN MOLECULAR GENETICS*

The study of cognitive processes underlying scientific discovery has traditionally proceeded by close examination of laboratory notebooks and post facto interviews. This process of historical reconstruction can now be supplemented by the experimental methods of cognitive psychology, which bring the cognition of scientific discovery into the laboratory. This cognitive science approach, the study of scientific reasoning, is exemplified in the recent important research of Kevin Dunbar, as described in the present chapter.

## STUDYING THE COGNITIVE PROCESSES UNDERLYING DISCOVERY IN MOLECULAR GENETICS: OVERVIEW

The logic underlying Dunbar's interesting research is first to provide experimental subjects with the same knowledge that molecular genetic scientists possess just prior to their discoveries, then to pose a problem of discovering mechanisms of genetic control, and then to observe how strategies of experimentation and hypothesis formation facilitated or inhibited problem solution. Dunbar (1993) presents the following overview of his important cognitive science research:

The scientific reasoning strategies used to discover a new concept in a scientific domain were investigated in two studies. An innovative task in which subjects discover new concepts in molecular biology was used. The task was based on one set of experiments that Jacob and Monod used to discover how genes are controlled, and for which they were awarded the Nobel Prize. In the two studies reported in this article, subjects were taught some of the basic facts and experimental techniques in molecular biology, using a simulated molecular genetics laboratory on a computer. Following their initial training, they were asked to discover how genes are controlled by other genes. In Study 1, subjects found no evidence that was consistent with their initial hypothesis. Subjects then set one of two goals for conducting experiments and evaluating data. One goal was to search for evidence consistent with the current hypothesis (and they did not attend to the features of discrepant findings); none of the subjects who had this goal succeeded at discovering how the genes were controlled. Other subjects in Study 1 used a different goal: Upon noticing evidence inconsistent with their current hypothesis, these subjects set a new goal of attempting to explain the cause of the discrepant findings. Using this goal, a subset of these subjects discovered the correct solution to the problem. Study 2 was conducted to test the hypothesis that subjects' goals of finding evidence consistent with their current hypothesis blocks consideration of alternate hypotheses and generation of new goals. It was predicted that if subjects could achieve their initial goal of discovering evidence consistent with their current hypothesis, they would then attend to particular features of discrepant evidence and solve the problem. To test this prediction, an additional mechanism of genetic control that was consistent with subjects' initial goal was added to the genes. Here, subjects had to discover two mechanisms of control: one mechanism consistent with their current hypothesis, and one inconsistent with their hypothesis. Twice as many subjects reached the correct solution in Study 2 than in Study 1. The findings of the two studies indicate that goals provide a powerful constraint on the cognitive processes underlying scientific reasoning and that the types of goals that are represented determine many of the reasoning errors that subjects make. (Dunbar, 1993, p. 397)

## MONOD AND JACOB'S DISCOVERY OF THE MECHANISMS OF GENE CONTROL

In order to understand the discovery task facing experimental subjects in Dunbar's research, a summary of the original discovery of the mechanisms of gene control made by Monod and Jacob is now presented.

In 1965 Jacques Monod and François Jacob were awarded the Nobel Prize for making a major discovery. They provided an answer to one of the most impor-

**Figure 1.1**
**The Cycle of Inhibitory Regulation of Genes in *E. coli***

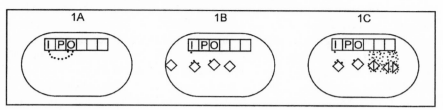

*Note:* In Figure 1A the *E. coli* is in an inhibited state: The I gene sends an inhibitor to the O gene, and the inhibitor binds to the O gene; this blocks production of β-gal from the three β-gal-producing genes (the three unlabeled genes). In Figure 1B, lactose (diamonds) enters the *E. coli*. The inhibitor binds to the lactose and not to the O gene. In Figure 1C, the β-gal-producing genes are no longer inhibited and the beta genes produce β-gal (small dots). The β-gal cleaves the lactose into glucose, which can then be utilized as an energy source. When all the lactose has been used up, the inhibitor binds to the O gene and the β-gal genes are inhibited from producing β-gal, as in Figure 1A.

*Source:* Dunbar, K. (1993). Concept discovery in a scientific domain. *Cognitive Science, 17*, p. 400.

tant questions in biology: Monod and Jacob discovered a mechanism for how genes are controlled. Many scientists had assumed that genes must somehow be controlled, but the mechanism by which genes were controlled was a complete mystery. Monod and Jacob were able to answer this question by studying very simple organisms such as the bacterium *Escherichia coli (E. coli)*, and a virus that attacks the bacterium. They made the novel and unexpected discovery that groups of genes control other genes and keep many genes inhibited until particular enzymes are needed. . . .

One of the most significant achievements in biology has been to determine how the genes on a chromosome are regulated, and in turn, regulate cells in living organisms. Jacob and Monod demonstrated that in the bacterium *E. coli*, there are regulator genes that control the activity of other genes. They discovered this by investigating the utilization of energy sources, such as glucose, in *E. coli*. *E. coli* need glucose to live and the most common source of glucose for *E. coli* is lactose. When lactose is present, the *E. coli* secrete enzymes that break down the lactose into glucose. The *E. coli* then use the glucose as an energy source. The *E. coli* secrete the beta-galactosidase enzyme (henceforth called β-gal) that breaks down lactose. The β-gal is secreted only when lactose is present. When there is no lactose present, β-gal is not secreted. Jacob and Monod discovered that a set of regulator genes inhibits the genes that produce β-gal until β-gal is needed. The mechanism that Monod and Jacob proposed was very simple: There are two genes designated I and O. These genes regulate the activity of the β-gal-producing genes. When there is no lactose present, the I gene sends out an inhibitor that binds to the O gene [Figure 1.1, 1A]. The O gene is beside the β-gal-producing genes and when the inhibitor is bound to the O gene, it prevents the β-gal-producing genes from functioning. When there is lactose present (represented by diamonds in Figures 1B and 1C), the inhibitor binds to the lactose, thereby preventing the inhibitor from binding to the O gene [Figure 1.1, 1B]. When there is no inhibition, the β-gal-producing genes start to produce the β-gal that breaks down the lactose into glucose [Figure 1.1, 1C]. When all of the lactose is exhausted, the inhibitor again binds to the O gene and the β-gal-producing gene stops producing β-gal [Figure 1.1, 1A]. Monod and Jacob thus proposed that the production of β-gal is controlled by an *inhibitory regulation* mechanism. It is now known that the P gene is also involved in the production of β-gal: The P gene is needed to switch on β-gal production. However, this was not discovered until after Monod and Jacob proposed the inhibitory mechanism of genetic regulation.

The discovery of the inhibitory mechanism was based on a number of very simple, but elegant, techniques that were developed. One was the use of mutant *E. coli*. In reproduction, *E. coli* often fail to copy their genes properly and mutations arise. That is, a particular gene will be copied incorrectly and it will cease to function in the normal way, often appearing not to function at all. When Monod and Jacob were investigating the genes that control the breakdown of lactose, they discovered a number of different types of mutants suggesting that the I and O genes regulated β-gal production. They discovered that *E. coli* with a mutant I gene or O gene (called I- and O- mutants) produced β-gal regardless of whether lactose was present or not. To Monod and Jacob, these findings indicated that the I and O genes controlled the β-gal-producing genes. Because I- and O- mutants produced a large output of β-gal, even when no lactose was added, they concluded that the I and O genes must inhibit β-gal production: When the I and O genes are mutant, the β-gal genes are no longer inhibited and a large output of β-gal occurs. When the I and O genes are present, they inhibit β-gal production and no β-gal is produced.

Another technique that was developed was to use mutants that have two chromosomes (diploid *E. coli*) rather than the normal one chromosome (haploid *E. coli*). By using diploid mutants it is possible to test the hypothesis that a particular gene causes certain events to occur: If a gene (e.g., I) is mutant on one chromosome, but normal on the other chromosome, and if the diploid *E. coli* performs normally, then the results would be consistent with the hypothesis that the I gene is the controlling gene. Diploid *E. coli* are made by mating male *E. coli* with female *E. coli*. The male *E. coli* donates genes to the female. For example, in [Figure 1.2, 2B], the I gene is missing from the haploid *E. coli* and a large amount of β-gal is produced. In [Figure 1.2, 2C], the I gene is missing from the female chromosome, but is present on the male chromosome. In this situation, the β-gal enzymes are not produced, even though the I gene is present only on the male chromosome. No β-gal is produced because the I gene is sending an inhibitory signal to the O gene. This mechanism is one of chemical

**Figure 1.2**
**Using Haploid and Diploid *E. coli* to Discover Inhibition**

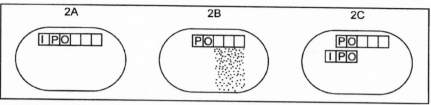

*Note:* Figure 2A shows a normal haploid *E. coli* in its resting state; here there is no production of β-gal because the I and O genes inhibit β-gal production. Figure 2B shows a haploid I- mutant; here there is a continuous production of β-gal due to the mutant I gene (the I- mutant does not produce an inhibitor). Figure 2C shows a diploid *E. coli*. The inhibitor binds to the lactose and not to the O gene. In Figure 1C, the β-gal-producing genes are no longer inhibited and the beta genes produce β-gal (small dots). The β-gal cleaves the lactose into glucose, which can then be utilized as an energy source. When all the lactose has been used up, the inhibitor binds to the O gene and the β-gal genes are inhibited from producing β-gal, as in Figure 1A.

*Source:* Dunbar, K. (1993). Concept discovery in a scientific domain. *Cognitive Science, 17*, p. 400.

inhibition. Thus, diploid *E. coli* can be used to determine the mechanism of control: When a particular controlling gene still controls when it is placed on another chromosome, this result indicates that the gene is sending a signal. The use of diploid *E. coli* also reveals that the O gene inhibits in a different manner: When the female chromosome has no O gene, but there is an O gene on the male chromosome, large amounts of β-gal are still produced (i.e., there is no inhibition when O is only present on the male). The O gene must be on the same chromosome as the β-gal genes for the O to inhibit β-gal production. Monod and Jacob proposed that the O gene must be beside the β-gal-producing genes, and physically blocks the production of β-gal. Thus, by using diploid *E. coli* Monod and Jacob were able to discover different mechanisms of inhibition for the I and O genes. They proposed that the I gene constantly sends out an inhibitor and this inhibitor binds to the O gene, which physically blocks production of β-gal. (Dunbar, 1993, pp. 398–401)

## EXPERIMENTAL REDISCOVERY OF MONOD AND JACOB'S ORIGINAL GENE DISCOVERIES

In order to understand Monod and Jacob's reasoning processes and strategies of experimentation, the task they faced was simulated by a computer-controlled genetics laboratory that permitted the selection from the screen of experiments to be conducted and the results that would be obtained. Although it took 20 years for Monod and Jacob to reach their solutions, undergraduates in the molecular genetics laboratory attained solutions within one hour. A general description of the experimental tasks and the reasons for the accelerated pace of the experimental redis-covery (1 hour versus 20 years) are given by Dunbar (1993) in the following interesting passage.

The purpose of this investigation is to extend our knowledge of how new theories are discovered by using tasks that involve giving subjects both knowledge of a real scientific domain and the opportunity to design and interpret experiments: Subjects were given a problem and a set of experimental tools that placed subjects in a similar context to that of Monod and Jacob immediately prior to their proposal that genes are controlled by inhibition. Subjects had to discover the mechanism by which a set of genes are controlled in the bacterium *E. coli*. They conducted experiments on genes and generated genetic mutations using a computer-simulated molecular genetics laboratory. By using a simulated molecular genetics laboratory, it is possible to construct a task that is similar to the one that experimental scientists face. The use of a complex molecular genetics domain makes it possible to investigate how old hypotheses are discarded and new hypotheses are proposed. Subjects' strategies used to design experiments, test hypotheses, and modify hypotheses can be investigated. In particular, the question of how previously acquired knowledge of a domain influences (a) subjects' hypothesis generation, (b) experimental strategies, and (c) evaluation of evidence can now be addressed. In the studies reported in this article, subjects were taught some initial concepts and experimental techniques prior to being given the problem. Thus, subjects begin the problem with basic knowledge of a domain that predisposes them to certain types of hypotheses much like scientists start research with a set of initial hypotheses. . . .

The work of Monod and Jacob provides a problem that can be readily transposed to the cognitive laboratory. A simulated molecular genetics laboratory was designed that makes it possible for subjects to propose and test hypotheses about genetic regulation. Moreover, the laboratory provides an environment to conduct genetics experiments and keeps a record of experimental manipulations and results.

In the studies reported in this article, one set of experiments that were crucial to Monod and Jacob's discovery were taken into the cognitive laboratory. The subjects performed this crucial set of experiments on a simulated molecular genetics laboratory on a computer. Clearly, bringing a major scientific discovery into a cognitive laboratory requires a simplification of the original problem. However, as will be seen later, the task that the subjects were given was very difficult and required conceptual shifts in thinking that paralleled the conceptual shifts required in the original discovery. The problem that subjects were given was to discover the mechanism by which a set of genes are controlled. Monod and Jacob and their numerous colleagues spent over 20 years attempting to discover this mechanism (cf. Jacob and Monod, 1961). The actual problem given to subjects was possible to solve in less than 1 hour. The reasons that subjects could solve this problem in 1 hour—rather than the 20 years that it took Monod and Jacob—are as follows:

1. The problem was highly constrained for the subjects. Only the key aspect of the Monod and Jacob discoveries was given to the subjects: How do genes control other genes? Monod and Jacob first had to discover that genes control other genes before discovering the mechanism by which genes control other genes.

2. Monod and Jacob had to invent many different techniques and conduct hundreds of experiments, during which they perfected their techniques to make their discovery. In the studies reported in this article, the subjects did not have to invent new instruments, methodologies, or chemicals for their experiments. The subjects were given tools to conduct experiments similar to the crucial experiments that Monod and Jacob conducted immediately prior to their discovery.

3. Subjects were not expected to propose the concept of the lactose operon per se, but were expected to propose the concept of an inhibitory mechanism that has the same functions as the inhibitory mechanisms in Monod and Jacob's discovery. That is, subjects were not asked to propose a concept of genetic control that could apply to all genetic systems, but were asked to discover the concept of genetic control for the genetic system that they had been introduced to in the study.

*Indeed, the purpose of the studies reported in this article was to place subjects in one knowledge state, allow them to design crucial experiments that produce results inconsistent with this knowledge state, then monitor the subjects' reactions to the inconsistent evidence and determine whether subjects will change their representations and how they propose a new mechanism. Thus, despite the fact that the subjects were working in a very simplified domain, the mechanisms that the subjects had to discover were identical to those uncovered by Jacob and Monod (see Jacob, 1988; Judson, 1979, for an account of how the discovery was made).* (Dunbar, 1993, pp. 398–402, italics added)

## STUDY 1 AND STUDY 2: METHOD

In the following section, Dunbar (1993) describes experimental procedures for Study 1 and Study 2.

Twenty McGill undergraduates were paid to participate in a 90-minute study for Study 1; 20 McGill undergraduates participated in Study 2 (N=40). All subjects had taken one introductory biology course. Students knew about DNA and RNA, and that DNA was transcribed to produce RNA, which in turn, served as templates for the production of proteins. However, subjects knew nothing about genetic regulation: This was ensured by using only students who had taken

**Figure 1.3**
**Starting an Experiment**

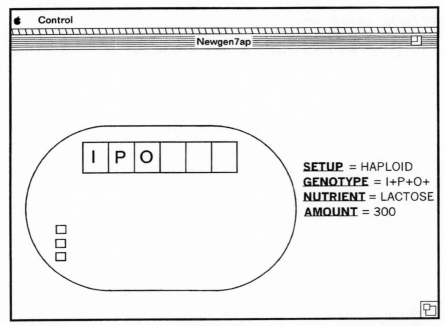

*Note:* This is what a subject sees when an experiment is conducted using a Haploid *E. coli* with 300 micrograms of lactose added. Each of the 3 small squares on the left represents 100 micrograms of lactose. Lactose travels across the screen until it is under the three β-gal genes.

*Source:* Dunbar, K. (1993). Concept discovery in a scientific domain. *Cognitive Science, 17*, p. 403.

an introductory biology course that does not cover the topic of genetic regulation. . . .

The simulated molecular genetics laboratory was written in the cT programming language (B. Sherwood & J. Sherwood, 1988) on a Macintosh II computer. Using this laboratory, subjects are able to design simulated molecular genetics experiments, watch the experiment unfold, and see a table of experimental results. To design an experiment a HAPLOID or DIPLOID *E. coli* is chosen from a DIP/HAP menu. Then, the type of mutant that the subject wants to use is selected from the GENE menu. Finally, the amount of lactose added is selected from the AMOUNT OF LACTOSE menu. This completes the design phase of the experiment. A subject might design an experiment using a haploid *E. coli* that is normal (has no mutant genes), and has 300μg of lactose added. To conduct this experiment, the LOOK option from the START REACTION menu is selected. Subjects then see an animated experiment on the

**Figure 1.4**
**β-gal Breaking Down Lactose**

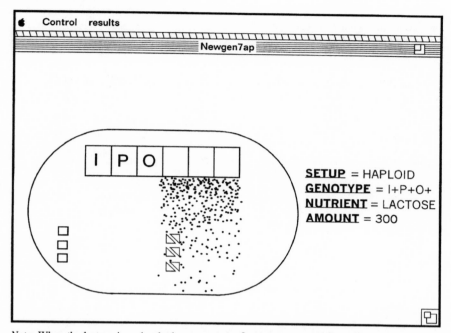

*Note:* When the lactose is under the beta genes, the β-gal genes secrete β-gal. β-gal is represented by the small black dots. The β-gal then breaks down the lactose into glucose (the glucose is represented by triangles).

*Source:* Dunbar, K. (1993). Concept discovery in a scientific domain. *Cognitive Science, 17,* p. 404.

screen. [Figures 1.3 and 1.4] show the types of screens that subjects see once they have started an experiment. In [Figure' 1.3], the lactose enters the *E. coli* (lactose is represented by a small square; each square corresponding to 100µg of lactose). The lactose travels across the screen until it is under the β-gal-producing genes. The β-gal-producing genes produce β-gal, which pours down on the lactose and cleaves it apart ([Figure 1.4]). A reaction takes about 12s.

Once an experiment has been conducted, subjects are obligated to look at a table of experimental results by selecting SHOW RESULTS from the RESULTS menu. As can be seen from [Figure 1.5], this table gives a complete record of experiments and results. The rows correspond to a particular experiment and the columns correspond to the variables manipulated during the experiment. The SETUP column shows whether the *E. coli* was haploid or diploid. GENE 1 shows which gene was mutated on the female chromosome. GENE 2 shows which gene was mutated on the male chromosome of a diploid *E. coli*. NU-

**Figure 1.5**
**Experimental Results Screen**

| | | | | | |
|---|---|---|---|---|---|
| ⬤ Control  new experiment | | | | | |
| 〰〰〰〰〰〰〰〰〰〰〰〰〰〰〰〰〰〰〰〰〰〰〰〰〰〰〰〰〰〰〰〰 | | | | | |
| | | Newgen7ap | | | ⬚ |

| SETUP | GENE 1 | GENE 2 | NUTRIENT | AMOUNT | OUTPUT |
|---|---|---|---|---|---|
| haploid | I+P+O+ | | LACTOSE | 100 | 50 |
| haploid | I+P+O+ | | LACTOSE | 0 | 0 |
| haploid | I+P-O+ | | LACTOSE | 200 | 100 |
| haploid | I-P+O+ | | LACTOSE | 200 | 876 |
| haploid | I+P+O- | | LACTOSE | 200 | 527 |
| haploid | I-P+O+ | I+P+O+ | LACTOSE | 200 | 100 |

*Note:* This screen displays the results of the current experiment and all previous experiments. The rows correspond to an experiment, and the columns correspond to each variable that was manipulated. Thus, the first experiment was a normal haploid *E. coli* with 100 micrograms of lactose added and an output of 50 micrograms of β-gal. Subjects see this screen after every experiment.

*Source:* Dunbar, K. (1993). Concept discovery in a scientific domain. *Cognitive Science, 17*, p. 405.

TRIENT specifies the type of nutrient given. In this study, the nutrient was always lactose. AMOUNT specifies the amount of lactose added. OUTPUT specifies the amount of β-gal produced in the experiment. Row 1 shows a haploid experiment with a normal *E. coli* in which 100 µg of lactose were added. This produced 50µg of β-gal. Both the results of the current experiment and all previous experiments are displayed. Subjects can only view this table after an experiment is conducted. When a subject wishes to conduct a new experiment, NEW is selected from the NEW EXPERIMENT menu. Subjects were also given a pen and paper to write down notes. . . .

In the two studies presented below, subjects were given an initial learning phase where they were taught about genetics and shown how to conduct simulated molecular genetics experiments on the computer. This was followed by

**Figure 1.6**
**Genetic Mechanism Used in the Learning Phase**

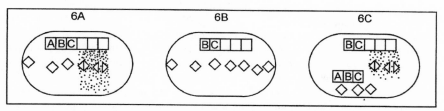

*Note:* In Figure 6A a normal *E. coli* produces delta to break down tryptoline. In Figure 6B, an A-mutant does not produce delta, even when the tryptoline is present, suggesting that the A gene switches on the delta-producing genes. In Figure 6C, a diploid *E. coli* with an A- chromosome and a normal chromosome is displayed. Here the *E. coli* works normally, suggesting that the A gene switches on delta production by sending a chemical message.

*Source:* Dunbar, K. (1993). Concept discovery in a scientific domain. *Cognitive Science, 17*, p. 406.

the discovery phase where the subjects were given the task of discovering how the β-gal genes are controlled.

## Learning Phase

In this phase, subjects are given some initial knowledge about possible mechanisms of genetic control using an example where a gene switches on (activates) enzyme production. They are told that the bacterium *E. coli* needs tryptoline to live. When tryptoline is present, a set of genes on the *E. coli* chromosome secretes a delta enzyme that breaks the tryptoline down into a substance that can be utilized by the bacterium. When there is no tryptoline present the genes do not secrete delta. They are told that three genes probably control the delta-producing genes. The genes are labeled A, B, and C as in [Figure 1.6]. Subjects are shown three experimental techniques for discovering how genes are controlled.

1. *Amount of nutrient*: Subjects could choose either 0, 100, 200, 300, 400, or 500 units of tryptoline to give to the *E. coli*. Then the subjects could conduct the experiment. They can see whether the *E. coli* produces the delta and how much delta it produces ([Figure 1.6, 6A]).

2. *Types of mutations*: A particular mutant can be chosen from a menu on the computer: a normal *E. coli*, a mutant with malfunctioning A gene (A−), B gene (B−), or C gene (C−). Subjects were only allowed to mutate one gene on a chromosome. That is, subjects could not generate chromosomes with two mutant genes such as an A−B−C+ mutant. This made the problem more difficult than being able to isolate a particular gene and see what the effect of one gene is, but mirrors the state of the technology at the time that Jacob and Monod made their discovery.

3. *Number of chromosomes*: Haploid or diploid *E. coli* could be used. In diploid *E. coli*, a new set of genes is introduced into the bacterium and the genetic makeup of the *E. coli* can be manipulated. For example, the haploid female *E. coli* could be A−B+C+ and it cannot produce delta ([Figure 1.6, 6B]). This would suggest that the A gene is responsible for the production of the delta. This hypothesis can be tested by making the *E. coli* diploid: a male chromosome with the A gene present can be added to the female A−B+C+ *E. coli* and the output of delta monitored ([Figure 1.6, 6C]). When the A gene is present, the *E. coli* then produce the delta. This result provides evidence in favor of the hypothesis that the A gene activated the delta-producing genes. Diploid *E. coli* can be used to determine the mechanism of genetic control. If a gene is mutant on the female and normal on the male and a normal output occurs, this indicates that the gene is sending a chemical message to the delta-producing genes.

*In sum, the mechanism shown to the subjects in the learning phase is as follows. When there is no tryptoline present, the regulator genes do nothing. When tryptoline is present, the A gene secretes a substance that binds to the delta-producing genes. This switches on delta production and the delta breaks down the tryptoline. This is a form of positive regulation or activation, where one gene activates or switches on another gene. After learning this mechanism, subjects' hypotheses about genetic control should be in an activation mode: Subjects should think that genes switch other genes on, that the target genes are in a quiescent state until they are switched on, that there are many potential genes that can switch genes on, and that an enzyme secreted by the controller genes activates target genes* [italics added].

## Discovery Phase

In this phase subjects are presented with a new type of *E. coli* also having six genes. The first three genes on the chromosome are labeled I, P, and O and the second three genes are not labeled (as in [Figure 1.3 and 1.4]). The subjects are told that the last three genes secrete an enzyme (β-gal) when lactose is present and do not secrete β-gal when lactose is absent. Subjects are told that scientists think that the I, P, and O genes might control β-gal production. The subjects are then asked to discover how the β-gal-producing genes are controlled. In this case, the I, P, and O genes work very differently from the examples that the subjects encounter in the learning phase. In the learning phase, the A gene activates the delta-producing genes, whereas in the discovery phase, the I and O genes inhibit the β-gal producing genes. That is, the mechanism in the learning phase is activation, whereas the to-be discovered mechanism is inhibition. Subjects were given sheets of paper and a pencil to keep any notes that they wanted.

In Study 1 the P gene plays no role, whereas in Study 2, the P gene is an activator. There are two reasons why the P gene plays no role in Study 1. First, Monod and Jacob proposed that the production of β-gal is controlled by an *inhibitory regulation* mechanism and did not have any type of activation in their original model, and thus, did not specify a role for the P gene. It is now known that the P gene is needed to switch on β-gal production. However, this was not discovered until after Monod and Jacob proposed the inhibitory mechanism of genetic regulation. The second reason for the P gene having no role was to allow the subjects to discover one control mechanism (i.e., inhibition) rather than two (i.e., inhibition and activation). It was expected that the task would be easier for the subjects when only one control mechanism was involved. However, as the results of Study 2 will demonstrate, this was not the case. . . .

## Collection

To determine the precise nature of the subjects' (a) hypotheses, (b) experimental goals and strategies, and (c) experimental procedures and results, a detailed analysis of each subject's protocol was conducted. The entire verbal protocols that subjects produced while conducting their experiments were audiotaped. At the same time, the computer automatically saved all of the experiments that the subjects conducted as well as all experimental results they obtained; this information was saved in the same format as is seen in [Figure 1.5].

## Transcription

All of the subjects' verbal statements were transcribed, and all of the experiments that the subjects conducted were also included in each subject's transcriptions. The entire transcription for each subject was then coded in the following manner.

## Coding

For every experiment that the subjects conducted, each and every statement that they produced regarding the following topics were identified in the transcriptions and entered into a computer database: (1) current hypothesis, (2) explicit statements of goals, (3) precise experiment being conducted, and (4) explicit comments evaluating experimental outcomes. Each subject's statements in which they evaluated their experimental outcomes were further coded in terms of whether: (a) the subject used inconsistent evidence to reject the current hypothesis (use inconsistent); (b) the subject ignored evidence inconsistent with the current hypothesis (ignore inconsistent); and (c) whether a subject changed the logic of the interpretation of his or her results to fit a current hypothesis (distortions).

This coding system yielded an extremely rich source of information, particularly regarding the subjects' initial and final hypotheses, their goals and strategies for solving the problem, and the differences between those who succeeded in solving the problem and those who did not. (Dunbar, 1993, pp. 402–408)

## STUDY 1: RATIONALE

The general rationale and specific expectations concerning hypothesis generation in Study 1 are summarized in the following section.

The subjects' initial hypotheses should be derived from the mechanism that they were shown in the learning phase. Subjects should analogically map knowledge of the A, B, C genes onto the I, P, O genes: As far as the subjects are concerned, both the structure of the concept acquired during the learning phase and the goals given to them are identical to that in the discovery phase, and therefore, analogical mapping should occur [cf. Gentner, 1989; Holyoak & Thagard, 1989; Novick & Holyoak, 1991]. Specifically, subjects should retrieve the A, B, C problem, map the A, B, C genes onto the I, P, O genes, and adapt the concept of activation onto the I, P, O genes. As a result, subjects should begin with the hypothesis that the I, P, O genes switch on or activate the β-gal-producing genes when the lactose is present just like the A gene did in the learning phase. However, after creating mutation experiments, the subjects should soon discover that the P gene has no effect and that the I and O genes do not switch on or activate the β-gal-producing genes. In particular, subjects should quickly notice that with I- or O- mutations there is a large output of β-gal nonetheless.

Given that subjects will not obtain results consistent with their initial hypothesis, the expectation was that subjects should be concerned with either (a) modifying their current hypothesis about the mechanism that controls β-gal production (i.e., genes *activate* other genes), or (b) generating a new hypothesis to account for the discrepant findings. In particular, one correct conclusion that subjects could draw from the preceding experimental results would be that the I and O genes function as inhibitors. Given that the subjects will be biased towards an activation hypothesis, the critical questions of this study are as follows: How will the subjects deal with evidence that is inconsistent with their current hypothesis, and how will inconsistent evidence influence the subjects' final hypotheses and the strategies used to achieve them? (Dunbar, 1993, pp. 408–409)

## STUDY 1: METHOD

The procedures of Study 1 are given in the following account.

Twenty McGill University undergraduates participated in this study (described previously). . . .

The study was carried out in three phases. First, subjects were taught some basic facts about molecular biology and were shown how a gene could be switched on (or activated) by another gene (described previously). Second, the

subjects were instructed on how to give a verbal protocol [cf. Ericsson & Simon, 1984]. To accomplish this, the subjects were given the 15 puzzle [Ericsson, 1975] and were asked to think aloud while they solved the puzzle. Third, subjects were shown a new set of genes that produced a chemical called β-gal when lactose was present and no β-gal when lactose was not present. They were told that the I, P, and O genes were potential candidates for controlling the β-gal genes and that their task was to discover the mechanism by which the β-gal genes were controlled. The subjects were told to state everything that they were thinking while they were performing the task. They were given 60 min to work on the problem. They were told that they could finish (a) when they felt that they had discovered how the β-gal genes were controlled; (b) when they felt that they could not discover how the β-gal genes were controlled; or (c) when 60 min had elapsed.

## The Experiment Space

As stated before, one aspect of experimental science is the searching of an experiment space in which hypotheses are tested, and/or new hypotheses are induced from the experimental results [e.g., Klahr & Dunbar, 1988]. In this task, the experiment space consisted of 120 possible experiments: 6 different amounts of lactose × 20 different types of mutations. The different attributes of the possible experiments are explained in the following:

1. *Amount of lactose*: The six amounts of lactose that the subjects could select were 0, 100, 200, 300, 400, and 500 μg.

2. *Types of mutations*: There are four types of *E. coli*: (1) normal *E. coli* (N) produce an amount of β-gal that is half the amount of lactose added; (2) I- mutants produce 876 units of β-gal regardless of how much lactose is added; (3) O- mutants produce 527 units of β-gal regardless of how much lactose is added; and (4) the P gene has no effect, therefore, P- mutants produce the same amount of β-gal as in the normal *E. coli* (half). The production of different amounts of β-gal for I- and O- mutants reflects the fact that the I- and O- mutants inhibit in different ways: I by sending an inhibitor, and O by physically blocking β-gal production. Subjects were told that there could only be one mutant gene on any chromosome: For example, subjects were not allowed to construct an I-O-P mutant. As stated earlier, by allowing subjects to only have one mutation on a particular chromosome, the task more closely resembles the types of experiments that Monod and Jacob were able to conduct with the technology that they had available at the time.

3. *Number of chromosomes*: Haploid or diploid *E. coli* could be used to determine how a gene is controlled. Subjects were told that if a gene were sending a chemical signal to the enzyme-producing genes, then the controller gene should work when it is present on a haploid *E. coli* and when it is present on a diploid *E. coli*. That is, the gene can send its signal to the enzyme-producing genes no matter which chromosome it is on. However, if the mechanism of activation is physical rather than chemical, then activation will only occur when the activator gene is on the same chromosome as the

**Table 1.1**
**Output of β-gal for Each of the 16 Diploid Types of *E. coli***

|                  | Female Chromosome | | | |
| Male Chromosome  | N     | I-    | P-    | O-   |
| --- | --- | --- | --- | --- |
| N                | half  | half  | half  | 527  |
| I-               | half  | 876   | half  | 527  |
| P-               | half  | half  | half  | 527  |
| O-               | half  | half  | half  | 527  |

*Note:* The columns correspond to the genetic makeup of the female chromosome and the rows correspond to the genetic makeup of the male chromosome: normal (N), I mutant (I-), P mutant (P-), and O mutant (O-).

*Source:* Dunbar, K. (1993). Concept discovery in a scientific domain. *Cognitive Science, 17*, p. 411.

enzyme-producing genes. Thus, by comparing a diploid version of the *E. coli* on which the gene is only present on the male chromosome with a haploid *E. coli*, it is possible to determine the mechanism by which the enzymes are controlled.

Diploid mutants are made by adding an extra set of genes from the male *E. coli* to the female *E. coli*. There are 16 types of diploid mutations. All 16 types of diploid mutants are displayed in [Table 1.1]. The rows of [Table 1.1] show the genetic structure of the male *E. coli*, and the columns show the genetic structure of the female *E. coli*. The intersection of a particular row and column shows the output of β-gal for that type of diploid mutant. For example, an I-female crossed with an I- male will produce 876μg of β-gal, whereas an I-female and a normal (N) male will produce an amount of β-gal equivalent to half the amount of lactose added. This latter diploid combination is the same as that displayed in [Figure 1.2, 2C].

## Generating Hypotheses from the Experimental Results

Different types of experimental results make it possible for the subjects to induce different types of hypotheses. For haploid *E. coli*, the fact that both I- and O- mutants produce a constant large output of β-gal regardless of the amount of lactose added, is not consistent with an activation hypothesis. Furthermore, the fact that P- haploids and normal *E. coli* produce an amount of β-gal equivalent to half the lactose added is not consistent with the hypothesis that the P gene is an activator. The three most important results for diploid *E. coli* are as follows:

1. If the I gene is present on either chromosome, then the *E. coli* will function normally. This result is consistent with the hypothesis that the I gene is sending a chemical message that inhibits β-gal production.

2. The O gene must be present on the female chromosome; if it is absent on the female but present on the male, then it will not function normally. This type of result is consistent with the hypothesis that the O gene physically blocks β-gal production.

3. P- mutations on either chromosome produce the same amount of β-gal as normal *E. coli*. This indicates that the P gene plays no role in β-gal production. . . .

Each subject's experimental hypotheses and strategies for solving the problem were determined by conducting the data analyses detailed before. (Dunbar, 1993, pp. 409–412)

## STUDY 1: RESULTS

The results of Study 1 are summarized in the following section.

Subjects spent, on average, 51 min on the task and the mean number of experiments conducted was 16.7. Four of the 20 subjects succeeded at discovering that the I and O genes inhibit the production of β-gal and that P has no role, and 16 subjects did not succeed. . . . There was not a significant difference in the amount of time spent on the problem by those who succeeded and those who did not. . . . There was no difference in the number of haploid experiments . . . but there was a difference in the number of diploid experiments conducted. . . .

### Type of Initial Hypotheses

All 20 students' initial hypothesis was that a gene switches on or activates β-gal production. That is, in expecting activation, the 20 subjects initially hypothesized that either the I, O, or P gene must switch on the β-gal-producing genes when lactose was present. To test this hypothesis, 18 of the 20 subjects began by conducting haploid experiments where the I, P, and O genes were mutant (the other 2 subjects began with a diploid experiments); 18 of the 20 subjects' first 4 experiments consisted of I-, O-, and P- haploid experiments. When subjects conducted these experiments with mutant I-, O-, or P- genes, they fully expected that there would be no production of β-gal. Instead, they discovered that all three types of mutants still yielded an output of β-gal. Because the I and O genes work by inhibition, subjects never did find a situation where there was no output of β-gal with a mutant gene (see [Table 1.1] for a list of all possible outcomes). Instead, subjects discovered that when the I or O genes were mutant, there was a large output of β-gal, and when the P gene was mutant, the *E. coli* behaved normally. If any of the three genes had been activators, then a mutant should have produced no output. However, as there was always a production of β-gal, rather than no production of β-gal, none of the experimental results were consistent with their activation hypothesis. Subjects then conducted further experiments to determine the roles of the three genes.

### Types of Final Hypotheses

Subjects proposed two different types of final hypotheses. One type was where subjects hypothesized that activation was the only mechanism that controlled β-gal production (Activation-Only Final Hypothesis); 13 of the 20 subjects proposed this type of final hypothesis. Twelve of the 13 subjects concluded that all three genes worked in combination as activators, and 1 of the 13 concluded that the I and O genes were activators and that the P gene played no role. A second type of final hypothesis was one that included inhibition (Inhibition Final Hypotheses); 7 of the 20 subjects proposed this type of final hypothesis. That is, 7 subjects stated that the I and O genes worked as inhibitors. Four of the 7 subjects in this group proposed that the P gene has no role, thereby reaching the correct conclusion. The 3 remaining subjects, although hypothesizing that the I and O genes worked as inhibitors, also concluded that the P gene worked by activation. Thus, only 7 of the 20 subjects generated an inhibition hypothesis, and only 4 of these 7 achieved an entirely correct solution.

After considering the subjects' initial and final hypotheses, the immediate question is, *How* did subjects arrive at their final hypotheses? What were the subjects' goals and strategies for solving the problems, and how did subjects interpret the results of each of their experiments? Importantly, how did the subjects react to evidence inconsistent with their hypothesis? To address these questions, the different strategies employed by those subjects who proposed activation only in their final hypotheses versus those who proposed inhibition hypotheses will be analyzed. . . .

### Activation-Only Versus Inhibition Groups

. . . [Comparisons] reveal that there were no significant differences between the groups in terms of numbers of haploid experiments . . . or diploid experiments conducted. . . . The two groups differed with respect to the subjects' statements about goals. Whereas a number of different goals were mentioned by subjects (e.g., trying to determine whether the amount of lactose makes a difference, or whether the O gene needs to be on the male), 88% of statements about goals were of two types: subjects stating that their goal was to find a situation where there is no output of β-gal, and stating a goal of trying to discover why I- and O- mutants produce large outputs of β-gal. The inhibition group conducted more experiments where they stated that their goal was to discover the cause of a large β-gal output. . . . However, there was no significant difference between subjects in both groups in terms of statements of a goal of finding no β-gal output. . . . To investigate the roles of these two types of goals in performance further, a comparison of the number of subjects in each group stating that their goal was to find no output versus explaining the large output for I- and O- mutants, was conducted. This analysis also indicates significant differences in goals between the two groups: 10 of the 13 activation subjects explicitly stated that their goal was to find no output, whereas 2 of the 7 subjects in the inhibition group explicitly stated that their goal was to find no output. Conversely, 6 of the 7 inhibition subjects stated an explicit goal was that they were trying to discover the cause of the large output, whereas only 1 of the 13 activation subjects stated that their goal was to discover the cause of the large output. . . .

The verbal protocols provided a more rounded picture of the different strategies that the activation-only and inhibition groups used. Segments that are representative of the protocols obtained from activation-only and inhibition subjects will now be presented. These brief segments are representative of all the subjects in a particular group in terms of what they said while conducting experiments and responding to experimental outcomes.

The initial and final hypotheses of the 13 subjects in the activation-only group changed in the following way: Rather than hypothesizing that one of the three genes switched on β-gal production, they hypothesized that some unknown combination of all three genes (I, O, P) switched on or activated β-gal production; as stated before, only 1 subject differed and concluded that two of the genes (I, O) switched on β-gal production, and 1 gene (P) had no role. Following the initial results inconsistent with a simple activation hypothesis, these subjects started to search for other ways of accounting for their results, while, at the same time, maintaining the activation hypothesis. To prove that their activation hypothesis was correct, 10 of the 13 subjects explicitly stated that they wanted to find a result where there was no output of β-gal when some combination of I-, O-, and P- mutants were present. For example, clear statements of this goal can be seen in the protocol of subject AS. The first two experiments conducted by subject AS were a P- and I- haploid, both with 100µg of lactose. (In the following protocol excerpts, italicized material appearing in parentheses represents the subjects' actions only). While setting up the third experiment AS stated:

> Haploid cell (*chooses a haploid*). This time we will have minus (*selects O-*) and hopefully we will not have any [beta-gal] produced, we will not have any enzyme produced with the amount of lactose the same. Start reaction (*starts experiment, then watches the experiment unfold on the screen*). So much for that theory (*looks at experimental results screen*). OK, so it must be a combination.

Similarly, after conducting his first three experiments (P-, I-, and O- haploids with 200µg of lactose), subject PG stated:

Right now, my objective is to find a way such that nothing is produced (*looking at results screen*). That's my objective. Um. Ok. So, so far I've tried the combinations of O absent. I've tried the combination of I absent. O absent, I absent. Uh . . . I present, O present, P absent gives me 200. If I take away the P, it gives me 876. No, if I take away I it gives me much greater amount. . . . Question: how to . . . how to make nothing appear. Have I tried all the combinations? P absent, I absent, O absent. I've tried all the three combinations, and all three cases it gave me . . . it gave me . . . it gave me . . . um . . . it gave me. . . . Therefore I conclude that it's not an isolated . . . the I's are not isolated to one. The site is a combination.

To be clear, both subjects, and all other activation-only subjects, demonstrated an awareness that their experimental results were inconsistent with their initial activation hypothesis. However, they turned from this inconsistent evidence (i.e., large β-gal output for I- and O- mutants), and instead, continued with a goal of finding *no output* of β-gal with *combinations* of I-, O-, and P- mutants. As with all subjects in the activation-only group, the subjects AS and PG had set a goal of finding no β-gal output and initially tried all three haploid experiments. To their surprise, however, the β-gal output still occurred. Also, like the other subjects in the activation-only group, these 2 subjects went on to conduct diploid experiments in pursuit of their activation hypothesis. Following their initial experiments, the subjects in this group concluded that the genes must work in some unknown combination to achieve activation; 6 of the 13 subjects reached this conclusion after finishing their experiments, and 7 of the 13 reached this conclusion when the experiment was terminated after 60 min.

The 7 subjects in the inhibition group performed very differently from the activation-only subjects. Following their initial discovery that all mutants nonetheless produce β-gal, these subjects set a new goal of discovering *why* this was the case. These subjects' goal was to find out why there was a large output of β-gal with I- and O- mutants. For example, after conducting his fourth experiment subject AC stated that:

(*looks at results screen*) As long as there's lactose present there's beta; you can break it down into glucose. In this case (*points to result for an I- mutant*), they seem to be unregulated. They produce this much (*points to an output of 876*). Why do they produce 876?

While conducting his third experiment (I- haploid with 100μg of lactose), subject RM stated:

Make it a haploid gene (*selects haploid*). Choose one with O negative gene (*selects O-*). Amount of lactose must be the same (*chooses same amount of lactose as in the previous experiment*). We look at the experiment and start it and see if any beta (*starts experiment*). Oh! Now that's interesting (*watches experiment unfold on the screen*)! Oh. . . . Oh. . . . They all seem to . . . uh . . . oh that's fun! Ok, so the O negative doesn't . . . uh . . . create the . . . um . . . beta enzyme, and what this seems to suggest perhaps is that my initial hypothesis of how these perform is incorrect. This is also producing a hellova . . . a hell of a lot of enzyme too. That's a real pain. Let's have a look at what's happening (*selects the show results screen*). That produces 527 amount of the enzyme. That's a bit more than the . . . uh . . . that's definitely more than the . . . uh . . . uh. . . . Oh, so that's definitely more than the control, but not as much as the I. Ok so let's make a new experiment. We're obviously going to have to go into the diploid . . . uh . . . field of the world.

## Use of Inconsistent Evidence

As the preceding excerpts demonstrate, there was a striking difference between the activation-only and inhibition subjects' responses to inconsistent evidence. Subjects in the inhibition group both attended to the inconsistent evidence and used this evidence to set up new goals to understand the discrepant findings that resulted from their experiments. Conversely, although all subjects in the activation-only group noted the inconsistent evidence, they proposed activation as the mechanism for the control of β-gal production, even though none of the data were consistent with this type of hypothesis. Subjects also distorted inconsistent evidence to fit their hypothesis. Subjects who distorted evidence also explicitly ignored inconsistent evidence. All *explicit* statements concerning the ignoring of inconsistent evidence only occurred in the context of a distortion and will be discussed in the context of distortions. Both the activation-only and the inhibition groups of subjects produced distortions, with all 13 subjects in the activation-only group explicitly distorting their results to fit their current hypothesis, and 3 of the subjects in the inhibition group explicitly distorting their results. This difference is significant. . . . The three inhibition subjects who concluded that the P gene is an activator, all distorted information, whereas none of the inhibition subjects who concluded that the I and O genes were inhibitors distorted the evidence.

Initially, all subjects used the inconsistent evidence to search for genes that produced activation. When a result was obtained that was inconsistent with a particular activation hypothesis (e.g., the I gene is the activator), they switched to another type of activation hypothesis (e.g., the O gene is the activator). Once subjects had conducted all their haploid experiments, differences among the activation-only and inhibition subjects appeared. Activation-only subjects kept the goal of discovering activation and started distorting evidence to fit their hypothesis. In order to maintain the activation hypothesis, these subjects had to *distort* the findings that resulted from their experimental studies: Recall that when the I and O genes are mutated, there is still a large output of β-gal. Rather than focusing on this fact, the activation-only subjects persisted in believing that some gene must be activating the production of β-gal. They then reasoned that the P gene must be the activation gene because it was common to both situations where a large output of β-gal was produced. However, in coming to this conclusion, these subjects ignored inconsistent evidence from their previous experiments, which demonstrated that regardless of whether the P gene was mutated, the *E. coli* produced the identical normal amount of β-gal. As such, these subjects distorted the interpretation of their results to fit their activation hypothesis. Indeed, all of the 13 subjects in the activation-only group explicitly distorted evidence to be consistent with an activator hypothesis. They noticed that I-mutants produced 876 and O- mutants produced 527. They also noted that both types of mutations have (a) a P gene present, and (b) a large output of β-gal occurred. They then concluded that the P gene was an activator because it was common to both, ignoring the fact that a normal *E. coli* also has the P gene present and only a small amount of β-gal was produced.

The seven subjects who proposed inhibition in their final hypothesis can be subdivided into two further subgroups: those who conclude that the P gene plays no role (*n=4*) and those who conclude that the P gene is an activator (*n=3*). The inhibition subjects noticed that large output of β-gal in the context of mutant genes, and consequently, set a new goal to account for the large outputs for the I and O genes. They then proposed that the I and O genes control the size of the output. However, when they realized that the amount of lactose added had no effect on the amount of β-gal produced by I- and O- mutants, they then proposed that the I and O genes work by inhibition. The 4 subjects who proposed that P had no role all mentioned that the P gene could possibly be an activator, but noted that P- mutants produced the same output as normal *E. coli* and rejected the hypothesis that P was an activator. Despite the fact that they did not explicitly state an activation goal, these subjects did not abandon the idea that some form of activation was present until late in their experimentation. The mean number of experiments conducted before these subjects ceased to mention activation was 11.

The 3 inhibition-group subjects who proposed that the I and O genes are inhibitors and that the P gene is an activator also distorted evidence to fit the P gene as activator hypothesis. They argued that some form of activation *must* be present and proposed that it was the P gene. Thus, although the subjects in this group did hypothesize that inhibition was involved, they did not drop the goal of finding activation. These subjects could not see a way that the *E. coli* could work by inhibition alone. They continued to search for a gene that could switch on or activate the β-gal genes and stated that this was their goal. Given that they had determined that I and O genes were inhibitors, they reasoned that the only gene that could possibly be an activator was the P gene.

## More on Successful Inhibition Subjects

Importantly, the subjects who proposed that the I and O genes were inhibitors and that the P gene played no role, also discovered some of the more subtle features of the genetic mechanisms. Two subjects proposed that the I gene could be present on the female or the male chromosome and proposed that the I gene sends out an inhibitory signal. These 2 subjects also discovered that the O gene has to be on the female chromosome. On the basis of this finding, 1 subject proposed that the O gene physically blocks production of β-gal and assumed that, because the O gene is adjacent to the β-gal genes, it must block β-gal production. *Thus, although all 4 subjects in this group proposed that the I and O genes were inhibitors and that the P gene had no role, only 1 subject proposed a complete mechanism by which the inhibition is achieved.* (Dunbar, 1993, pp. 412–419, italics added)

## STUDY 2: RATIONALE

The interesting rationale for Study 2 is set forth in the following account.

Two potential sources of difficulty may underlie the subjects' performance in Study 1: First, the subjects' goal of finding evidence in favor of their current hypothesis may prevent them from both setting up a new goal and from searching for alternative ones. Second, subjects may be unwilling to abandon the old hypothesis if they have a strong belief in it. Study 2 was conducted to investigate these issues further.

In Study 1, the subjects' goal of finding evidence in support of their initial hypothesis appeared to influence their ability to attend to and/or use inconsistent evidence and to set new experimental goals. What if the task were changed and subjects were now permitted to find evidence in support of their initial hypothesis? Once subjects had found evidence consistent with their favored hypothesis, would the subjects then be more inclined to attend to the other evidence inconsistent with their favored hypothesis? Would subjects then set new goals? To examine these questions, the genetic mechanism was changed so that the P gene works by activation and the I and O genes work by inhibition. That is, one gene works as an activator and the other two genes as inhibitors. In this situation, subjects should first discover activation and then set a new goal of explaining the findings that are inconsistent with an activation hypothesis. Once this goal is set, subjects should be able to generate an inhibitory hypothesis. The design of this study is virtually identical to that of Study 1. The only change is that the P gene must be present for the *E. coli* to secrete β-gal. When the P gene is absent, no β-gal is produced. The subjects now have to discover that the P gene works by activation and the I and O genes work by inhibition. *If correct, significantly more subjects should propose inhibition than in Study 1.* (Dunbar, 1993, p. 419, italics added)

## STUDY 2: METHOD

The procedures for Study 2 are described in the following section.

Twenty new subjects participated in the experiment. . . .

The procedures were identical to those employed in Study 1. There were three phases: training, giving protocols, and discovering the mechanism of genetic control. The only difference between this study and Study 1 was that in this study, the P gene was an activator gene. The P gene must be present for an output to occur. Furthermore, the P gene must be on the female gene for output to occur. Thus, for all mutants with a P- mutant on the female, there was no production of β-gal. . . .

Each subject's experimental hypotheses and strategies for solving the problem were determined in the manner specified in Study 1. (Dunbar, 1993, pp. 419–420)

## STUDY 2: RESULTS

The results of Study 2 are described in the following section.

Subjects spent, on average, 38 min on the task and the mean number of experiments conducted was 14. Nineteen of the 20 subjects discovered that the P gene was an activator gene. Fourteen subjects proposed that both inhibition and activation were involved, and 1 subject proposed that only inhibition was involved. Ten of the 14 subjects discovered activation before inhibition. For the 14 subjects who proposed activation and inhibition, two types of final hypotheses were proposed. Nine subjects proposed that I and O are inhibitors and that the P gene is an activator. Five subjects proposed that I was an inhibitor and O and P were activators. Both of these inhibitory hypotheses are consistent with subjects' experimental results. . . .

All of the 20 subjects initially proposed that one or more genes activate β-gal production. Nineteen of the 20 subjects discovered that the P gene switches on β-gal production. They then switched their focus to the I and O genes; subjects who succeeded at finding activation then set a new goal of accounting for the large outputs of β-gal with the I- and O- mutant genes. As in Study 1, two major types of final hypotheses were proposed by subjects: activation only and inhibition. . . . Five of the 20 subjects concluded with an activation-only hypothesis; 4 said all three genes were activators and 1 said that the P gene was an activator and I and O had no role. Fifteen of the 20 subjects concluded with inhibition hypotheses; all but 1 of these subjects proposed both inhibition and activation mechanisms. Fourteen of the 15 subjects in the inhibition group achieved a correct solution to the problem.

In the next section, the different strategies used by the activation-only versus inhibition groups, as well as their use of inconsistent evidences, will be discussed. Following this, differences among subjects who generated hypotheses containing inhibition will be further considered. Finally, a comparison between the overall results of Studies 1 and 2 will be made.

## Activation-Only Versus Inhibition Groups

The working hypothesis for Study 2 was that once subjects discovered the mechanism that corresponded to their own initial hypothesis (i.e., activation), they should then be more inclined to set a new goal of accounting for unusual findings, thereby freeing them to discover inhibition. Specifically, once activation had been discovered, the subjects should then attempt to account for the large output of $\beta$-gal with I- and O- mutants, and therefore, more subjects should achieve the final solution to the problem (P gene = activator, I and O genes = inhibitors). An analysis of subjects' explicit statements about their goals reveals that 14 of the 19 subjects discovered activation, then explicitly set a new goal of accounting for the large output of $\beta$-gal with I- and O- mutants. . . .

The only significant differences in performance were in terms of goals. None of the 5 subjects in the activation-only group stated that they had set a new goal of explaining the large output of $\beta$-gal for I- and O- mutants after discovering that the P gene was an activator. Their verbal statements indicate that they did not set a new goal of explaining the large output of $\beta$-gal. These 5 subjects did not use the results for I- and O- mutants to generate new goals, and assumed that all three genes were activators. With regard to the inhibition group, 13 of the 15 subjects explicitly stated that their goal was to explain the large output of $\beta$-gal. Thus, subjects' verbal statements indicate the main difference between the activation-only and the inhibition groups is that none of the subjects in the activation-only group set a new goal of explaining why I- and O- mutants produce more output of $\beta$-gal, whereas the inhibition group did. . . . None of the other differences in performance measures between the two groups were statistically significant.

## Differences Within the Inhibition Group

Subjects in the inhibition group employed the following general strategy. Once they had discovered that the P gene is an activator, they all attempted to account for the finding that there was increased output of $\beta$-gal for I- and O- mutants. Two main types of final hypotheses were proposed by these subjects. Note that both of these conclusions are consistent with all the data that the subjects obtained. Nine subjects proposed that the I and O genes are inhibitors; the other 5 subjects proposed that the O gene is an activator, and that the I gene is an inhibitor. That these 5 subjects assigned an inhibitory role for the I gene and an activation role for the O gene demonstrates that these subjects were using a different induction strategy. These 5 subjects reasoned that the P and O work together, with O helping P to activate more β-gal production. They reached this conclusion by focusing on the genes that are present, rather than the mutation that they had used. For example, rather than regarding an I- as an *E. coli* with a malfunctioning I gene, they regarded it as an *E. coli* with the P and O genes working correctly. They then argued that mutants with an I and a P produce 876μg of β-gal, whereas mutants with an I and a P produce 527μg. Thus, the two inhibition subgroups focused upon different aspects of the data and induced different types of hypotheses for the O gene.

## STUDIES 1 AND 2: COMPARISON

Dunbar (1993) presents an analytic comparison of Studies 1 and 2 in the following section.

Several key differences exist between the subjects' performance in Study 1 and that of Study 2. As predicted, more subjects generated an inhibition hypothesis in Study 2 ($n = 15$) than in Study 1 ($n = 7$). . . . In addition, 14 subjects in Study 2 determined the correct roles in all three genes, whereas only 4 subjects in Study 1 assigned the correct roles for all 3 genes. . . . In Study 2, only 2 subjects explicitly stated that their goal was to generate a finding with no output of β-gal, whereas in Study 1, 11 subjects explicitly stated that their goal was to find no output of β-gal. . . . Similarly, more subjects stated an explicit goal of explaining the large output in Study 2 ($n = 13$) than in Study 1 ($n = 7$). . . . In addition, fewer subjects distorted evidence in Study 2 ($n = 4$) than in Study 1 ($n = 16$). . . . (Dunbar, 1993, pp. 420–423)

## STUDIES 1 AND 2: SUMMARY

A lucid précis of the research is given in the following passage.

The two studies reported in this article investigated the discovery of a complex concept in a scientific domain. Subjects in both studies used the knowledge that they acquired in the learning phase to propose an initial working hypothesis. All subjects initially hypothesized that the genes were activators and explicitly stated that they had a goal of finding which genes worked in a way that was consistent with this hypothesis.

In Study 1, subjects found no evidence that was consistent with an activation hypothesis: All experimental results were inconsistent with an activation hypothesis. At this point, Study 1 subjects employed one of two strategies for dealing with the inconsistent evidence before them. One strategy was to continue using the current goal of finding activation. Other subjects in Study 1 used a second strategy: Upon noticing inconsistent evidence against an activation hypothesis, they stated that they had set a new goal of attempting to explain the cause of the discrepant findings. These subjects were able to generate a new hypothesis to account for the discrepant findings. A relatively small subset of these subjects discovered the correct solution to the problem.

In Study 2, it was predicted that once subjects had achieved their initial goal of discovering activation, they would then be more inclined to attend to inconsistent evidence, thereby permitting more subjects to discover the concept of inhibition. This was the case: Twice as many subjects proposed inhibition in Study 2 than in Study 1, and more subjects reached the correct conclusion. (Dunbar, 1993, p. 423)

## STUDIES 1 AND 2: DISCUSSION

The goals set by experimental subjects were central to the hypotheses they deployed and experiments they conducted.

These studies lay bare the critical ways in which subjects' goals influence their generation of hypotheses, strategies for conducting experiments, and evaluation of experimental evidence before them, including inconsistent evidence. Importantly, this research further reveals key components of the mental processes underlying the subjects' use of goals. The goals that the subjects set for themselves had a large effect on their ability to discover new concepts in the simulated scientific domains of Studies 1 and 2, and these results indicate that goals play an important role in the process of scientific discovery. . . .

A variety of goals (representation of a desired end state) were employed by subjects while working on the problem; goals led to the subjects' initiation of processes (or strategies) to reach the end state. In these studies, the subjects' goals affected both (a) the types of hypotheses (explanatory mechanisms) that they generated to account for the experimental findings, and (b) the types of strategies that they used to discover a new concept.

### Goals and Hypotheses

The overarching goal that all subjects stated at the start of the problem was the goal derived from the problem statement (i.e., find how genes are controlled); this goal constituted the stable goal around which all experimental activity initially began. However, two additional goals were stated by the subjects that proved to be critical to their ability or inability to solve the problem. One goal was to find data consistent with the current type of hypothesis (e.g., activation), and the other goal was to find a hypothesis consistent with the data; the former will be termed the "find-evidence goal" and the latter the "find-hypothesis goal."

No other goals were stated as frequently, or by all subjects, indicating that these were critical components of their reasoning.

Using both the find-evidence and find-hypothesis goals, subjects noticed that data were inconsistent with the current hypothesis. However, when subjects had a find-evidence goal, rather than assuming that the inconsistent data ruled out the current type of hypothesis, these subjects merely noted the inconsistency and continued to search for any data that were consistent with the current type of hypothesis. That is, these subjects assumed that the current type of hypothesis was correct (i.e., one or more of the genes is an activator) and then attempted to generate data that were consistent with a particular version of the hypothesis (e.g., the I gene is an activator); when subjects had this goal they did not attempt to change the type of hypothesis they were working on even in the face of inconsistent evidence. However, subjects did use inconsistent evidence to change from one instantiation of their hypothesis to another instantiation of their hypothesis (e.g., switching from the I gene is an activator, to the P gene is an activator), rather than switching from one type of hypothesis to another type of hypothesis (e.g., switching from activation to inhibition).

Using the find-hypothesis goal, subjects not only noted that the data were inconsistent with the current hypothesis, but they also assumed that the data ruled out the current type of hypothesis and thereupon attempted to generate new hypotheses that could account for the range of experimental data. Subjects only switched from a find-evidence to a find-hypothesis goal following the accumulation of evidence inconsistent with any simple activation hypothesis.

The critical difference between the preceding goals lies in the aspects of the experimental data that the subjects attend to. When the goal is to find evidence that allows subjects to specify values of the current type of hypothesis (find-evidence goal), the strategy employed is to focus upon the general nature of the experimental data relative to this hypothesis (i.e., whether an experimental result allows them to further specify the features of their hypothesis). They do not focus on specific aspects of the evidence or why the evidence is inconsistent with their hypothesis. Conversely, when the goal is to propose a new hypothesis (find-hypothesis goal), subjects focus upon specific features of the outcomes of their experiments and induce the new hypothesis from the key features of the experimental data. . . .

## Blocking

As was demonstrated earlier, all subjects began by stating an activation hypothesis. At the close of Studies 1 and 2, the activation-only group of subjects stated an activation goal, and this was their main goal. Given that they never discovered any simple form of activation mechanism, their search remained wholly unsuccessful. This suggests that initial goals can *block* the generation of new goals and hypotheses, and, consequently, subjects can distort or bias the interpretation of results to fit a current goal. The blocking process was investigated in Study 2. Recall that in Study 2 it was predicted that once subjects had achieved their initial goal of discovering activation, they would then be more inclined to attend to inconsistent evidence, thereby permitting more subjects to discover the concept of inhibition. In this study, it was found that once subjects achieved their initial goal of discovering activation, they then set a new goal of accounting for the discrepant findings and consequently proposed inhibition. Thus, only when their initial goal was achieved were they able to set up new goals.

Another possible explanation for blocking is that subjects stay with their current hypothesis because they are unable to think of alternative hypotheses. Einhorn and Hogarth [1986] argued that subjects will maintain a hypothesis even when it is disconfirmed, that is, if they cannot think of alternative hypotheses. Another version of this unable-to-think-of-an-alternative-hypothesis explanation is that subjects do not have heuristics for generating new goals and/or hypotheses when their current hypothesis is disconfirmed. For example, Kaplan and Simon [1990] argued that subjects fail to find solutions to problems because they lack various heuristics for generating new solutions. Whereas such explanations may be consistent with the findings of Study 1 (e.g., subjects may have stayed with activation because they could not think of any other hypotheses or do not have heuristics for generating new hypotheses), these explanations cannot account for the findings of Study 2. Recall that in Study 2, many more subjects discovered inhibition than in Study 1, and these subjects discovered inhibition after achieving the goal of finding evidence consistent with their activation hypothesis. Thus, the unable-to-think-of-an-alternative-hypothesis explanation cannot account for this finding: If the subjects' problem was merely one of being unable to think of alternative hypotheses, then the Study 2 manipulation should not have led to better performance.

## Dropping

The finding that other subjects in Studies 1 and 2 proposed final hypotheses containing inhibition (be they inhibition only or inhibition and activation) suggests another locus of difficulty of subjects: *dropping* an original goal. Whereas activation-only subjects did not drop their original goal, subjects whose final hypotheses contained inhibition did so. Indeed, all subjects whose final hypotheses contained inhibition demonstrated a clear attention to, and use of, inconsistent evidence to set a new goal of accounting for the nature of the inconsistent evidence. However, even here, not all of these subjects reached the correct final solution. Study 1 was especially revealing in this regard. To succeed at Study 1, subjects had to drop completely the hypothesis of activation. This proved difficult for the subjects. Some subjects failed to drop activation—even though they had discovered inhibition—and instead proposed hybrid activation and inhibition hypotheses. Even the subjects who dropped the activation-only hypothesis did so fairly late in their experimentation. Thus, these findings provide additional support for the claim that, in addition to blocking, the ability to drop an original goal is an essential process underlying the discovery of novel concepts in a scientific domain. . . .

The tasks used in research in "confirmation bias" (cf. Klayman and Ha, 1987; Tweney, Doherty, and Mynatt, 1981) bear a superficial resemblance to the studies reported here. Typically, subjects in confirmation bias tasks are asked to discover an arbitrary concept in a domain constructed by the experimenter. For example, in the "artificial universe" task (Mynatt, Doherty, and Tweney, 1977, 1978), subjects had to discover the rule that governs the motion of "particles" in a computer screen consisting of squares, circles, and triangles of various sizes. Subjects fired particles at shapes on the screen, and had to discover the arbitrary rule that the experimenters built into the task. Based on these types of tasks, researchers have concluded that subjects have a number of confirmation biases: (a) subjects conduct experiments that will confirm rather than disconfirm their current hypothesis (e.g., Klayman and Ha, 1987; Wason, 1968b); (b) subjects ignore evidence inconsistent with their current hypothesis (e.g., Mynatt et al., 1977, 1978); (c) subjects distort evidence to their current hypothesis (e.g., Mynatt et al., 1978); and (d) subjects fail to consider alternate hypotheses (Mynatt et al., 1977, 1978). However, there are important differences between the research reported here and the work on confirmation bias in both (a) the nature of the studies, and (b) the conclusions reached.

In the artificial universe and other studies, the universe was arbitrary, the relationships among the features were arbitrary, and the rule to be discovered was also arbitrary. It is well known that content has a large effect upon reasoning (e.g., Cheng and Holyoak, 1985). In the current research, subjects discovered a real concept, in a real scientific domain in which the features of hypotheses were causally related to each other. Furthermore, the conclusions reached from the artificial universe studies were that subjects display confirmation biases, although the actual reasons for these biases were not explained. Except for asserting that these biases exist, little is offered regarding why subjects demonstrate these biases and the conditions under which they will or will not use them (save "cognitive limited capacity"). Here, the specific factors that underlie subjects' biases and the conditions under which they use them are directly addressed.

In the artificial universe studies, if subjects ignored inconsistent evidence, they were classified as demonstrating a confirmation bias. To make this attribution, any changes that subjects made to their hypotheses following inconsistent evidence appears to have been set aside, because of the researchers' observation that subjects maintained the same overarching type of hypothesis. A close examination of such data, however, reveals that subjects do make small changes to their hypotheses in light of inconsistent evidence. Crucially, the novel claim advanced here is that subjects do not ignore inconsistent evidence. Subjects use inconsistent evidence, and they do so in different ways depending upon their goals. For example, in this study, subjects with the overarching class or type of activation hypothesis, formulated a *goal* to find evidence consistent with specific exemplars of this overarching activation hypothesis (find-evidence goal), such as "the I gene is an activator." When faced with inconsistent evidence regarding their specific (or "local") exemplar hypothesis, subjects changed their local hypothesis—for example, from "the I gene is an activator" to one involving "the P gene is an activator"—while, at the same time, leaving untouched their overarching type of hypothesis (i.e., activation).

Artificial universe studies have further failed to offer an account of why or when subjects start to consider or propose alternative hypotheses on the basis of inconsistent evidence. Using the present approach, I advance an account of how subjects begin to consider and propose alternative hypotheses. Specifically, when evidence inconsistent with all of the subjects' specific (or local) hypotheses had accumulated, they demonstrated that they realized that no specific (local) hypothesis was tenable, at which point they set a *new goal* to generate a new and/or alternate hypothesis (find-hypothesis goal). This changing of goals is crucial to understanding why subjects do not readily propose alternate overarching *types* of hypotheses in the face of inconsistent evidence. It is only when subjects change goals to determine the cause of inconsistent findings that subjects begin to consider new hypotheses. Thus, the hypothesis offered here is that subjects' ability to consider other overarching hypotheses—as well as their failure to do so—is directly affected by their current goal. (Dunbar, 1993, pp. 425–428)

## STUDIES 1 AND 2: COMPARISONS OF MODELS OF SCIENTIFIC DISCOVERY

In the following section, the results of Studies 1 and 2 are compared with other research that has demonstrated the types of constraints and heuristics that occur in the process of scientific discovery.

Recently, a number of models of scientific discovery have been proposed that have specified general heuristics that are used in reasoning scientifically (e.g., Holland, Holyoak, Nisbett, and Thagard, 1986; Klahr and Dunbar, 1988; Kulkarni and Simon, 1988; Langley, Simon, Bradshaw, and Zytkow, 1987; Shrager and Langley, 1990). All of these models incorporate mechanisms for inducing hypotheses from data. A major challenge for all these models has been to characterize the constraints that operate on the types of hypotheses proposed, experiments conducted, and data to make inductions over. One approach to the issue of what types of experiments to conduct and what types of data should be used to induce new hypotheses has been to build in heuristics that will take advantage of surprising results (e.g., Kulkarni and Simon, 1988). When an experimental result falls outside the bounds of those predicted by the current hypothesis, the model will focus on the surprising results and attempt to explain the cause of the puzzling event. Although Kulkarni and Simon built this heuristic into their model to simulate the scientific reasoning strategies that Krebs used in his research, it is interesting to ask whether nonscientists would also use this heuristic. The results of these studies indicate that few subjects spontaneously adopted this heuristic.

One possible reason why the exploit-surprising-results heuristic was not used is that it is not necessarily advantageous to follow up a surprising result, as the result may be due to a wide variety of reasons such as errors in the observation or measurement. The two studies reported in this article indicate that subjects will identify results as surprising only after they have conducted a *series* of experiments that provide results that are inconsistent with the current hypothesis. Surprising results will only be followed up once it has been discovered that the current hypothesis cannot be modified to fit the data. Subjects will not treat every anomalous result as worthy of being followed up until their current hypothesis has been totally rejected or has been confirmed. In Study 1, subjects only attempted to explain inconsistent results after they had conducted all their haploid experiments. In Study 2, the majority of subjects only attempted to explain the inconsistent or surprising results once they had discovered activation. Thus, the application of the exploit-surprising-results heuristic is conservative: Subjects' initial reaction to a result that is inconsistent with their current hypothesis is not to focus on the finding, but to search elsewhere for evidence that is consistent with their hypothesis.

Another possible explanation for subjects' unwillingness to use inconsistent data is that subjects treated inconsistent evidence as errors in the data, and this "insulated" their hypotheses against inconsistent evidence. That is, subjects could argue that any result that was inconsistent with their hypothesis was an error. Gorman (1986) demonstrated that when subjects are told that there is a possibility of error in data, the subjects assume that inconsistent evidence is due to error (see also Kern, 1983). However, in the studies reported here, subjects were not told that there was error in the data and no subject explicitly stated or implicitly indicated that they thought there was error in the data. Furthermore, this explanation would not account for the finding that performance improved between Studies 1 and 2.

The work of Qin and Simon (1990) is also relevant to the research reported in this article. They demonstrated that by giving subjects that data on planetary motion that Kepler had access to (i.e., a set of numbers), it is possible for some subjects to propose a rule that is equivalent to Kepler's law. Furthermore, they argued that the strategies subjects used to induce the rule was equivalent to the heuristics that the BACON series of programs uses (cf. Langley et al., 1987).

Thus, their research demonstrated that with the appropriate data, subjects can induce an appropriate rule, and that it is possible to investigate the cognitive mechanisms involved in a particular scientific discovery. The work reported in this article took a different, but related approach: Subjects actually had to design experiments and collect their own data, rather than being given the data. Furthermore, subjects were working within a real scientific domain that is influenced by knowledge of the domain. In the Qin and Simon study, subjects were not told that the numbers that they were dealing with were the positions of planets: They were only told that they were a set of numbers. Thus, there was no opportunity for hypotheses about planetary motion to influence the discovery process. As the results of both studies reported in this article demonstrate, prior knowledge of the domain had a large effect upon the goals that subjects instantiated and the design and interpretation of their experimental results.

In the Klahr and Dunbar (1988) article on scientific reasoning strategies, we argued that scientific discovery could be considered as a search in two problem spaces: a space of hypotheses and a space of experiments (see also Klahr, Dunbar, and Fay, 1989; Simon and Lea, 1974). Using this framework, we identified two different strategies for generating new hypotheses about how a new key works on a programmable device. One was to search memory for possible hypotheses (hypothesis space search) and the other was to conduct experiments until a new hypothesis could be generated from the data (experiment space search). When the same type of analysis is applied to the current set of studies, it can be seen that subjects used both types of search, rather than using one type of search exclusively. The subjects who proposed inhibition conducted experiments to collect data, and then searched memory for a mechanism that could explain their results. The subjects who proposed activation did search the experiment space, but with the find-evidence goal, rather than searching for evidence to induce new hypotheses from. The different findings obtained here indicate that subjects switched between the two spaces. Furthermore, the goals that the subjects set constrained the search of both spaces, determining the types of information retrieved from memory and the types of experiments conducted. *These findings indicate that when subjects reason in a complex domain, their strategies also become more complex, requiring the use of different strategies that necessitate a coordinated search of a hypothesis space and an experiment space* [italics added]. . . .

The primary reason for using a simulated genetics environment in these studies was to investigate scientific reasoning in a context that would be more similar to real science than those that are currently used in cognitive research on this topic. By using this approach, it was hoped that the conceptual processes underlying scientific discovery in real scientific domains could be identified.

The research approach taken here may appear related to historical approaches to scientific discovery, but is, in fact, very different in content and motivation. Usually, researchers using historical data have analyzed historical accounts of scientific discoveries to uncover the mechanisms involved in scientific reasoning. For example, Nersessian (1992) and others (e.g., Gooding, 1992; Holmes, 1985; Tweney, 1985) conducted detailed analyses of diaries and notebooks that make it possible to infer some of the cognitive processes involved in particular scientific discoveries. *The limitations of this approach are that only* indirect *and selective access to the cognitive processes underlying scientists' discoveries can be obtained. However, in the research reported in this article, a different, more direct approach was taken. Here, on-line access to the cognitive processes that underlie components of a scientific discovery can be obtained. Specifically, I drew from a variety of historical sources to construct a task that made it possible to investigate a number of important features underlying scientific reasoning. These tasks provided key insights into the cognitive processes involved in the representation of hypotheses and the change in hypotheses in the course of discovering a new scientific concept. Such insights are not obtainable from diary and notebook studies because they do not have access to on-line cognitive processes, but to selective components of particular discoveries.* (Dunbar, 1993, pp. 428–431, italics added)

## STUDIES 1 AND 2: COMPARISON WITH MONOD AND JACOB

In the following section, interpretive comparisons are drawn between the "experiment on-line" research that permitted undergraduate students to rediscover specific genetic mechanisms and the original discovery by Jacob and Monod.

Despite the differences between the original discovery of Monod and Jacob and that observed in the studies reported here, clear similarities exist between the conceptual processes employed by the subjects and those employed by Jacob and Monod: A key element in Jacob and Monod's discovery of the lactose operon was their use of the concept of inhibition, which they already know of (cf. Judson, 1979), in a new concept (i.e., genetic regulation). This was not merely the application of the concept of inhibition to a new domain, but was the generation of a concept of mutually interacting components that worked by inhibition. This was the same problem facing the subjects in the two studies reported here. Undoubtedly, all subjects had, at some point, used the concept of inhibition (e.g., subjects had all taken an introductory course in psychology in which the concept of inhibition had been discussed). The problem for the subjects was to conceive of a new mechanism that could be applied to genetic regulation. That is, the subjects generated a new concept of mutually interacting genes that regulate enzyme production by inhibition. These subjects behaved just like Monod and Jacob. Furthermore, just like the subjects in the experiments reported in this article, Monod and Jacob had difficulty in formulating the concept of inhibitory control due to their belief in activation: In the 1940s, Monod began investigating the conditions under which *E. coli* could be *induced* to produce certain enzymes. Monod hypothesized that this induction of enzymes was an activation mechanism, or a positive process. (Note that in molecular biology, induction refers to the conditions that initiate a biological process, such as the conditions under which *E. coli* produce the β-gal enzyme). Judson (1979), in his account of the Jacob and Monod discovery, stated that Monod and Jacob continued to think of the mechanism underlying the induction of enzymes as activation. That is, they saw the mechanism underlying enzyme induction as a positive induction process where enzyme production is switched on (i.e., positive induction or activation), rather than turned off (i.e., negative induction or inhibition):

> . . . Monod's persistent sense of the logic of induction as a positive process: he was convinced that the inducer turned something on. The only universal mechanism for enzyme synthesis that had been suggested so far was Monod's own extension of positive induction—his idea that production of a constitutive enzyme [*E. Coli* producing β-gal even when no lactose is present] was kept on by an inducer made internally by the cell itself. . . . The mental set continued even when the enzymes normally constitutive were shown to be repressible systems, turned off by an abundance of their own end product. (Judson, 1979, p. 403)

The types of conclusions that the subjects came to using I- mutants were similar of those of Monod and Jacob. Both the subjects in this study, and Monod and Jacob, thought that an I- was sending out more activation than the normal *E. coli*. It was only when experiments were conducted that crossed I- females with I+ males, that the idea of activation and proposed inhibition were abandoned (cf. Judson, 1979). Similarly, it was only when the subjects began to conduct the same types of experiments as Monod and Jacob (I−P+O+ female with I+O+P+ male) that they then proposed inhibition.

In Study 1, the 4 subjects who proposed only inhibition used a similar logic as that of Monod and Jacob. They realized that the I gene must be sending out a repressor by using diploid mutations. However, only 1 of the 40 subjects across the two studies proposed a mechanism that provided a complete mechanism of control. Clearly, the problem was very difficult for the subjects here, as it was for the scientists who originally discovered the mechanism.

*In conclusion, the results reported in this article demonstrate that by using a complex problem taken from real science, fundamental insights into the conceptual processes underlying scientific discovery can be revealed: The findings of these studies provide evidence supporting the conclusion that the goals subjects set affected all aspects of the discovery of new concepts in a scientific domain, including the generation of new hypotheses, the strategies for conducting experiments, and the evaluation of consistent and inconsistent evidence* [italics added]. An examination of scientists at work on related problems reveals that they, too, exhibited similar patterns of discovery as those uncovered here.

Clearly, other conceptual processes must be involved in scientific discovery. François Jacob, in his account of the discovery of the mechanism of genetic regulation in *E. coli*, commented that "Evidently, the world of science, like that of art or religion, was a world created by the human imagination, but within very strict constraints imposed by nature and the human brain" (Jacob, 1988, p. 306). My ongoing research on real scientists engaged in research in their laboratories (cf. Dunbar, 1992), further addresses the constraints and imagination underlying the process of scientific discovery. (Dunbar, 1993, pp. 430–432)

# 2

# Scientific Discovery Heuristics and Developmental Level

## *SCIENTIFIC REASONING AND DEVELOPMENTAL DIFFERENCES: OVERVIEW*

Klahr, Fay, and Dunbar (1993) summarize their research in the following account.

Scientific discovery involves search in a space of hypotheses and a space of experiments. We describe an investigation of developmental differences in the search constraint heuristics used in scientific reasoning. Sixty-four subjects (technically trained college students, community college students with little technical training, sixth graders, and third graders) were taught how to use a programmable robot. Then they were presented with a new operation, provided with a hypothesis about how it might work, and asked to conduct experiments to discover how it really did work. The suggested hypothesis was always incorrect, as subjects could discover if they wrote informative experiments, and it was either plausible or implausible. The rule for how the unknown operation actually worked was either very similar or very dissimilar to the given hypothesis. Children focused primarily on plausible hypotheses, conducted a limited set of experiments, designed experiments that were difficult to interpret, and were unable to induce implausible (but correct) hypotheses from data. Adults were much better than children in discovering implausible rules. The performance deficits we found were not simply the result of children's inadequate encoding or mnemonic skills. Instead, the adults appear to use domain-general skills that go beyond the logic of confirmation and disconfirmation and deal with the coordination of search in two spaces: a space of hypotheses and a space of experiments. (Klahr, Fay, and Dunbar, 1993, p. 111)

## SCIENTIFIC REASONING AND DEVELOPMENTAL DIFFERENCES: BACKGROUND

Klahr, Fay, and Dunbar (1993) provide the following introduction to their research.

Scientific discovery requires the integration of a complex set of cognitive skills, including the search for hypotheses via induction or analogy, the design and execution of experiments, the interpretation of experimental outcomes, and the revision of hypotheses (Klahr & Dunbar, 1988). There are two long-standing disputes about the developmental course of these skills: (a) the "child-as-scientist" debate asks whether or not it makes sense to describe the young child as a scientist; (b) the "domain-specific or domain-general" debate revolves around the appropriate attribution for whatever differences in children and adults may exist. The first issue is controversial because, although there is considerable evidence that young children possess some rudiments of scientific reasoning (Brewer & Samarapungavan, 1991; Karmiloff-Smith, 1988), there appears to be a long and erratic course of development, instruction, and experience before the component skills of the scientific method are mastered, integrated, and applied reliably to a wide range of situations (Fay, Klahr, & Dunbar, 1990; Kuhn, Amsel, & O'Loughlin, 1988; Mitroff, 1974; Kern, Mirels, & Hinshaw, 1983; Siegler & Liebert, 1975).

The second issue derives from a lack of consensus about the extent to which developmental differences in performance on scientific reasoning tasks results from domain-specific or domain-general acquisitions. . . . On the one hand, acquisition of domain-specific knowledge influences not only the substantive structural knowledge in the domain (by definition) but also the processes used to generate and evaluate new hypotheses in that domain (Carey, 1985; Keil, 1981; Wiser, 1989). On the other hand, in highly constrained discovery contexts, young children correctly reason about hypotheses and select appropriate experiments to evaluate them, even when the context is far removed from any domain-specific knowledge (Sodian, Zaitchik, & Carey, 1991).

The two principal ways (aside from direct instruction) in which children acquire such domain-specific knowledge are observation and experimentation. Analysis of children's performance as *observational* scientists is exemplified by Vosniadou and Brewer's [1992] investigations of children's mental models of the earth. Such studies involve assessments of children's attempts to integrate their personal observations (e.g., the earth looks flat) with theoretical assertions conveyed to them by adults and teachers (e.g., the earth is a sphere). Similarly, children's understanding of illness concepts (see Hergenrather & Rabinowitz, 1991) is based primarily on their observations in the domain, rather than on their experiments. Issues of experimental design do not arise in this context. *Experimental* science adds to the demands of observational science the burden of formulating informative experiments. Studies investigating young children's ability to design factorial experiments (Case, 1974; Siegler & Liebert, 1975) focus on experimental aspects of science, as do studies of children's performance in experimental microworlds (e.g., Schauble, 1990).

We have approached the study of developmental differences in scientific reasoning by attempting to disentangle these different aspects of scientific discovery, while using a context that provides a plausible laboratory microcosm of real-world scientific discovery. We view scientific discovery as a type of problem solving (Klahr & Dunbar, 1988; Simon, 1977) in which domain-general heuristics for constraining search in a problem space play a central role. *In this paper, we describe a study that illustrates some important developmental differences in subjects' use of several domain-general search heuristics. We compare the ability of children and adults to reason in a context designed to simulate some of the key problems faced by an experimental scientist. In our task, subjects' domain-specific knowledge biases them to view some hypotheses as plausible and others as implausible. However, they must rely on domain-general heuristics to guide them in designing experiments. In summary, our focus is on developmental differences in domain-general heuristics for experimental design, in a context where domain-specific knowledge influences the plausibility of different hypotheses.* (Klahr, Fay, and Dunbar, 1993, pp. 112–113, italics added)

In the following section, Klahr, Fay, and Dunbar (1993) present their theory of scientific discovery processes.

We view scientific discovery as a problem-solving process involving search in two distinct, but related, problem spaces. Our work is based on Klahr and Dunbar's (1988) SDDS framework (Scientific Discovery as Dual Search), which elucidates a set of interdependent processes for coordinating search in a space of experiments and a space of hypotheses. The three main processes are:

*1. Searching the hypothesis space.* SDDS characterizes the process of generating new hypotheses as a type of problem-solving search, in which the initial state consists of some knowledge about a domain, and the goal state is a hypothesis that can account for some or all of that knowledge in a more concise or universal form. Several mechanisms have been proposed to account for the way in which initial hypotheses are generated. These include memory search, analogical mapping, remindings, and discovery of effective representations (Dunbar & Schunn, 1990; Gentner, 1983; Gick & Holyoak, 1983; Kaplan & Simon, 1990; Klahr & Dunbar, 1988; Ross, 1984; Shrager, 1987). Each of these mechanisms emphasizes a different aspect of the way in which search in the hypothesis space is initiated and constrained.

Once generated, hypotheses are evaluated for their initial plausibility. Expertise plays a role here, as subjects' familiarity with a domain tends to give them strong biases about what is plausible in the domain. Plausibility, in turn, affects the order in which hypotheses are evaluated: highly likely hypotheses tend to be tested before unlikely hypotheses (Klayman & Ha, 1987; Wason, 1968a). Furthermore, subjects may adopt different experimental strategies for evaluating plausible and implausible hypotheses.

*2. Searching the experiment space.* Hypotheses are evaluated through experimentation. But it is not immediately obvious what constitutes a "good" or "informative" experiment. In constructing experiments, subjects are faced with a problem-solving task paralleling their search for hypotheses. However, in this case search is in a space of experiments rather than in a space of hypotheses. Ideally, experiments should discriminate among rival hypotheses. Subjects must be able to plan ahead by making predictions about which experimental results could support or reject various hypotheses. This involves search in a space of experiments that is only partially defined at the outset. Constraints on the search must be added during the problem-solving process.

One of the most important constraints is to produce experiments that will yield interpretable outcomes. This, in turn, requires domain-general knowledge about one's own information-processing limitations, as well as domain-specific knowledge about the pragmatic constraints of the particular discovery context. Furthermore, utilization of this knowledge to design experiments capable of producing interpretable outcomes requires a mapping from hypotheses to experiments and an ability to predict what results might occur.

*3. Evaluating evidence.* This involves a comparison of the predictions derived from a hypothesis with the results obtained from the experiment. Compared to the binary feedback provided to subjects in the typical psychology experiment, real-world evidence evaluation is not so straightforward. Relevant features must first be extracted, potential noise must be suppressed or corrected, and the resulting internal representation must be compared with earlier predictions. Theoretical biases influence not only the strength with which hypotheses are held in the first place—and hence the amount of disconfirming evidence necessary to refute them—but also the features in the evidence that will be attended to and encoded (Wisniewski & Medin, 1991).

Each of the components listed above is a potential source of developmental change, and most investigators have studied them in isolation. . . . *We have approached the study of scientific reasoning by using tasks that require coordinated search in both the experiment space and the hypothesis space, as well as the evaluation of evidence produced by subject-generated experiments. Rather than eliminating search in either space, we have focused on the coordination of both, because we believe that it is an essential aspect of scientific reasoning.* (Klahr, Fay, and Dunbar, 1993, pp. 113–115, italics added)

## SCIENTIFIC REASONING AND DEVELOPMENTAL DIFFERENCES: DESIGN

### Rationale

Klahr, Fay, and Dunbar (1993) summarize the rationale for their research in the following account.

In this paper, we focus on developmental differences in the heuristics used to constrain search in the experiment space. We were interested in the extent to which such heuristics would vary according to age, amount of formal scientific training, and the plausibility of the hypotheses under investigation. Although most studies demonstrate that subjects tend to attempt to confirm, rather than disconfirm, their hypotheses (cf. Klayman & Ha, 1987), such studies typically use hypotheses about which subjects have no strong prior beliefs about plausibility or implausibility. In contrast, we used a context in which plausibility played an important role.

Results from earlier investigations (Dunbar & Klahr, 1989) suggested that, in the domain in which we planned to test them, subjects at all ages and technical levels would be likely to share *domain-specific* knowledge that would bias them in the same direction with respect to the relative plausibility of different hypotheses. This allowed us to determine how search in the experiment space was influenced by the hypothesis' plausibility. We expected the effects of age and scientific training to reveal differences in the *domain-general* heuristics used to constrain search in the experiment space. Such domain-general heuristics might include rules for effecting normative approaches to hypothesis testing as well as pragmatic rules for dealing with processing limitations in encoding, interpreting, and remembering experimental outcomes. (Klahr, Fay, and Dunbar, 1993, p. 115)

### Subjects

Klahr, Fay, and Dunbar (1993) describe the research subjects in the following section.

Four subject groups participated: 12 Carnegie Mellon (CM) undergraduates, 20 community college (CC) students, 17 "sixth" graders (a mixed class of fifth to seventh graders, mean age 11 years) and 15 third graders (mean age, 9 years).

The adult groups were selected to contrast subjects with respect to technical and scientific training. Sixth graders were selected because they represent the age at which many of the components of "formal reasoning" are purported to be available, and the third graders were chosen because pilot work had indicated they were the youngest group who could perform reliably in our task. In addition, the two younger groups match the ages of children studied in many other investigations of children's scientific reasoning skills (e.g., Kuhn, Amsel, & O'Loughlin, 1988).

CMs were mainly science or engineering majors. . . . They reported having taken about two programming courses, and they rated themselves between average and above average on technical and scientific skills. All CCs were non-science majors (General Studies, Paralegal, Communications, Pre-nursing, etc.). . . . CCs had little training in mathematics or physical sciences beyond high school, and less than half of them had taken a college course in Biology or Chemistry. While 70% of them had used computer-based word processors and 45% had used spreadsheets, only 3 of the 20 had ever taken a programming course.

Children were volunteers from an urban private school and came primarily from academic and professional families. They were selected to be young "equivalents" of the CMs with respect to both the likelihood of ultimately attending college and age-appropriate computer experience. All sixth graders had at least 6 months of Logo experience, and most had more than a year of experience. All but one of the third graders had at least 1 month of Logo, with the majority having 6 months to a year of experience. Note that CCs had less programming experience than the third graders. (Klahr, Fay, and Dunbar, 1993, pp. 115–116)

## Material: The BT Microworld

Klahr, Fay, and Dunbar (1993) describe the experiment material in the following section.

We used a computer microworld—called BT—in which subjects enter a sequence of commands to a "spaceship" which then responds by carrying out various maneuvers. The discovery context was established by first instructing subjects about all of BT's basic features and then asking them to extend that knowledge by discovering how a new—and uninstructed—function works in the microworld. Subjects proposed hypotheses and evaluated them by experimenting, i.e., by writing programs to test their hypotheses. . . .

The spaceship moves around in the left-hand panel according to instructions that are entered in its memory when subjects "press" (point and click) a sequence of keys on the keypad displayed on the right. The basic execution cycle involves first clearing the memory and returning BT to "base" with the CLR/HOME key and then entering a series of up to 16 instructions, each consisting of a function key (the command) and a 1- or 2-digit number (the argument). The five command keys are: ↑, move forward; ↓, move backward; ←, turn left; →, turn right; and FIRE. When the GO key is pressed BT executes the program. For example, one might press the following series of keys:

CLR ↑ 5 ← 7 ↑ 3 → 15 FIRE 2 ↓ 8 GO.

When the GO key was pressed, BT would move forward 5 units, rotate counterclockwise 42° (corresponding to 7 min on an ordinary clock face), move forward 3 units, rotate clockwise 90°, fire (its "laser cannon") twice, and back up 8 units. (Klahr, Fay, and Dunbar, 1993, p. 116)

## Experimental Procedure

Klahr, Fay, and Dunbar (1993) provide the following details of the experimental procedure.

The study had three phases. In the first, subjects were introduced to BT and instructed on the use of each basic command. During this phase, the display did not include the RPT key. . . . Subjects were trained to criterion on how to write a series of commands to accomplish a specified maneuver. In the second phase, subjects were shown the RPT key. They were told that it required a numeric parameter (N) and that there could only be one RPT N in a program. They were told that their task was to find out how RPT worked by writing at least three programs and observing the results. At this point, the Experimenter suggested a specific hypothesis about how RPT might work.

One way that RPT might work is: [one of the four hypotheses described in the next section]. Write down three good programs that will allow you to see if the repeat key really does work this way. Think carefully about your program and then write the program down on the sheet of paper. . . . Once you have written your program down, I will type it in for you and then I will run it. You can observe what happens, and then you can write down your next program. So you write down a program, then I will type it in, and then you will watch what the program does. I want you to write three programs in this way.

Next, the third—and focal—phase began. Subjects wrote programs (experiments) to evaluate the given hypothesis. After each program had been written, but before it was run, subjects were asked to predict the behavior of BT. Subjects had access to a record of the programs they had written (but not to a record of BT's behavior).

Subjects were instructed to give verbal protocols. This gave us a record of

(a) what they thought about the kinds of programs they were writing while testing their hypotheses, (b) what they observed and inferred from the device's behavior, and (c) what their hypotheses were about how RPT actually worked. When subjects had written, run, and evaluated three experiments, they were given the option of either terminating or writing additional experiments if they were still uncertain about how RPT worked. The entire session lasted approximately 45 min. (Klahr, Fay, and Dunbar, 1993, pp. 116–117)

## Experimental Task Analysis: The Hypothesis Space

Klahr, Fay, and Dunbar (1993) present an analysis of the experimental hypothesis space in the following account.

In previous studies with adults and grade school children (Klahr & Dunbar, 1988), we found that there were two very "popular" hypotheses about the effect of RPT $N$ in a program:

A: Repeat the entire program $N$ times.

B: Repeat the last step $N$ times.

Subjects devoted a large proportion of their effort to exploring these two hypotheses. In contrast, there were two hypotheses that subjects were unlikely to propose at the outset:

C: Repeat the $N$th step once.

D: Repeat the last $N$ steps once.

The preference for A and B and the disinclination to propose C and D was found at all ages.

These four hypotheses about RPT $N$ (as well as many others) can be represented in a space of "frames" (Minsky, 1975). The basic frame consists of four slots, corresponding to four key attributes: (1) The role of $N$; does it *count* a number of repetitions (as in A and B) or does it *select* some segment of the program to be repeated (as in C and D)? We call A and B *Counter* hypotheses and C and D *Selector* hypotheses. (2) The unit of repetition; is it a step (as in B and C), the entire program (as in A), or a group of steps (as in D)? (3) Number of repetitions; 1, $N$, some other function of $N$, or none? (4) Boundaries of repeated segment; beginning of program, end of program, $N$th step from beginning, or end? Of the four slots, $N$-role is the most important, because a change in $N$-role from *Counter* to *Selector* mandates a change in several other attributes. For example, if $N$-role is *Counter*, the number of repetitions is $N$, whereas, if $N$-role is *Selector*, then the number of repetitions is 1. (Klahr, Fay, and Dunbar, 1993, pp. 118–119)

## Experimental Task Analysis: The Experiment Space

Klahr, Fay, and Dunbar (1993) provide an analysis of the experiment space in the following section.

Subjects could test their hypotheses by conducting experiments, i.e., by writing programs that included RPT and observing BT's behavior. The BT experiment space can be characterized in many ways: the total number of commands in a program, the location of RPT in a program, value of $N$, the specific commands in a program, the numerical arguments of specific commands, and so on. (For example, counting only commands, but not their numerical arguments, as distinct, there are over 30 billion distinct programs [$5^{15}$] that subjects could choose from for each experiment. Even if we consider only programs with 4 or fewer steps, there are nearly 800 different experiments to choose from [$5^4 + 5^3 + 5^2 + 5$].) In this paper, we characterize the experiment space in terms of just two parameters. The first is the length of the program preceding the RPT. The second is the value of $N$—the argument that RPT takes. Because both parameters must have values less than 16, there are 225 "cells" in the space. Within that space, we identify three distinct regions. Region 1 includes all programs with $N = 1$. Region 2 includes all programs in which $1 < N < \lambda$. Region 3 includes all programs in which $N \geq \lambda$. The regions are depicted in [Figure 2.1] together with illustrative programs, from the (4,1) cell in Region 1, the (3,2) cell in Region 2, and the (1,4) cell in Region 3.

Programs from different regions of the experiment space vary widely in how effective they are in supporting or refuting different hypotheses. (A complete analysis of the interaction between experiment space regions and hypotheses is given in Klahr, Dunbar, & Fay, 1990). Here we summarize the major differences between the regions.)

1. Region 1 programs have poor discriminating power. . . .

2. Region 2 programs provide maximal information about all of the common hypotheses, because they can distinguish between Counters and Selectors, and they can distinguish *which* Selector or Counter is operative. Region 2 produces different behavior under all four rules for any program in the region, and varying $N$ in a series of experiments in this region always produces different outcomes.

3. Region 3 experiments may yield confusing outcomes. For rules C (Repeat the $N$th step once) and D (Repeat the last $N$ steps once), programs in this region are executed under the subtle feature that values of $N$ greater than $\lambda$ are truncated to $N = \lambda$. Therefore, varying $N$ from one experiment to the next may give the impression that $N$ has no effect. For example, Rule D would generate the same behavior for ↑4 Fire 2 RPT 3 and ↑4 Fire 2 RPT 4. Some of the programs in this region are discriminating, but others either don't discriminate at all, or they depend on the truncation assumption to be fully understood. (Klahr, Fay, and Dunbar, 1993, pp. 118–119)

**Figure 2.1**
**Regions of the Experiment Space, Showing Illustrative Programs**

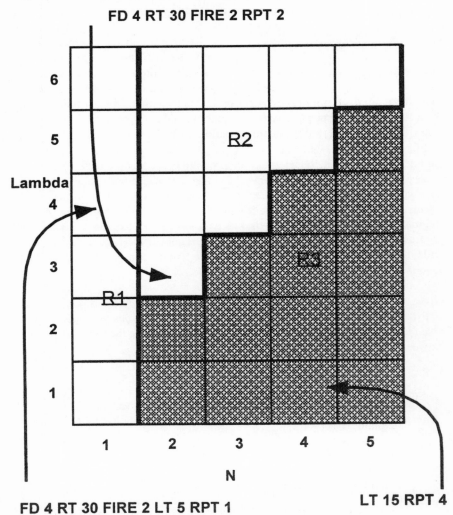

**FD 4 RT 30 FIRE 2 RPT 2**

**FD 4 RT 30 FIRE 2 LT 5 RPT 1**

**LT 15 RPT 4**

*Note:* Shown here is only the 6 × 5 subspace of the full 15 × 15 space.

*Source:* D. Klahr, A. L. Fay, and K. Dunbar (1993). Heuristics for scientific experimentation: A developmental study. *Cognitive Psychology, 25*, p. 119.

**Table 2.1**
**Design of Given-Actual Conditions**

| | Actual Rule | |
|---|---|---|
| | Counter | Selector |
| Given Hypothesis Counter | B: Repeat last step N times ↓ A: Repeat entire program N times | A: Repeat entire program N times ↓ D: Repeat the last N steps once |
| Selector | D: Repeat the last N steps once ↓ A: Repeat the entire program N times | C: Repeat step N once ↓ D: Repeat the last N steps once |

*Source:* D. Klahr, A. L. Fay, and K. Dunbar (1993). Heuristics for scientific experimentation: A developmental study. *Cognitive Psychology, 25*, p. 120.

## Experimental Controls

Klahr, Fay, and Dunbar (1993) provide details of the experimental conditions in the following section.

One consequence of domain-specific knowledge is that some hypotheses about the domain are more plausible than others. In this study we explored the effect of domain-specific knowledge by manipulating the role of plausible and implausible hypotheses. Our goal was to investigate the extent to which prior knowledge—as manifested in hypothesis plausibility—affected the types of experiments designed and the interpretation of results.

We provided each subject with an initial hypothesis about how RPT might work. The suggested hypothesis was always wrong. However, depending on the condition, subjects regarded it as either plausible or implausible (recall that both children and adults in earlier studies regarded Counter hypotheses as highly plausible and Selector hypotheses as implausible). In some conditions the suggested hypothesis was only "somewhat" wrong, in that it was from the same frame as the way that RPT actually worked. In others, it was "very" wrong, in that it came from a different frame than the actual rule.

The BT simulator was programmed so that each subject worked with a RPT command obeying one of the two Counter rules or two Selector rules described above. We used a between-subjects design, depicted in [Table 2.1]. The Given hypothesis is the one that was suggested by the experimenter, and the Actual Rule is the way that BT was programmed to work for a particular condition. The key feature is that RPT *never worked in the way that was suggested.* In each Given-Actual condition, there were three CMs, five CCs, four sixth graders, and four third graders (except for the Counter-Counter condition, which had three third graders and five sixth graders).

*Changing from a hypothesis within a frame to another hypothesis from the same frame (e.g., from one Counter to another Counter) corresponds to theory refinement.* However, as noted earlier, a change in *N*-role requires a simultaneous change in more than one attribute, because the values of some attributes are linked to the values of others. *Changing from a hypothesis from one frame to a hypothesis from a different frame (e.g., from a Counter to a Selector) corresponds to theory replacement.* (Klahr, Fay, and Dunbar, 1993, pp. 119–120, italics added)

## Experimental Protocols

Klahr, Fay, and Dunbar (1993) describe general aspects of subject protocols and provide a specific subject protocol in the following section.

The raw protocols provided the basis for all performance measures. They are comprised of subjects' written programs as well as transcriptions of subjects' verbalizations during the experimental phase. Before presenting the quantitative analysis of subjects' behavior, we examine the verbal protocol of a single subject in order to illustrate a variety of interesting qualitative aspects of subjects' behavior. (The full protocol is listed in the Appendix.) Our goal is to convey a general sense of subjects' approach to the task and to illustrate how we encoded and interpreted the protocols. In subsequent sections, we provide a detailed analysis based on the full set of protocols.

DP was a male CM subject in the Counter-Selector condition, and he was given Rule A: *Repeat entire program N times.* The actual rule was Rule C: *Repeat Nth step once.* DP discovered the correct rule after five experiments. Two characteristics of DP's protocol make it interesting (but not atypical). First, even before the first experiment, DP proposed an alternative to the Given hypothesis (2: "I want to test to see if RPT repeats the statements before it"). Second, throughout the experimental phase, DP made many explicit comments about the attributes of the experiment space. He clearly attended to the properties of a "good" experiment.

DP's goal in his first experiment is unambiguous (2–9): to determine whether RPT acts on instructions before or after the RPT command. To resolve this question DP concluded an experiment with easily distinguished commands before and after the RPT key. (This ability to write programs that contain useful "markers" is an important feature of our subjects' behavior, and we will return to it later.) This experiment allowed DP to discriminate between these two rival hypotheses. However, with respect to discriminating between the Given hypothesis (A), the Current hypothesis (B) and the Actual hypothesis (C), the program yielded ambiguous results. DP extracted from the first experiment the information he sought (17–18: "it appears that the repeat doesn't have any effect on any statements that come after it").

For the second experiment DP returned to the question of whether the Given hypothesis (A), or the Current hypothesis (B) was correct, and he increased λ from 1 to 2. He also included one step following the RPT "just to check" that RPT had no effect on instructions that follow it (22–23). Thus, DP was in fact testing three hypotheses; A, B, and "after." Once again, he used commands that could be easily discriminated. He wrote another program from Region 3 of the experiment space (λ = 2, N = 2). DP observed that there were two executions of the ↑ 2 instruction, and he concluded (29–30) that "it only repeats the statement immediately in front of it." While this conclusion is consistent with the data that DP had collected so far, the hypothesis (B) was not in fact how the RPT key worked.

For the third experiment, DP continued to put commands after RPT just to be sure they were not affected. However, given that his Current hypothesis had been confirmed in the previous experiment, he next wrote a program that further increased the length of the program. This was his first experiment in Region 2. The goal of this experiment was to "see what statements are repeated" (33). He realized that the outcome of this experiment was inconsistent with his Current hypothesis (B), while the outcome of the previous experiment was consistent with B (47: ". . . it seemed to act differently in number two and number three"). The unexpected result led DP to abandon Hypothesis B and to continue beyond the mandatory three experiments.

For the fourth experiment, DP used a different value of N (53–54: ". . . repeat three instead of repeat two, and see if that has anything to do with it"). Here too, DP demonstrated another important characteristic of many of our subjects' approach to experimentation. He used a very conservative incremental strategy, similar to VOTAT (vary one thing at a time) strategies described by Tschirgi (1980) and the Conservative Focusing strategy described by Bruner, Goodnow, and Austin (1956). This approach still led him to put commands after the RPT, even though he was confident that RPT had no effect on them, and even though they placed greater demands on his observational and recall processes. (At the λ-N level, DP executed VOTAT consistently throughout his series of five experiments. The λ-N pairs were: 1–2, 2–2, 3–2, 3–3, 3–1. For the last three experiments, even the specific commands and their parameters remained the same, and only N varied.) This moved him from Region 2 into Region 3, and while analyzing the results of this experiment (59–69) in conjunction with earlier results, DP changed from the Counter frame to the Selector frame. First he noticed that "the number three" statement (i.e., the ↓ 1) was repeated twice in this case but that "the turning statement" was repeated (i.e., executed) only once (59–61). The implied comparison was with the previous experiment in which the turning statement (i.e., "the right 15 command" [43]) was the command that got repeated.

*The next sentence is of particular interest: ". . . because when I change the number not only did it change . . . it didn't change the uh . . . the number that it repeated but it changed the uh . . . the actual instruction" (64–67). We believe that DP was attempting to articulate a change from the Counter frame to the Selector frame, as the following paraphrase of his comments indicates: "When I changed the value of N, it didn't change the number of repetitions, but it did change which commands got repeated."*

*DP went on to clearly state two instantiated versions of the correct rule by referring to previous results with N = 2 and N = 3, and he designed his fifth experiment to test his prediction with N = 1. The outcome of this final experiment, from Region 1, in conjunction with earlier results, was sufficient to convince him that he had discovered how RPT worked.* (Klahr, Fay, and Dunbar, 1993, pp. 120–121, italics added)


## SCIENTIFIC REASONING AND DEVELOPMENTAL DIFFERENCES: RESULTS

### Differential Success Rates

Klahr, Fay, and Dunbar (1993) present their findings concerning success rates in the following section.


Domain-specific knowledge—as manifested in subjects' expectations about what "repeat" might mean in this context—played an important role in subjects' ability to discover the Actual rule. . . . Regardless of what the Given hypothesis was, subjects found it easier to discover Counters (81%) than Selectors (35%). . . . There was also a main effect for group: the correct rule was discovered by 83% of the CMs, 65% of the CCs, 53% of the sixth graders, and 33% of the third graders. . . . This group effect is attributable to the Actual = Selector conditions, in which 56% of the adults but only 13% of the children were successful. . . . For Counters, adults and children were roughly equal in their success rates (88% versus 75%). . . .

The main effect for plausibility can also be attributed primarily to the children's performance in the Actual = Selector condition. Whereas 75% of the children discovered the rule when it was a Counter, only 13% discovered the rule when it was a Selector. . . . Adults were also better at discovering Counters than Selectors (88% versus 56%), although the effect was not as strong as for children . . . due to the surprisingly poor performance by the CC subjects in the Counter-Counter condition. (Klahr, Fay, and Dunbar, 1993, p. 122)

## Hypothesis Interpretation and Search

Klahr, Fay, and Dunbar (1993) present their findings concerning the effect of hypothesis plausibility on search behavior in the following section.

The purpose of presenting subjects with a Given hypothesis was to determine the extent to which search in the hypothesis space was influenced by the plausibility of the hypothesis being considered. This is one of the points at which domain-specific knowledge (which determines plausibility) might affect domain-general knowledge about experimental strategies, such as attempts to disconfirm, discriminating between rival hypotheses, and so on.

Prior to running the first experiment, subjects were asked to predict what would happen. Their predictions indicated the extent to which they understood and/or accepted the Given hypotheses. Each subject's response to the Given hypothesis was assigned to one of three categories: I, accept the Given hypothesis; II, accept the Given, but also propose an alternative (see the protocol of Subject DP, presented earlier); and III, reject the Given, and propose an alternative. . . .

There was a main effect of Given hypothesis (Counter versus Selector) on type of response. . . . This effect was attributable entirely to the third graders, who almost always accepted Counters and rejected Selectors. . . . There was also a main effect for group. . . .

In both conditions, the two adult groups always accepted the Given hypothesis, either on its own (Category I) or in conjunction with a proposed alternative (Category II). . . .

In contrast, no third grader and only two sixth graders ever proposed an alternative to compare to the Given (Category II). Children were approximately evenly divided between accepting the Given (Category I) or rejecting it (Category III). . . . Overall, adults were more likely to consider multiple alternatives than children: 10 of 29 adults in Category II, versus 2 of 31 children. . . .

Of the 25 subjects who proposed alternatives to the Given hypothesis, three proposed alternatives that could not be coded as either Counters or Selectors. For the remaining 22, there was a strong effect of the type of Given hypothesis on the type of alternative proposed. . . . In each group, Given = Counter subjects who proposed alternatives always proposed another Counter, whereas, across all four groups, only two of the Given = Selector alternatives were from the Selector frame. . . .

*In summary, when responding to the Given hypothesis, adults were able to consider more than a single hypothesis, whereas children were not. When subjects did propose alternatives, they tended to propose plausible rather than implausible alternatives (i.e., Counters rather than Selectors). As we shall see in the next section, this propensity to consider multiple versus single hypotheses can affect the type of experimental goals set by the subjects, which in turn can be used to impose constraints on search in the experiment space.* (Klahr, Fay, and Dunbar, 1993, pp. 123–125, italics added)

## Experiment Space Search

Klahr, Fay, and Dunbar (1993) describe experiment search strategies in the following section.

Different experimental strategies can . . . be inferred by classifying experiments in terms of experiment space regions. . . . As noted earlier, Region 2 is the most informative region, and adults appear to have understood its potential informativeness better than the children. Eleven of 12 CMs, 15 of 20 CCs, 10 of 17 sixth graders, and 8 of 15 third graders wrote at least one Region 2 experiment. . . . Another way to extract useful information from the E-space is to write experiments from more than a single region. Adults were more likely to sample different regions than were children. Ninety-one percent of the adults (100% of the CMs and 85% of the CCs) wrote experiments from at least two different regions of the experiment space. In contrast, only 29% of the sixth graders and 6% of the third graders sampled from more than one region. . . . Staying in one region of the experiment space is only detrimental if the region fails to discriminate between hypotheses (e.g., Region 1 for hypothesis B versus D) or if it fails to adequately demonstrate the correct hypothesis (e.g., Region 3 for hypothesis D).

All of the third graders in Actual = Selector conditions who stayed in one region were in either Region 1 or 3. For the sixth graders in Actual = Selector conditions, 75% who stayed in one region were in Region 3. Thus, for the children, the failure to run experiments from different regions of the experiment space severely limited their ability to extract useful information from the outcomes of their experiments.

The common pattern here is that there is little or no difference between the CM and CC subjects, who, when combined, tend to differ from the two children's groups. For some measures, the sixth graders cluster with the adult subjects. Taken as a whole, this pattern suggests a developmental effect, rather than a training effect, for subjects' sensitivity to the potential informativeness of different types of experiments as a function of the Given hypothesis. Moreover, by some of our measures, this effect appears between third and sixth grades. (Klahr, Fay, and Dunbar, 1993, p. 129)

## Relating Experiment Outcomes to Hypotheses

Klahr, Fay, and Dunbar (1993) analyze subjects' ability to coordinate experiment outcomes and hypothesis modification in the following section.

In order to determine the effect of experiment space region on overall success rate, we calculated the probability of discovering the correct rule as a function of the Regions actually visited. When success rates are aggregated over all grades and conditions, there appears to be no benefit from having been in Region 2. Sixty-four percent of the 44 subjects who had one or more Region 2 experiments were successful, while 45% of the 20 who never entered Region 2 were successful. . . . However, as predicted, a closer analysis reveals a clear effect of Region 2's utility for discovering Selectors. . . . As just noted, most subjects in the Actual = Counter conditions were successful, regardless of whether or not they entered Region 2. However, for all but one subject in the Actual = Selector conditions, having at least one experiment in Region 2 is a necessary but not sufficient condition for success. (Klahr, Fay, and Dunbar, 1993, pp. 132–133)

## SCIENTIFIC DISCOVERY HEURISTICS AND DEVELOPMENTAL LEVEL: DISCUSSION

### Heuristics for Experiment Space Search

Klahr, Fay, and Dunbar (1993) discuss differences and similarities in subjects' use of heuristics to search in the experiment space in the following section.

Both CM and CC adults were effective at drastically pruning the experiment space. Over half of their experiments occurred within the $\lambda \leq 4$, $N \leq 3$ area of the experiment space, which represents only 5% of the full space. In contrast, less than one-third of the children's experiments were so constrained. Furthermore, the pattern of results described in the previous section revealed a developmental trend in the overall systematicity and effectiveness with which subjects searched the experiment space. Our interpretation of this pattern is that it is a consequence of developmental differences in the application of a set of domain-general heuristics for searching the experiment space. The four principle heuristics are:

1. *Use the plausibility of a hypothesis to choose experimental strategy.* . . . For implausible hypotheses, adults and young children used different strategies. Adults' response to implausibility was to propose hypotheses from frames other

than the Given frame and to conduct experiments that could discriminate between them. Our youngest children's response was to propose a hypothesis from a different, but plausible frame, and then to ignore the initial, and implausible, hypothesis while attempting to demonstrate the correctness of the plausible one. Third graders were particularly susceptible to this strategy, but by sixth grade, subjects appeared to understand the type of experiments that will be informative.

*2. Focus on one dimension of an experiment or hypothesis.* Experiments and hypotheses are both complex entities having many aspects on which one could focus. In this study, experiments could vary at the $\lambda$-$N$ level, at the command level, or even at the level of arguments for commands. . . .

Use of this focusing heuristic was manifested in different ways with respect to hypotheses and experiments. For hypotheses, it led all groups except the third graders to focus initially on the number of times something was repeated when given Counters, and what was repeated when given Selectors. . . .

For experiments, it led to a characteristic pattern of between-experiment moves that minimized changes at the command level. Here, the CM adults stood apart from the other three groups. They were much more likely than any of the three groups to make conservative moves—that is, to minimize differences in program content between one program and the next. Although there are few sequential dependencies in the informativeness of experiment space regions, CM adults may have used this heuristic to reduce the cognitive load imposed when comparing the outcomes of two programs.

Interestingly, only the third graders failed to use this heuristic when searching the hypothesis space, whereas only the CM adults used it effectively when searching the experiment space. It is possible that, because the hypothesis search aspect of the discovery task is so familiar, all but the third graders were able to use the focusing heuristic. In contrast, when confronted with the relatively novel experimental design aspect of the task, even adults, if untrained in science, remained unaware of the utility of a conservative change strategy.

*3. Maintain observability.* As BT moves along the screen from one location to another, it leaves no permanent record of its behavior. Subjects must remember what BT actually did. Thus, one heuristic is to write short programs in order to make it easy to remember what happened and to compare the results to those predicted by the Current hypotheses. At the level of individual commands, this heuristic produces small arguments for the ↑ and ↓ commands, so that BT does not go off the screen. There were clear differences in the use of this heuristic. Adults almost always used it, whereas the youngest children often wrote programs that were very difficult to encode. This heuristic depends upon knowledge of one's own information processing limitations as well as a knowledge of the device. . . .

*4. Design experiments giving characteristic results.* Physicians look for "markers" for diseases, and physicists design experiments in which suspected particles will leave "signatures." In the BT domain, this heuristic is instantiated as "use many distinct commands." This heuristic maximizes the interpretability of experimental outcomes. It is extremely difficult to isolate the cause of a particular piece of BT behavior when many of the commands in a program are the same. All four groups were roughly equivalent in their use of this heuristic; on average, about half of all programs did not contain any repeated commands.

Overall, adults and children differed widely in their use of these heuristics. Adults not only appeared to use each of them but also appeared to be able to deal with their inherent contradictions. No subject ever used the 1,1 cell, even though it would yield the easiest to observe behavior, because it is so uninformative with respect to discriminating among rival hypotheses. Additionally, in a related study (Klahr, Dunbar, & Fay, 1989), adults' experiments were significantly *over*-represented in the $\lambda = 3$, $N = 2$ cell of the experiment space. This cell represents the shortest possible Region 2 experiment, and its over-representation suggests a compromise between informativeness and simplicity. Adults' tendency to cluster their experiments in the $4 \times 3$ experiment space in the present study represents a similar compromise among competing heuristics.

In contrast, children either failed to use these heuristics at all or they let one of them dominate. For example, one approximation to the "characteristic result" heuristic would be to write long experiments that could generate unique behavior, although that would violate the "maintain observability" heuristic. Even on their first experiments, adults tended to write relatively short programs. Only one-third of them wrote first programs with $\lambda > 3$, whereas 80% of the children wrote programs with $\lambda > 3$. (Klahr, Fay, and Dunbar, 1993, pp. 134–136)

## Developmental Differences in Scientific Problem Solving

Klahr, Fay, and Dunbar (1993) compare the scientific reasoning behavior of adults and children in the following section.

Our study yielded a picture of both similarities and differences in the way that children and adults formulate hypotheses and design experiments to evaluate them. At the top level of the cycle of scientific reasoning—that is, the level of hypothesis formation, experimentation and outcome interpretation—older elementary school children approached the discovery task in an appropriate way. Most sixth graders and some third graders understood that their task was to produce evidence to be used in support of an argument about a hypothesis. Contrary to Kuhn et al. (1988), they were able to distinguish between theory (hypotheses) and evidence. However, when placed in a context requiring the coordination of search in two spaces, children's performances were markedly inferior to adults' (both with and without technical and scientific training).

An examination of the fine structure of the subjects' sequences of experiments and hypotheses revealed that their overall performance differences could be attributed to characteristic differences in how they searched both the hypothesis space and the experiment space. The most important difference in hypothesis space search was in the way that adults and children responded to plausible and implausible hypotheses. When adults were given an implausible hypothesis, they established a goal of designing an experiment that could discriminate between the given implausible hypothesis and a plausible hypothesis of their own creation (usually one of the standard Counters).

When children were given hypotheses to evaluate, they were not insensitive to whether they were plausible or implausible, but they responded by generating a different goal than the adults'. In the implausible case, rather than simultaneously considering two alternative hypotheses, children focused only on a plausible one of their own making (a Counter), and attempted to generate what they believed would be extremely convincing evidence for it. This was not an unreasonable goal, but it produced uninformative experiments. More specifically, in order to generate a convincing case for a Counter hypothesis, third graders chose large values of $N$, so that the effect of the number of repetitions would be unambiguous. Because their goal was demonstration, inconsistencies were interpreted not as disconfirmations, but rather as either errors or temporary failures to demonstrate the desired effect. When subsequent efforts to demonstrate the Counter hypothesis were successful, they were accepted as sufficient. Because the third graders did not seek global consistency, they extracted only local information from experimental outcomes. Analogous results with respect to lack of global consistency have been reported by Markman (1979). She demonstrated that children between 8 and 11 years old have difficulty noticing internal contradictions in relatively brief text passages. Markman suggested that children focus on the reasonableness of individual statements, rather than their collective consistency. Similarly, our youngest children selectively focused on specific experimental outcomes, rather than seeking a hypothesis that could account for all of them.

The BT context elicited behavior in our third graders that is characteristic of younger children in simpler contexts. Resistance to disconfirming evidence has been observed in studies of discrimination learning (Tumblin & Gholson, 1981), but it has been limited to much younger children. For example, Gholson, Levine, and Phillips (1972) found that kindergarten children maintained disconfirmed hypotheses on about half of the negative feedback trials, while by second grade the rate dropped to 10%. The complexity of the discovery context, in conjunction with strong plausibility biases, may have caused our third graders to function like kindergarten children in the simpler discrimination learning task.

With respect to search heuristics in the experiment space, children were less able than adults to constrain their search, they tended not to consider pragmatic constraints, and they were unsystematic in the way that they designed experiments. These findings indicate that one of the problems for the younger children is to apply effective search constraints on their experiments. This viewpoint is consistent with research on the effects of constraints on problem solving in younger children. When presented with "standard" puzzles (involving search in a single problem space), young children perform much better when the order of subgoals is constrained by the structure of the materials than when they have to decide for themselves what to do first (Klahr, 1985; Klahr & Robinson, 1981). Here too, we find the third graders in our dual-search situation behaving analogously to younger children in single-search contexts. That is, in our study, when given a task in which they had to impose multiple constraints on hypotheses and experimental design, children did not conduct appropriate experiments. However, in studies where both hypotheses and experimental choices are highly constrained, young children can select appropriate experiments (Sodian, Zaitchik, & Carey, 1991).

*Overall, the SDDS framework has helped us to begin to answer some enduring questions about the development of scientific discovery skills. The results of our analysis, when combined with the related work from other laboratories, clarify the conditions under which children's domain-general reasoning skills are adequate to successfully coordinate search for hypotheses and experiments: (a) hypotheses must be easily accessible (such as the highly plausible Counters in our study) or few in number (as in the two-alternative situations used by Sodian et al.), (b) the experimental alternatives must also be few in number (also as in Sodian et al.), and (c) the domain must provide feedback relevant to discriminating among plausible hypotheses (as in Region 2 experiments in BT studies). It is important to reiterate the point that the performance deficits we found were not simply the result of children's inadequate encoding or mnemonic skills. As shown earlier, when experimental outcomes were consistent with children's expectations, they were correctly encoded, even though they were three times as long as those incorrectly encoded, but discrepant from children's expectations. Instead, the adult superiority appears to come from a set of domain-general skills that go beyond the logic of confirmation and disconfirmation and deal with the coordination of search in two spaces.* (Klahr, Fay, and Dunbar, 1993, pp. 139–141, italics added)

## CONCLUSIONS

Beyond the interesting specific results of the experimental research, it is important to inquire into generalizations that can be drawn.

Scientific and technical training facilitated success in the experimental task. The central heuristic of varying one thing at a time is an efficient problem-solving strategy acquired during formal university training in scientific laboratory procedures.

The conceptual account of scientific discovery as the coordination of search in hypothesis and experiment spaces is a highly valuable contribution to the philosophy of science. The validity of scientific explanation depends on the establishment of coherence between hypothesis and evidence, and the competence of scientific prediction depends on the establishment of correspondence between experimental expectation and experimental outcome. Discovery, explanation, and prediction all require the interpenetration of knowledge in the space of hypotheses and the space of experiments.

# PART II

## COMPUTER SCIENTIFIC DISCOVERY PROCESSES

# 3

# Mathematical Discovery

## *MATHEMATICAL DISCOVERY AND ARTIFICIAL INTELLIGENCE*

### THE GENERAL LOGIC OF AM

The intelligence of Lenat's Automatic Mathematician (AM) program, guided by mathematical aesthetics, seeks the discovery of new concepts and conjectures in elementary mathematics and set theory. The logic of AM is not directed toward the attainment of preassigned goals such as characterize problem-solving systems. AM does not know what goals it will reach, what concepts it will discover, or how these concepts will be defined and related to other concepts. The general logic of AM's creative acts are motivated and carried along by the type of ideation that characterizes human research mathematicians, namely, ideas of what might be interesting to explore (e.g., converses, maxima, minima, boundary conditions, exceptions, extrema). In this section, AM structures and operations will be described, the mathematical discoveries that it made will be summarized, and an analysis of AM's strengths and limitations will be offered. AM was developed by Lenat (1976).

### CHARACTERISTICS OF AM

The nature of AM's initial concepts is summarized in Section 2 of Table 3.1. AM discovered over 200 concepts during a run of several

**Table 3.1**
**AM and Its Basic Characteristics**

1.  AM as a heuristic search program

    AM is initially supplied with a few facts about some simple math concepts. AM

    then explores mathematics by selectively enlarging that basis. One could say

    that AM consists of an active body of mathematical concepts plus enough

    "wisdom" to use and develop them effectively (for "wisdom," read "heuristics").

    Loosely speaking, then, AM is a heuristic search program.

2.  AM's concepts and heuristic rules

    Initially, AM is given the definitions of 115 simple set-theoretic concepts (like

    "Delete" or "Equality"). Each concept is represented internally as a data

    structure with a couple dozen slots or facets (like "Definition," "Examples,"

    "Worth"). Initially, most facets of most concepts are blank, and AM uses a

    collection of 250 heuristics--plausible rules of thumb--for guidance, as it tries to

    fill in those blanks. Some heuristics are used to select which specific facet of

    which specific concept to explore next, while others are used to actually find

    some appropriate information about the chosen facet. Other rules prompt AM

    to notice simple relationships between known concepts, to define promising new

    concepts to investigate, and to estimate how interesting each concept is.

*Source:* Adapted from Davis, R., and Lenat, D. (1982). *Knowledge-based Systems in Artificial Intelligence.* New York: McGraw-Hill, pp. 3–4, 8–11.

hours. It discovered the significant concept of prime numbers. Table 3.2 displays the primes concept and filled-in slots for concept definition, concept examples, concept generalization and concept specialization, analogies, interest of the primes concept, and significant conjectures that involved the concept of primes.

AM's production system contains many heuristic rules. The nature of AM as a heuristic search program is summarized in Section 1 of Table 3.1. The discovery process in AM consists of an agenda mechanism. The control mechanism ensures that AM gives priority in task selection to the task with the highest interest rating. Thus, the mathematical aesthetics of tasks guide the discovery process in AM. The mathematical aesthetics in AM are achieved by a set of 59 heuristic rules that evaluate concepts and tasks with respect to their interest and worth.

The creative process in AM makes use of an extensive set of general methods that can result in new mathematical concepts:

**Table 3.2**
**The PRIMES Concept Produced by AM**

NAME: *Prime Numbers*
DEFINITIONS:
    ORIGIN: *Number-of-divisors-of(x)* = 2

    PREDICATE-CALCULUS: $Prime(x) \leftrightarrow (\forall z)(z \mid x \rightarrow (z = 1 \otimes z = x))$
    ITERATIVE: (*for* $x > 1$): *For i from 2 to* $\sqrt{x}, i \nmid x$
EXAMPLES: 2, 3, 5, 7, 11, 13, 17
    BOUNDARY: 2, 3
    BOUNDARY-FAILURES: 0, 1
    FAILURES: 12
GENERALIZATIONS: *Number, numbers with an even number of divisors*
SPECIALIZATIONS: *Odd primes, prime pairs, prime uniquely addables*
CONJECS:   *Unique factorization, Goldbach's conjecture, extrema of number-of-divisors-of*
INTUS:    *A metaphor to the effect that primes are the building blocks of all numbers*
ANALOGIES:
    *Maximally divisible numbers are converse extremes of number-of-divisors-of*
    *Factor a nonsimple group into simple groups*
INTEREST: *Conjectures tying primes to times, to divisors of, to related operations*
WORTH: 800
*Source:* Rich, E. (1983). *Artificial Intelligence.* New York: McGraw-Hill, p. 376.

1. *Generalization.* The domain and range of an existing concept can be expanded.

2. *Specialization.* The domain and range of an existing concept can be contracted (restricted).

3. *Inversion.* The inverse of an existing relation can be created. AM can also create interesting concepts such as the inverse image of an interesting subset of the range and the inverse image of an interesting value in the range.

4. *Composition.* Two functions F(x) and G(y) can be composed to obtain the new functions F(G(y)) and G(F(x)).

5. *Projection.* An existing multiple-argument function F can be projected onto a set of its argument. For example, Proj2(F(x,y)) is just y. (Cohen and Feigenbaum, 1982, p. 445)

The creation of mathematical conjectures in AM results from a set of heuristic rules whose function (like that of a scrutinizing human mathematician) is to discern confirming and negating patterns in the empirical data. In AM, conjectures can be proposed and represented as follows:

1. C1 is an example of C2;

2. C1 is a specialization (generalization) of C2;

3. C1 is equivalent to C2;

4. C1 is related by X to C2 (where X is some predicate);

5. Operation C1 has domain D or range R.

Most of these conjectures are discovered by performing rough statistical comparisons of examples. If all of the examples of C1 are also examples of C2, then AM conjectures that C1 is a specialization of C2. If AM is unable to find negative examples of C1, it conjectures that C1 is trivially true. If all examples of elements in the range of C1 seem to be numbers, then AM conjectures that C1 has numbers as its range. If all of the range elements of C1 are equal to corresponding domain elements, then perhaps C1 is the same as the identity function. (Cohen and Feigenbaum, 1982, p. 446)

## THE DISCOVERIES OF AM

A developmental account of AM's mathematical work is presented below. In Table 3.3, the account is organized in two sections, each summarizing a significant aspect of AM's achievements in mathematical discovery (adapted from Davis and Lenat, 1982, pp. 10–12).

## COMMENTARY ON AM

Discovery in mathematics has been variously represented as the sudden and spontaneous product of mysterious unconscious processes (Poincaré, 1913) and as the gradual and deliberate product of critical and inductive conscious processes (Lakatos, 1970). Neither account would encourage the representation of mathematical discovery as automated heuristic search. Yet the AM program explored a mathematical realm by means of its heuristic rules and its initial body of concepts (Table 3.1) and discovered new and significant concepts and conjectures (Table 3.3). That the concepts and conjectures discovered by AM had been previously discovered by human mathematicians working over a period of several millennia does not diminish the originality of AM's achievement.

AM's major strength was its reliance on heuristic rules, but this reliance was also its Achilles' heel, as the concepts it developed retreated more and more from the scope of its original set of heuristics and lacked the power to create appropriate new heuristics. AM's successor, EURISKO, synthesizes new heuristics and has been applied not only to the

**Table 3.3**
**AM as a Mathematician**

1.    AM and arithmetic operations

AM rediscovered multiplication in three ways: as repeated addition, as the

numeric analog of the Cartesian product of sets, and by studying the cardinality

of power sets. These operations were defined in different ways, so it was an

unexpected (to AM) discovery when they all turned out to be equivalent.

2.    Conjecture of the fundamental theorem of arithmetic

AM conjectured the fundamental theorem of arithmetic and Goldbach's conjecture in

a surprisingly symmetric way. The unary representation of numbers gave way to a

representation as a bag of primes (based on unique factorization).

*Source:* Adapted from Davis, R., and Lenat, D. (1982). *Knowledge-based Systems in Artificial Intelligence.* New York: McGraw-Hill, pp. 10–12.

field of mathematics but also to the fields of VLSI (very large scale integration) circuit architecture and naval fleet design (Lenat, 1982, 1983a, 1983b; Lenat and Brown, 1984).

## *FUNCTIONAL TRANSFORMATIONS IN SCIENTIFIC DISCOVERY SYSTEMS*

### FUNCTIONAL TRANSFORMATION: INTRODUCTION

Shen (1990) sets forth the general characteristics and objectives of the function transformation mechanism in the following introductory account.

In order to discover unknown concepts, a system has to start with a certain amount of knowledge. For example, a problem solving system may start with problem states, legal operators, and search control knowledge. A concept learning system may start with a language describing concept instances, a language describing concepts, and, perhaps, a domain theory.

Consider a discovery system aimed at the domain of elementary mathematics. The system's initial knowledge may include a variety of data structures, such as *set, list*; a set of primitive functions, such as *union, intersection, difference*; a set of mechanisms to create new functions and domains, such as *composition* and *substitution*. At the outset, we wish to give the system as little knowledge as possible. *When comparing two discovery systems of comparable power, we will prefer the one that does its work with the fewest assumptions.*

*The first goal of this project is to propose a parsimonious set of primitive functions and a uniform mechanism for discovering elementary mathematical functions. A second goal is to construct a system capable of pursuing new discoveries without any boundary that was foreseeable when the system was designed. A third, long-term, goal is to see to what extent such a discovery system can be independent of particular domains of application, and how system interaction with external information ("the outside world") could influence the discovery process* [italics added].

The function-creating mechanism discussed here is called *functional transformation* (FT). As we shall see, a FT may contain functions, functional variables, and functional forms (ways to combine or construct functions). A FT can specify the transformation from one function to another; hence can represent relations between functions. *A FT containing functional variables can also create new functions by instantiating the variables with specific functions. Although FT is rooted in the ideas of functional programming [Backus, 1978], it is not a programming language, but a functional language of functions.* (Shen, 1990, pp. 257–258, italics added)

## FUNCTIONAL TRANSFORMATION SYSTEMS: GENERAL CONCEPTS

Shen (1990) delineates the basic concepts of functional transformation and functional transformation systems in the following section.

A functional transformation system consists of *objects, functions, functional variables* and a fixed set of combining forms called *functional forms*. All the functions are of one type: they map objects into objects and always take a single argument. All the functional variables are variables that can have functions as their values. The functional forms are the sole means, using simple definitions, of building new functions from existing ones. A *functional transformation* is defined as a formula of functional forms containing functions as well as some functional variables. We give as an example of the functional transformation systems the following:

### Example

(1) A set *O* of *objects;* an object is either an element or a sequence of elements, where an element is either a capital English letter, a positive number or a special symbol $\perp$ meaning "undefined." Some examples of objects are: $\perp$, $T$, 5, $\langle A,B \rangle$, $\langle A, \langle 2,C \rangle, D \rangle$ (notation $\langle \ldots \rangle$ means a sequence of objects).

(2) A set $F$ of *functions f* that map objects into objects; e.g. *add, id* (identify), *distr* (distribute from right), *distl* (distribute from left), *2nd* (the second element).

(3) A set of *functional forms;* these are used to combine existing functions, or objects, to form new functions in $F$; for example, consider five such functional forms:

- *compose ( ° )* means
  $(f°g):x \equiv f:(g:x)$ ;
- *construct ( [ . . . ] )* means
  $[f_1, \ldots, f_n]:x \equiv \langle f_1 :x, \ldots, f_n:x \rangle;$
- *apply-to-all ( & )* means
  $\&f:\langle x_1, \ldots, x_n \rangle \equiv \langle f:x_1, \ldots, f:x_n \rangle;$
- *reduce ( / )* means
  $/f:x \equiv$ **if** $x = \langle x_1 \rangle$ **then** $x_1,$
    **if** $x = \langle x_1, \ldots, x_n \rangle$ $n>1$
    **then** $f:\langle x_1, /f:\langle x_1, \ldots, x_n \rangle \rangle,$
- *invert ( ~ )* means
  $f:\langle x \rangle \equiv f^{-1}:x.$

(4) A set of *functional variables*, notated by *"flv,"* whose values are functions.

(5) An operation, **Def**, that permits new functions to be defined in the terms of old ones, and assigns a name to each:

e.g.  **Def** *double* $\equiv$ *add* $\circ$ *[id, id]*

(6) An operation, *application* ( : );
e.g.
*add:* $\langle 2,2 \rangle = 4;$
*id:* $\langle D, \langle 2 \rangle \rangle = \langle D, \langle 2 \rangle \rangle;$
*distl:* $\langle \langle A \rangle, \langle C,D \rangle \rangle = \langle \langle \langle A \rangle, C \rangle, \langle \langle A \rangle, D \rangle \rangle;$
*&2nd* $\circ$ *distr:* $\langle \langle A,B \rangle, \langle C,D \rangle \rangle$
  $= \&2nd:$ *(distr:* $\langle \langle A,B \rangle, \langle C,D \rangle \rangle)$
  $= \&2nd:$ $\langle \langle A, \langle C,D \rangle \rangle, \langle B, \langle C,D \rangle \rangle \rangle$
  $= \langle 2nd:$ $\langle A, \langle C,D \rangle \rangle, 2nd:$ $\langle B, \langle C,D \rangle \rangle \rangle$
  $= \langle \langle C,D \rangle, \langle C,D \rangle \rangle.$

In the functional transformation system defined above, we can define new functions such as *"double."* For **Def** *double* $\equiv$ *add* $\circ$ *[id,id]*, we have

$double:x$  $= (add \circ [id,id]): x$
        $= add: ([id,id]: x)$
        $= add: \langle id: x, id: x \rangle$
        $= add: \langle x,x \rangle,$

which is exactly what we mean by *"double."*

*Notice that a* functional transformation *is a formula of functional forms containing functions as well as some functional variables. Thus, a functional transformation can be used as a tool for specifying relations between functions* [italics added]. For example, for the function pair *(add, double)*, the functional trans-

**Table 3.4**
**Some Applications of FT** *flv* ∘ *[id,id]*

| Given | FT *flv* ∘ *[id,id]* creates |
|:---:|:---:|
| + | double |
| * | square |
| - | zero |
| exclusive-or | false |
| set-union | identify |
| set-intersect | identify |

*Source:* Shen, W. M. (1990). Functional transformations in AI discovery systems. *Artificial Intelligence, 41*, p. 260. Reprinted with the permission of Elsevier Science Publishers.

formation *flv* ∘ *[id,id]* expresses the transformation from *add* to *double*, since instantiating the functional variable *flv* by *add*, we get the function *add* ∘ *[id,id]*, which is equivalent to *double* as we showed before. (Shen, 1990, pp. 258–260)

The most salient feature of functional transformation is its capacity to create new functions.

The interesting aspect of functional transformation lies not only in its ability to specify relations between functions, but also in its usefulness for creating new functions. For example, if we apply the above transformation, *flv* ∘ *[id,id]*, to the function *multiply* rather than *add*, we then build the new function *square*. Similarly, applying the transformation to the function *subtract*, we get the function *zero*. [Table 3.4] lists some examples of applications of the transformation *flv* ∘ *[id,id]*.

[Table 3.4] illustrates the application of FT. Notice that every function pair in the table is generated by the same transformation. Thus, if we were given any one of the pairs we could find the functional transformation that relates its members, replace the given function in the transformation by a functional variable, and then use the new FT to create new functions from existing ones. Using this idea, we have applied FT to the discovery of elementary mathematical functions, as we shall now demonstrate. (Shen, 1990, pp. 260–261)

## FUNCTIONAL TRANSFORMATION: DISCOVERY OF MATHEMATICAL FUNCTIONS

Shen (1990) demonstrates the application of functional transformation to the objective of discovering elementary mathematical functions, in the following section.

Applying FT to the task of discovering functions, we find that, from a small set of primitive functions, with the aid of a few functional transformations . . . , we can discover all the common functions in elementary mathematics. *Such functions as addition, subtraction, multiplication, division, exponentiation, and logarithm can be constructed using only five functional transformations derived from the relations between simple functions in set theory* [italics added]. Suppose we have given basic functions like *bag-union* (a function that appends two bags together, where a *bag* is a set that allows duplicated elements), *bag-difference, cross-product* (cross-product: $\langle\langle A, B \rangle, \langle 1, 2 \rangle\rangle = \langle\langle A, 1 \rangle, \langle A, 2 \rangle, \langle B, 1 \rangle, \langle B, 2 \rangle\rangle$) and *identity*, then, for example, the same FT that transforms *bag-union* to *cross-product* also transforms addition to multiplication and multiplication to exponentiation; the FT from *bag-union* to *identity* constructs double from addition and square from multiplication; the FT from *bag-union* to *bag-difference* constructs subtraction from addition, half from double, division from multiplication, square root from square and logarithm from exponentiation. *Moreover, repeated use of these functional transformations can yield additional useful functions, such as* $x^{x}$ *and so on, although these are not as well known as the others* [italics added]. We have tried to capture these phenomena in [Figure 3.1].

*Functional transformation can do more than just constructing elementary mathematical functions in a parsimonious way. It can also be used to expand the domain of numbers, following a path that somewhat imitates the history of the subject's development* [italics added]. A FT applied to a particular function, may define only a partial function, which does not have values in the domain of the argument for all values of the argument. For example, subtraction, which can be obtained by applying the FT *invert* to addition, does not always produce a natural number (a positive integer); and division, obtained by applying *invert* to multiplication, does not always produce an integer. Similarly, square root, the inverse of squaring, may not produce a value in the domain of the rationals; while taking a square root of a negative number will not produce a value in the domain of the reals. When a FT defines a partial function in this way, this signals that a new set of objects is needed to extend the range of the function and complete it. Research on this matter is currently under way. (Shen, 1990, pp. 261–262)

## THE ARE SYSTEM: CHARACTERISTICS AND COMPARISONS WITH THE AM SYSTEM

Shen (1990) developed the ARE system as an implementation of the concepts of functional transformation. The ARE system is then compared with the classic AM system (Lenat, 1976).

In order to demonstrate the power of functional transformations, a system ARE is implemented to discover new functions and concepts in the domain of elementary mathematics, which is the primary domain of AM and one of the do-

**Figure 3.1**
**The FT's among Elementary Mathematics Functions**

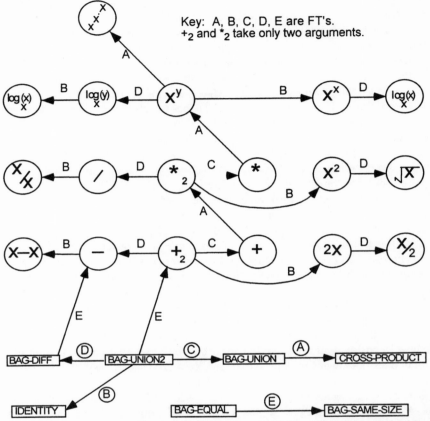

Key: A, B, C, D, E are FT's.
$+_2$ and $*_2$ take only two arguments.

*Source:* Shen, W. M. (1990). Functional transformations in AI discovery systems. *Artificial Intelligence, 41*, p. 261. Reprinted with the permission of Elsevier Science Publishers.

mains of EURISKO. *The use of FT's makes possible the elimination of the numerous special-purpose creative operations employed by AM, allowing these operations to be defined in terms of a few general ones along the route of discovery* [italics added]. Unfortunately, it is not clear how many creative operations are pre-programmed in EURISKO, otherwise it would be interesting to compare ARE with EURISKO too. (Shen, 1990, p. 262)

In the following paragraph, Shen (1990) presents a succinct account of AM's initial knowledge, its heuristics, and, most importantly, its creative operations.

AM is a computer program written by Douglas Lenat [Lenat, 1976; Michalski, Carbonell, and Mitchell, 1983] that discovers concepts in elementary mathematics and set theory. Searching in a space of mathematical concepts, it seeks to define and evaluate interesting concepts under the guidance of a set of heuristics. The system is data-driven, and its main control structure is an agenda of tasks with priorities.

*As its search control knowledge, AM starts with about 243 heuristics spread throughout the whole initial concept network. As its creative operators, it has a set of 11 operators coded in schemes and heuristics* [italics added]. By creative operations we mean the operations that can actually create new concepts. So *set-union* is not a creative operation while *coalesce*, which will be discussed shortly, is.

Among AM's creative operations, some are used only for special purposes. For instances, the creative operation *parallel-join2* is so powerful that it creates the *multiplication* operation in just one step; the creative operation *canonize*, which is implemented as a group of heuristics, creates the crucial concept *number* but the operation is never useful again. As an overview of AM's starting knowledge, we list AM's initial creative operations in [Figure 3.2], but we will examine only one of them, *coalesce*, more closely.

*The operation* coalesce *is very powerful. It is essential to most of the new concepts created by AM, as shown in a run trace in [Lenat, 1976]* [italics added]. Its actual implementation contains several heuristics, but the main idea is:

**if** *f: A\*A → B;*
    **then** *define g: A → B as g(x) ≡ f(x,x).*

It says that if a function f takes a pair of A's as arguments, then it is often worth the time and energy to define $g(x) = f(x,x)$. Some of the contributions of this heuristics are shown in [Table 3.5].

*From our point of view,* coalesce *is not an essential creative operation, since it can be synthesized by the FT technique from simpler primitive functions, as we will see later. Other creative operations in AM that we can dispense with in ARE are*: canonize, parallel-replace2, repeat2, parallel-join2, *and* parallel-join [italics added]. We list all such nonessential creative operators in AM and their possible FT constructions in [Table 3.6]. (Shen, 1990, pp. 262–264)

In the following section Shen (1990) presents an interesting account of the creative operations in the ARE system.

Like AM, the ARE system represents concepts by schemata, and employs an agenda mechanism with tasks as its control structure. However, ARE needs far

**Figure 3.2**
**AM's Initial Operations**

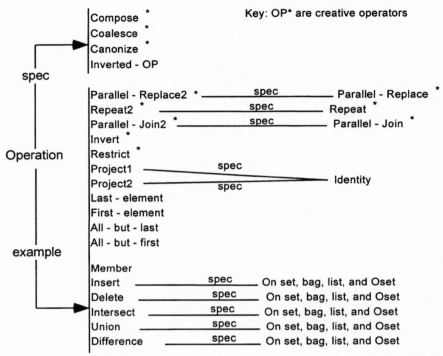

*Source:* Shen, W. M. (1990). Functional transformations in AI discovery systems. *Artificial Intelligence, 41*, p. 263. Reprinted with the permission of Elsevier Science Publishers.

fewer heuristics (at present 23) for controlling the search process. ARE has only six creative operations initially, five of them are implemented as functional forms. . . . They are: *compose* $\circ$ *; construct* $[f_1, \ldots , [f_n]$*; invert* $\sim$*; reduce* /; and *apply-to-all* &. The sixth creative operation, *substitution*, implemented by heuristics, can create new functions by replacing an old function's domain with new ones. [Figure 3.3] shows the entire initial concept hierarchy of ARE.

There are several terms in [Figure 3.3] that need explanation. *Constant-t* is a function that turns every element in its argument into the constant *t*, e.g.

$$constant\text{-}t: \langle D, \langle F \rangle, \langle \rangle \rangle = \langle t, t, t \rangle.$$

*Union₂* is the same as function *union* except it takes only arguments with two components. The function *distr (distl)* means distribute from right (left), taking

**Table 3.5**
**Some Contributions of *Coalesce***

| Given | *Coalesce* creates |
|---|---|
| + | double |
| * | square |
| - | zero |
| set-union | identify |
| set-intersect | identify |
| compose | self-compose |

*Source:* Shen, W. M. (1990). Functional transformations in AI discovery systems. *Artificial Intelligence, 41*, p. 264. Reprinted with the permission of Elsevier Science Publishers.

two objects and combining the second (first) object with every element of the first (second) one. For example,

*distr:* $\langle\langle X, Y\rangle, \langle A, B\rangle\rangle = \langle\langle X, \langle A, B\rangle\rangle, \langle Y, \langle A, B\rangle\rangle\rangle.$

Finally, the data structure *bag* is a set that allows duplicate elements, or in other words, an unordered list.

*The heart of the ARE system is its means for creating useful creative operations with which new mathematical concepts can be constructed. This is accomplished by first proposing some functions as interesting pairs, such as* (bag-union, bag-difference) *and* (bag-union, cross-product), *then searching for functional transformations between the paired functions. At present, two simple heuristics are used for proposing function pairs. One says that if a function has just been generalized, then propose the function with its generalization as an interesting pair. The other says that if many examples of a function have been found, then propose to pair it with all those functions that have many examples* [italics added]. Once an interesting pair is chosen, the search space for a transformation would be huge because there could be a great number of primitive functions and functional forms. At present, the system employs a best-first approach to control the search. A depth-first search might not be suitable in this situation, because there is no way to specify maximum depth of search. This paper will not discuss the criteria for choosing the next node from which to search; the criterion problem has not yet been explored, and the present criteria are crude. The search stops if a functional transformation is found or its given time is exhausted. To illustrate the synthesis procedure, let us consider how ARE creates the *coalesce* operation by searching from the FT that transforms the function *intersect* into *identity*.

**Table 3.6**
**AM's Nonessential Creative Operators and Their FT Construction**

| AM's operator | FT construction |
| --- | --- |
| Coalesce | flv ∘ [id, id] |
| Canonize | flv ∘ &&constant-t |
| Parallel-replace2 | &flv ∘ distr |
| Repeat2 | /(flv ∘ [1st ∘ 1st, 2nd] ∘ distr) |
| Parallel-join2 | Bag-union ∘ &flv ∘ distr |
| Parallel-join | Bag-union ∘ &flv |

Source: Shen, W. M. (1990). Functional transformations in AI discovery systems. *Artificial Intelligence, 41,* p. 264. Reprinted with the permission of Elsevier Science Publishers.

When given the function pair: *intersect*, the base function, and *identity*, the target function, ARE starts a generate and test process. The target function need not have an algorithm but it is required to have a set of positive examples for testing FT hypotheses. New hypotheses are generated according to the properties of the base and target, then the hypotheses are tested against the examples of the target function. If a hypothesis, which includes the base function as one of its components, matches all the examples of the target, the search is terminated. For example, in [Figure 3.4], the search is terminated after the test of *intersect ∘ [id, id]*, since this hypothesis is satisfied by all the examples of function *identity* and it contains the base function *intersect*. The hypothesis is then generalized by replacing the base function with a functional variable. The generalized hypothesis is then returned as the transformation from *intersect* to *identity*, namely *flv ∘ [id, id]. This functional transformation is equivalent to AM's powerful operation*, coalesce [italics added].

Ideally, once a new FT is created, the system should apply it to all the functions that are analogous to the base function, but at present this analogy test is not fully implemented. So ARE blindly applies a newly created FT to every existing function. *In a run, ARE had created all the creative operations that AM generated, and produced new functions and concepts as AM did* [italics added]. [Figure 3.5] shows the running trace, and now we give a brief description.

Given the initial concept hierarchy (see [Figure 3.3]), ARE starts to generate examples for its initial concepts and functions. When it notices that too few examples are found for the function *equal*, a task is proposed to generalize the function. When the generalized function *same-size* is defined (in AM-like fash-

**Figure 3.3**
**ARE's Initial Concept Hierarchy**

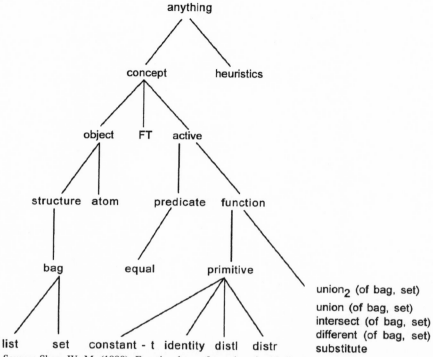

*Source:* Shen, W. M. (1990). Functional transformations in AI discovery systems. *Artificial Intelligence, 41*, p. 265. Reprinted with the permission of Elsevier Science Publishers.

ion), one of the heuristics for proposing an interesting function pair is fired and suggests to search a functional transformation between *equal* and *same-size*. The search results in a functional transformation FT1 (*flv ○ &&const-t*). This new FT is then applied to the existing functions, and *add2* and *sub2*, among others, are created. At this point, since applying FT to every *"bag-"* function produced a new function, the system decides to create a new domain by abstracting these new functions (isolating the common parts of their definitions). Such abstraction creates a new function, *all-t (&&const-t)*, which can be viewed as the generator of the new domain. When applied to *bag* (the domains of the functions that can be abstracted), the function *all-t* creates a new concept, *number*.

Continuing on filling examples for concepts and functions, ARE also proposes, among others, the following pairs of functions to search functional trans-

**Figure 3.4**
**The Search Tree for FT** *Coalesce*

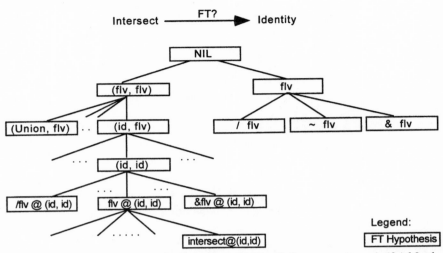

*Source:* Shen, W. M. (1990). Functional transformations in AI discovery systems. *Artificial Intelligence, 41*, p. 266. Reprinted with the permission of Elsevier Science Publishers.

formations: *(bag-union2, bag-diff), (bag-union2, identity), (bag-union2, bag-union), and (bag-union, cross-product).* These searches produce respectively the following new functional transformations: FT2 *( ~ flv)*, FT3 *(flv ○ [id, id])*, FT4 *(/flv)*, and FT5 *(flv ○ &distr ○ distl)*. Every time a new FT is created, it is applied to the existing functions, and whenever a new function is successfully produced, all existing functional transformations will be applied to it again. Notice that the interestingness of newly created functions declines when applying FT's further, so that the creation process will stop when a newly created function's interestingness is below some threshold. (Shen, 1990, pp. 264–268)

In the following section, Shen (1990) provides a technical comparative analysis of the ARE with the AM and the EURISKO systems.

So much has been said about AM in the AI literature [Lenat and Brown, 1984; Ritchie and Hanna, 1984]. Here, we would like to briefly compare the behaviors of ARE and AM (according to Lenat [Lenat, 1983b], EURISKO performed the same as AM when working on AM's domain), then point out two important differences between the two systems, namely, knowledge representation and the mutation operators [Lenat and Brown, 1984] (a term equivalent to the creative operator in this paper).

Examining AM's running trace, as shown in [Figure 3.6], we notice that the

**Figure 3.5**
**The Main Thread of ARE's Running Trace**

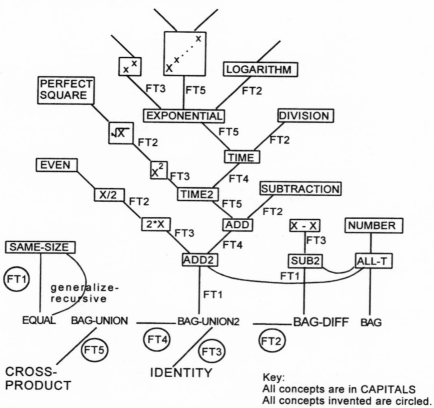

*Source:* Shen, W. M. (1990). Functional transformations in AI discovery systems. *Artificial Intelligence, 41*, p. 267. Reprinted with the permission of Elsevier Science Publishers.

concept *number* is the bottleneck and it is created by a powerful yet nonessential operation called *canonize* before any arithmetical function is defined. In contrast, ARE defines the *number* concept by creating arithmetical functions first (these functions take *bag* as domain but treat it as if all the elements are the same), then abstract these functions and generalize their domain. We think this is a powerful and general method to define new concepts. . . .

Since ARE is just an implementation to demonstrate the power of functional transformation, we did not intend to duplicate everything AM does. In fact, we did not implement the discovery of *prime* and there are no "conjecture" slots in ARE's concepts.

*It is well known that the success of AM is mainly due to its lucky represen-*

**Figure 3.6**
**A Typical Running Trace of AM**

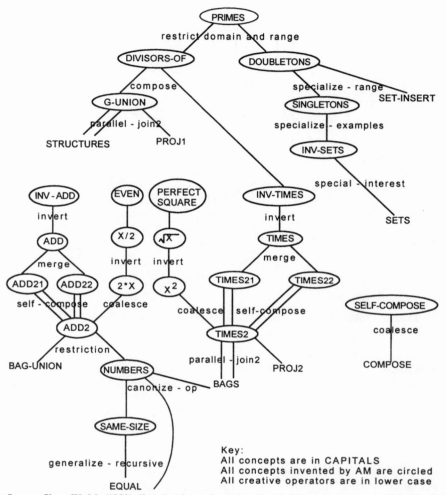

*Source:* Shen, W. M. (1990). Functional transformations in AI discovery systems. *Artificial Intelligence, 41*, p. 269. Reprinted with the permission of Elsevier Science Publishers.

tation. As Lenat said in [Lenat and Brown, 1984], AM's representation language, LISP, was so closely related to mathematics that AM's mutation operators turned out to yield a high "hit rate" of viable, useful new math concepts. But when it comes to the mutation of heuristics, these mutation operators lost their power because the LISP representation of heuristics is not highly matched to the meaning of heuristics.

*Unlike AM, ARE uniformly represents both domain knowledge and heuristics in schemata. Therefore, it will not have problems, like AM did, if the heuristics need to be mutated too. Even though we did not test any mutation of heuristics in the ARE system, we think that such representation is a necessary condition to accomplish the primary objective of ARE, the objective to understand the nature of mutation operators and investigate methods to discover new and useful such operators. Moreover, the functional transformation is a new representation for mathematical functions. It allows us to have fine granulated "building blocks" and, at the same time, keep a high "hit rate" discovery.*

*EURISKO is an improvement of AM. Much of its power comes from its ability to create new heuristics to control the application of existing mutation operators so that the discovery process can keep a high "hit rate." But unlike the ARE system, EURISKO (and AM) did not address the issue of creating new and useful mutation operators* [italics added].

As we saw in the previous section, representing and discovering mutation operators is the main subject of ARE. Compared to AM and EURISKO, ARE's initial mutation operators are more primitive. Therefore, ARE created some mathematical functions, such as *logarithm, $x^x$*, and the Ackermann function, that were not, or could not be, created by AM. Moreover, since ARE can create new and useful mutation operators along the path of discovery, it managed to keep a high hit rate even if its search space is greater (due to the more primitive mutation operators). It is hoped that, as partially demonstrated in the ARE system, creating new and useful mutation operators may give us an alternative way to keep a discovery process with high hit rate for longer time. (Shen, 1990, pp. 268–269)

## FUNCTIONAL TRANSFORMATION AND GENERAL PROBLEM SOLVING CONCEPTS

In the following section Shen (1990) relates the concept of functional transformation to Simon and Lea's (1974) two-space model of problem solving, to the technique of macro operators, and to unit analogical problem solving.

When applying the functional transformation technique to the discovery of elementary mathematical functions, we notice that there are two search spaces involved: the space of domain concepts (including domain functions), and the space of creative operators. This is very similar to the *concept formulation systems* postulated by Simon and Lea [Simon and Lea, 1974]. To induce rules they use a space of instances and a space of rules. Problem solving can be viewed as a search through the spaces, with the search in one space guided by information available in the other. Under their framework, the space of creative operators in ARE corresponds to the rule space, and the space of domain concepts corresponds to the instance space. Search in the space of creative operators is triggered whenever an interesting function pair emerges from the space of domain concepts; search in the space of domain concepts is facilitated whenever a new creative operator is created in the space of creative operators. *The ARE system differs from Simon and Lea's concept formation systems only in the fact that a creative operator is automatically consistent with the instances in the space of domain concepts, because it creates them.*

*What we think is important in ARE is not the use of two search spaces, but the parsimonious nature of the primitives. In fact, they constitute a set that is closely related to the primitives for the class of primitive recursive functions [Davis and Weyuker, 1983]. In primitive recursive function theory the only two creative operators are: the composition rule and the recursive rule. In ARE, the function forms* compose *and* construct *can be thought of as equivalent to the composition rule;* apply-to-all *and* reduce *can be considered as together possessing most of the power of the recursion rule.*

*The functional transformation technique is related to a standard AI technique: macro-operators. But they are different in two aspects. Firstly, macro-operators are only formed by composition, where FT's generalize this to the other functional forms. Secondly, the macro-operator technique does not deal with creative operations. Therefore a macro-operator can be used to achieve certain states quickly, but cannot be used to create new operations. In contrast, an FT is a template for creating many different macro-operators because instantiating an FT with different existing operators will produce new and different operators.*

*Functional transformation also captures some properties of human discovery by analogy* [italics added]. For example, if one discovers the transformation from addition to multiplication, he will most likely try the transformation on anything analogous to addition. *Although to define this analogy precisely is a difficult task, we could consider any functions analogical to each other if they have the same structure, or the same primitives, or the same number of components* [italics added]. In the example above, multiplication can be one of the functions analogous to addition because they have the same structure. Then, applying the transformation to multiplication produces exponentiation. (Shen, 1990, pp. 270–271)

## FUNCTIONAL TRANSFORMATION AND THE ARE SYSTEM: SUMMARY

Shen (1990) provides the following concise summary of the research.

*It is crucial for a discovery system to have a productive set of creative operators as well as an effective set of heuristics to control the search. Although both sets* can be treated as assumptions, we prefer to use as few assumptions as possible while preserving a system's original power. *This paper proposes a functional transformation mechanism as a tool to create new creative operators during exploration, thereby making the search for new concepts more productive while based on fewer built-in creative operators.* We have implemented a system called ARE to apply the FT technique to the same tasks explored by AM and the results are promising. *Besides showing a way to meet the criticisms of lack of parsimony that have been leveled against AM, the ARE system provides a route to discovery systems that are capable of "refreshing" themselves indefinitely by continually creating new operators.*

Several important questions have emerged during this research. One is whether the FT technique can be applied to domains other than mathematics. Others include how to locate an interesting function pair in order to find a useful FT, and how to define "analogy" more precisely so that an FT can produce meaningful functions efficiently. (Shen, 1990, p. 271, italics added)

# 4

# Explanatory Systems and Scientific Discovery Processes

## *EXPLANATORY COHERENCE AND THE ECHO SYSTEM*

### THE THEORY OF EXPLANATORY COHERENCE: OVERVIEW

Thagard (1989) has developed an important theory of intelligent explanatory reasoning. The theory of explanatory coherence has been implemented in the ECHO system. Thagard (1989) presents a summary of his theory and his research program in the following account.

This target article presents a new computational theory of explanatory coherence that applies to the acceptance and rejection of scientific hypotheses as well as to reasoning in everyday life. The theory consists of seven principles that establish relations of local coherence between a hypothesis and other propositions. A hypothesis coheres with propositions that it explains, or that explain it, or that participate with it in explaining other propositions, or that offer analogous explanations. Propositions are incoherent with each other if they are contradictory. Propositions that describe the results of observation have a degree of acceptability on their own. An explanatory hypothesis is accepted if it coheres better overall than its competitors. The power of the seven principles is shown by their implementation in a connectionist program called ECHO, which treats hypothesis evaluation as a constraint satisfaction problem. Inputs about the explanatory relations are used to create a network of units representing propositions, while coherence and incoherence relations are encoded by excitatory and inhibitory links. *ECHO provides an algorithm for smoothly integrating theory evaluation based on considerations of explanatory breadth, simplicity, and analogy. It has been applied to such important scientific cases as Lavoisier's argument for oxygen against the phlogiston theory and Darwin's argument for evolution against creationism, and also to cases of legal reasoning* [italics added]. The theory of explanatory coherence has implications for artificial intelligence, psychology, and philosophy. (Thagard, 1989, pp. 435–436)

## THE THEORY OF EXPLANATORY COHERENCE: PRINCIPLES

Thagard (1989) states the basic principles of the theory of explanatory coherence in the following terms.

I now propose seven principles that establish relations of explanatory coherence and make possible an assessment of the global coherence of an explanatory system S. S consists of propositions P, Q, $P_1 \ldots P_n$. Local coherence is a relation between two propositions. I coin the term "incohere" to mean more than just that two propositions do not cohere: To incohere is to *resist* holding together. The principles are as follows:

**Principle 1. Symmetry**.

(a) If P and Q cohere, then Q and P cohere.
(b) If P and Q incohere, then Q and P incohere.

**Principle 2. Explanation**.

If $P_1 \ldots P_m$ explain Q, then:
(a) For each $P_i$ in $P_1 \ldots P_m$, $P_r$ and Q cohere.
(b) For each $P_i$ and $P_j$ in $P_1 \ldots P_m$, $P_i$ and $P_j$ cohere.
(c) In (a) and (b), the degree of coherence is inversely proportional to the number of propositions $P_1 \ldots P_m$.

**Principle 3. Analogy**.

(a) If $P_1$ explains $Q_1$, $P_2$ explains $Q_2$, $P_1$ is analogous to $P_2$, and $Q_1$ is analogous to $Q_2$, then $P_1$ and $P_2$ cohere, and $Q_1$ and $Q_2$ cohere.
(b) If $P_1$ explains $Q_1$, $P_2$ explains $Q_2$, $Q_1$ is analogous to $Q_2$, but $P_1$ is disanalogous to $P_2$, then $P_1$ and $P_2$ incohere.

**Principle 4.  Data Priority**.

Propositions that describe the results of observation have a degree of acceptability on their own.

**Principle 5.  Contradiction**.

If P contradicts Q, then P and Q incohere.

**Principle 6.  Acceptability**.

(a) The acceptability of a proposition P in a system S depends on its coherence with the proposition in S.

(b) If many results of relevant experimental observations are unexplained, then the acceptability of a proposition P that explains only a few of them is reduced.

**Principle 7.  System Coherence**.

The global explanatory coherence of a system S of propositions is a function of the pairwise local coherence of those propositions. (Thagard, 1989, pp. 436–437)

Thagard (1989) discusses the preceding seven principles of explanatory coherence theory in the following account.

Principle 1, Symmetry, asserts that pairwise coherence and incoherence are symmetric relations, in keeping with the everyday sense of coherence as holding together. The coherence of two propositions is thus very different from the nonsymmetric relations of entailment and conditional probability. Typically, P entails Q without Q entailing P, and the conditional probability of P given Q is different from the probability of Q given P. But if P and Q hold together, so do Q and P. The use of symmetrical relation has advantages that will become clearer in the discussion of the connectionist implementation below.

Principle 2, Explanation, is by far the most important for assessing explanatory coherence, because it establishes most of the coherence relations. Part (a) is the most obvious: If a hypothesis P is part of the explanation of a piece of evidence Q, then P and Q cohere. Moreover, if a hypothesis $P_1$ is explained by another hypothesis $P_2$, then $P_1$ and $P_2$ cohere. Part (a) presupposes that explanation is a more restrictive relation than deductive implication, because otherwise we could prove that any two propositions cohere; unless we use relevance logic (Anderson & Belnap, 1975), $P_1$ and the contradiction $P_2$ & not-$P_1$ imply any Q, so it would follow that $P_1$ coheres with Q. *It follows from Principle 2 (a), in conjunction with Principle 6, that the more a hypothesis explains, the more coherent and hence acceptable it is. Thus, this principle subsumes the*

*criterion of explanatory breadth (which Whewell, 1840/1967, called "consili-*
*ence") that I have elsewhere claimed to be the most important for selecting the*
*best explanation* (Thagard, 1978, 1988a) [italics added].

Whereas part (a) of Principle 2 says that what explains coheres with what is
explained, part (b) states that 2 propositions cohere if together they provide an
explanation. Behind part (b) is the Duhem-Quine idea that the evaluation of a
hypothesis depends partly on the other hypotheses with which it furnishes explanations (Duhem, 1954; Quine, 1961; . . . ). I call two hypotheses that are used
together in an explanation "cohypotheses." Again I assume that explanation is
more restrictive than implication; otherwise it would follow that any proposition
that explained something was coherent with every other proposition, because if
$P_1$ implies Q, then so does $P_1$ & $P_2$. But any scientist who maintained at a
conference that the theory of general relativity and today's baseball scores together explain the motion of planets would be laughed off the podium. Principle
2 is intended to apply to explanations and hypotheses actually proposed by
scientists.

Part (c) of Principle 2 embodies the claim that if numerous propositions are
needed to furnish explanation, then the coherence of the explaining propositions
with each other and with what is explained is thereby diminished. Scientists tend
to be skeptical of hypotheses that require myriad *ad hoc* assumptions in their
explanations. There is nothing wrong in principle in having explanations that
draw on many assumptions, but we should prefer theories that generate explanations using a unified core of hypotheses. I have elsewhere contended that the
notion of *simplicity* most appropriate for scientific theory choice is a comparative
one preferring theories that make fewer special assumptions (Thagard, 1978,
1988a). Principles 2 (b) and 2 (c) together subsume this criterion. I shall not
attempt further to characterize "degree of coherence" here, but the connectionist
algorithm described below provides a natural interpretation. Many other notions
of simplicity have been proposed (e.g., Foster & Martin, 1966; Harman et al.,
1988), but none is so directly relevant to considerations of explanatory coherence as the one embodied in Principle 2.

The third criterion for the best explanation in my earlier account was analogy,
and this is subsumed in Principle 3. There is controversy about whether analogy
is of more heuristic use, but scientists such as Darwin have used analogies to
defend their theories; his argument for evolution by natural selection is analyzed
below. Principle 3 (a) does not say simply that any two analogous propositions
cohere. There must be an explanatory analogy, with two analogous propositions
occurring in explanations of two other propositions that are analogous to each
other. Recent computational models of analogical mapping and retrieval show
how such correspondences can be noticed (Holyoak & Thagard, [1989]; Thagard, et al., 1989). Principle 3 (b) says that when similar phenomena are explained by dissimilar hypotheses, the hypotheses incohere. Although the use of
such disanalogies is not as common as the use of analogies, it was important in

the reasoning that led Einstein (1952) to the special theory of relativity: He was bothered by asymmetries in the way Maxwell's electrodynamics treated the case of (1) a magnet in motion and a conductor at rest quite differently from the case of (2) a magnet at rest and a conductor in motion.

Principle 4, Data Priority, stands much in need of elucidation and defense. In saying that a proposition describing the results of observation has a degree of acceptability on its own, I am not suggesting that is indubitable, but only that it can stand on its own more successfully than can a hypothesis whose sole justification is what it explains. A proposition Q may have some independent acceptability and still end up not accepted, if it is only coherent with propositions that are themselves not acceptable.

From the point of view of explanatory coherence alone, we should not take propositions based on observation as independently acceptable without any explanatory relations to other propositions. As Bonjour (1985) argues, the coherence of such propositions is of a nonexplanatory kind, based on background knowledge that observations of certain sorts are very likely to be true. From past experience, we know that our observations are very likely to be true, so we should believe them unless there is substantial reason not to. Similarly, at a very different level, we have some confidence in the reliability of descriptions of experimental results in carefully refereed scientific journals. . . .

Principle 5, Contradiction, is straightforward. By "contradictory" here I mean not just syntactic contradictions like P & not-P, but also semantic contradictions such as "This ball is black all over" and "This ball is white all over." In scientific cases, contradiction becomes important when incompatible hypotheses compete to explain the same evidence. Not all competing hypotheses incohere, however, because many phenomena have multiple causes. For example, explanations of why someone has certain medical symptoms may involve hypotheses that the patient has various diseases, and it is possible that more than one disease is present. Competing hypotheses incohere if they are contradictory or if they are framed as offering *the* most likely cause of a phenomenon. In the latter case, we get a kind of pragmatic contradictoriness: Two hypotheses may not be syntactically or semantically contradictory, yet scientists will view them as contradictory because of background beliefs suggesting that only one of the hypotheses is acceptable. For example, in the debate over dinosaur extinction (Thagard, 1988b), scientists generally treat as contradictory the following hypotheses:

(1) Dinosaurs became extinct because of a meteorite collision.

(2) Dinosaurs became extinct because the sea level fell.

Logically, (1) and (2) could both be true, but scientists treat them as conflicting explanations, possibly because there are no explanatory relations between them and their conjunction is unlikely.

The relation "cohere" is not transitive. If $P_1$ and $P_2$ together explain Q, while $P_1$ and $P_3$ together explain not-Q, then $P_1$ coheres with both Q and not-Q, which incohere. Such cases do occur in science. Let $P_1$ be the gas law that volume is proportional to temperature, $P_2$ a proposition describing the drop in temperature of a particular sample of gas, $P_3$ a proposition describing the rise in temperature of the sample, and Q a proposition about increases in the sample's volume. Then $P_1$ and $P_2$ together explain a decrease in the volume, while $P_1$ and $P_3$ explain the increase.

Principle 6, Acceptability, proposes in part (a) that we can make sense of the overall coherence of a proposition in an explanatory system just from the pairwise coherence relations established by Principles 1–5. If we have a hypothesis P that coheres with evidence Q by virtue of explaining it, but incoheres with another contradictory hypothesis, should we accept P? To decide, we cannot merely count the number of propositions with which P coheres and incoheres, because the acceptability of P depends in part on the acceptability of those propositions themselves. We need a dynamic and parallel method of deriving general coherence from particular coherence relations; such a method is provided by the connectionist program described below.

Principle 6 (b), reducing the acceptability of a hypothesis when much of the relevant evidence is unexplained by any hypothesis, is intended to handle cases where the best available hypothesis is still not very good, in that it accounts for only a fraction of the available evidence. Consider, for example, a theory in economics that could explain the stock market crashes of 1929 and 1987 but that had nothing to say about myriad other similar economic events. Even if the theory gave the best available account of the two crashes, we would not be willing to elevate it to an accepted part of general economic theory. What does "relevant" mean here? [See Précis of Sperber and Wilson's *Relevance, BBS* 10 (4) 1987.] As a first approximation, we can say that a piece of evidence is *directly* relevant to a hypothesis if the evidence is explained by it or by one of its competitors. We can then add that a piece of evidence is relevant if it is directly relevant or if it is similar to evidence that is relevant, where similarity is a matter of dealing with phenomena of the same kind. Thus, a theory of the business cycle that applies to the stock market crashes of 1929 and 1987 should also have something to say about nineteenth-century crashes and major business downturns in the twentieth century.

The final principle, System Coherence, proposes that we can have some global measure of the coherence of a whole system of propositions. Principles 1–5 imply that, other things being equal, a system S will tend to have more global coherence than another if,

(1) S has more data in it;

(2) S has more internal explanatory links between propositions that cohere because of explanations and analogies, and;

(3) S succeeds in separating coherent subsystems of propositions from conflicting subsystems.

The connectionist algorithm described below comes with a natural measure of global system coherence. It also indicates how different priorities can be given to the different principles. (Thagard, 1989, pp. 437–438)

## COHERENCE AND THE COMPUTATIONAL ACCOUNT OF CREATIVITY

### ECHO: INPUT FORMULAS

The principles of explanatory coherence are represented in the connectionist program ECHO. In the following section, Thagard (1989) describes the input formulas to ECHO.

Let us now look at ECHO, a computer program written in Common LISP that is a straightforward application of connectionist algorithms to the problem of explanatory coherence. In ECHO, propositions representing hypotheses and results of observations are represented by units. Whenever Principles 1–5 state that two propositions cohere, an excitatory link between them is established. If two propositions incohere, an inhibitory link between them is established. In ECHO, these links are symmetric, as Principle 1 suggests: The weight from unit 1 to unit 2 is the same as the weight from unit 2 to unit 1. Principle 2(c) says that the larger the number of propositions used in an explanation, the smaller the degree of coherence between each pair of propositions. ECHO therefore counts the number of propositions that do the explaining and proportionately lowers the weight of the excitatory links between units representing coherent propositions. . . .

The following are some examples of the LISP formulas that constitute ECHO's inputs (I omit LISP quote symbols; see [Tables 4.1–4.4] for actual input):

1. (EXPLAIN (H1 H2) E1)

2. (EXPLAIN (H1 H2 H3) E2)

3. (ANALOGOUS (H5 H6) (E5 E6))

4. (DATA (E1 E2 E5 E6))

5. (CONTRADICT H1 H4)

Formula 1 says that hypotheses H1 and H2 together explain evidence E1. As suggested by the second principle of explanatory coherence proposed above, formula 1 sets up three excitatory links, between units representing H1 and E1, H2 and E1, and H1 and H2. Formula 2 sets up six such links, between each of the hypotheses and the evidence, and between each pair of hypotheses, but the weight on the links will be less than those established by formula 1, because there are more cohypotheses. In accord with Principle 3 (a), Analogy, formula 3 produces excitatory links between H5 and H6, and between

**Table 4.1**
**Input Propositions for Lavoisier (1862) Example**

*Evidence*
| | |
|---|---|
| (proposition 'E1 | "In combustion, heat and light are given off.") |
| (proposition 'E2 | "Inflammability is transmittable from one body to another.") |
| (proposition 'E3 | "Combustion only occurs in the presence of pure air.") |
| (proposition 'E4 | "Increase in weight of a burned body is exactly equal to the weight of the air absorbed.") |
| (proposition 'E5 | "Metals undergo calcination.") |
| (proposition 'E6 | "In calcination, bodies increase weight.") |
| (proposition 'E7 | "In calcination, volume of air diminishes.") |
| (proposition 'E8 | "In reduction, effervescence appears.") |

*Oxygen Hypotheses*
| | |
|---|---|
| (proposition 'OH1 | "Pure air contains oxygen principle.") |
| (proposition 'OH2 | "Pure air contains matter of fire and heat.") |
| (proposition 'OH3 | "In combustion, oxygen from the air combines with the burning body.") |
| (proposition 'OH4 | "Oxygen has weight.") |
| (proposition 'OH5 | "In calcination, metals add oxygen to become calxes.") |
| (proposition 'OH6 | "In reduction, oxygen is given off.") |

*Phlogiston Hypotheses*
| | |
|---|---|
| (proposition 'PH1 | "Combustible bodies contain phlogiston.") |
| (proposition 'PH2 | "Combustible bodies contain matter of heat.") |
| (proposition 'PH3 | "In combustion, phlogiston is given off.") |
| (proposition 'PH4 | "Phlogiston can pass from one body to another.") |
| (proposition 'PH5 | "Metals contain phlogiston.") |
| (proposition 'PH6 | "In calcination, phlogiston is given off.") |

*Source:* Thagard, P. (1989). Explanatory coherence. *Behavioral and Brain Sciences, 12*, p. 444. Reprinted with the permission of Cambridge University Press and Paul Thagard.

E5 and E6, if previous input has established that H5 explains E5 and H6 explains E6. Formula 4 is used to apply Principle 4, Data Priority, setting up explanation-independent excitatory links to each data unit from a special evidence unit. Finally, formula 5 sets up an inhibitory link between contradictory hypotheses H1 and H4, as prescribed by Principle 5. A full specification of ECHO's inputs and algorithms is provided in the Appendix. (Thagard, 1989, pp. 439–440)

**Table 4.2**
**Input Explanations and Contradictions in Lavoisier (1862) Example**

*Oxygen Explanations*
(explain '(OH1 OH2 OH3) 'E1)
(explain '(OH1 OH3) 'E3)
(explain '(OH1 OH3 OH4) 'E4)
(explain '(OH1 OH5) 'E5)
(explain '(OH1 OH4 OH5) 'E6)
(explain '(OH1 OH5) 'E7)
(explain '(OH1 OH6) 'E8)

*Phlogiston Explanations*
(explain '(PH1 PH2 PH3) 'E1)
(explain '(PH1 PH3 PH4) 'E2)
(explain '(PH5 PH6) 'E5)

*Contradictions*
(contradict 'PH3 'OH3)
(contradict 'PH6 'OH5)

*Data*
(data '(E1 E2 E3 E4 E5 E6 E7 E8))

*Source:* Thagard, P. (1989). Explanatory coherence. *Behavioral and Brain Sciences, 12*, p. 445. Reprinted with the permission of Cambridge University Press and Paul Thagard.

## ECHO: GENERAL CHARACTERISTICS

In the following section Thagard (1989) summarizes the chief characteristics and capabilities of ECHO.

Program runs show that the networks thus established have numerous desirable properties. *Other things being equal, activation accrues to units corresponding by hypotheses that explain more, provide simpler explanations, and are analogous to other explanatory hypotheses* [italics added]. The considerations of explanatory breadth, simplicity, and analogy are smoothly integrated. The networks are holistic, in that the activation of every unit can potentially have an effect on every other unit linked to it by a path, however lengthy. Nevertheless, the activation of a unit is directly affected by only those units to which it is linked. Although complexes of coherent propositions are evaluated together, different hypotheses in a complex can finish with different activations, depending on their particular coherence relations. The symmetry of excitatory links

**Table 4.3**
**Explanations and Contradictions for Darwin (1872/1962) Example**

*Darwin's Evidence*

(proposition 'E1    "The fossil record contains few transitional forms.")
(proposition 'E2    "Animals have complex organs.")
(proposition 'E3    "Animals have instincts.")
(proposition 'E4    "Species when crossed become sterile.")
(proposition 'E5    "Species become extinct.")
(proposition 'E6    "Once extinct, species do not reappear.")
(proposition 'E7    "Forms of life change almost simultaneously around the world.")
(proposition 'E8    "Extinct species are similar to each other and to living forms.")
(proposition 'E9    "Barriers separate similar species.")
(proposition 'E10   "Related species are concentrated in the same areas.")
(proposition 'E11   "Oceanic islands have few inhabitants, often of peculiar species.")
(proposition 'E12   "Species show systematic affinities.")
(proposition 'E13   "Different species share similar morphology.")
(proposition 'E14   "The embryos of different species are similar.")
(proposition 'E15   "Animals have rudimentary and atrophied organs.")

*Darwin's Main Hypotheses*

(proposition 'DH1   "Organic beings are in a struggle for existence.")
(proposition 'DH2   "Organic beings undergo natural selection.")
(proposition 'DH3   "Species of organic beings have evolved.")

*Darwin's Auxiliary Hypotheses*

(proposition 'DH4   "The geological record is very imperfect.")
(proposition 'DH5   "There are transitional forms of complex organs.")
(proposition 'DH6   "Mental qualities vary and are inherited.")

*Darwin's Facts*

(proposition 'DF1   "Domestic animals undergo variation.")
(proposition 'DF2   "Breeders select desired features of animals.")
(proposition 'DF3   "Domestic varieties are developed.")
(proposition 'DF4   "Organic beings in nature undergo variation.")
(proposition 'DF5   "Organic beings increase in population at a high rate.")
(proposition 'DF6   "The sustenance available to organic beings does not increase at a high rate.")
(proposition 'DF7   "Embryos of different domestic varieties are similar.")

*Creationist Hypothesis*

(proposition 'CH1   "Species were separately created by God.")

*Source:* Thagard P. (1989). Explanatory coherence. *Behavioral and Brain Sciences, 12*, p. 448.
        Reprinted with the permission of Cambridge University Press and Paul Thagard.

means that the active units tend to bring up the activation of units with which they are linked, whereas units whose activation sinks below 0 tend to bring down the activation of units to which they are linked. Data units are given priority, but can nevertheless be deactivated if they are linked to units that become deactivated. So long as excitation is not set too high . . . , the networks

**Table 4.4**
**Explanations and Contradictions for Darwin Example**

*Darwin's Explanations*
  (a) of natural selection and evolution
  (explain '(DF5 DF6) 'DH1)
  (explain '(DH1 DF4) 'DH2)
  (explain '(DH2) 'DH3)
  (b) of potential counterevidence
  (explain '(DH2 DH3 DH4) 'E1)
  (explain '(DH2 DH3 DH5) 'E2)
  (explain '(DH2 DH3 DH6) 'E3)
  (c) of diverse evidence
  (explain '(DH2) 'E5)
  (explain '(DH2 DH3) 'E6)
  (explain '(DH2 DH3) 'E7)
  (explain '(DH2 DH3) 'E8)
  (explain '(DH2 DH3) 'E9)
  (explain '(DH2 DH3) 'E10)
  (explain '(DH2 DH3) 'E11)
  (explain '(DH2 DH3) 'E12)
  (explain '(DH2 DH3) 'E13)
  (explain '(DH2 DH3) 'E14)
  (explain '(DH2 DH3) 'E15)
*Darwin's Analogies*
  (explain '(DF2) 'DF3)
  (explain '(DF2) 'DF7)
  (analogous '(DF2 DH2) '(DF3 DH3))
  (analogous '(DF2 DH2) '(DF7 E14))
*Creationist Explanations*
  (explain '(CH1) 'E1)
  (explain '(CH1) 'E2)
  (explain '(CH1) 'E3)
  (explain '(CH1) 'E4)
*Contradiction*
  (contradict 'CH1 'DH3)
*Data*
  (data '(E1 E2 E3 E4 E5 E6 E7 E8 E9 E10 E11 E12 E13 E14 E15))
  (data '(DF1 DF2 DF3 DF4 DF5 DF6 DF7))

*Source:* Thagard P. (1989). Explanatory coherence. *Behavioral and Brain Sciences, 12*, p. 449.
Reprinted with the permission of Cambridge University Press and Paul Thagard.

set up by ECHO are stable: In most of them, all units reach asymptotic activation levels after fewer than 100 cycles of updating. The most complex network implemented so far, comparing the explanatory power of Copernicus's heliocentric theory with Ptolemy's geocentric one, requires about 210 cycles before its more than 150 units have all settled. (Thagard, 1989, p. 440)

## ECHO: APPLICATIONS TO SCIENTIFIC EXPLANATORY REASONING

ECHO has been applied to the comparative evaluation of competing scientific explanations, as described by Thagard (1989) in the following section.

To show the historical application of the theory of explanatory coherence, I shall discuss two important cases of arguments concerning the best explanation: Lavoisier's argument for his oxygen theory against the phlogiston theory, and Darwin's argument for evolution by natural selection. ECHO has been applied to the following:

Contemporary debates about why the dinosaurs became extinct (Thagard, 1988b);

Arguments by Wegener and his critics for and against continental drift (Thagard & Nowak, 1988; [1990]);

Psychological experiments on how beginning students learn physics (Ranney & Thagard, 1988) and;

Copernicus's case against Ptolemaic astronomy (Nowak & Thagard, forthcoming). (Thagard, 1989, p. 444)

## ECHO APPLIED TO THE SCIENTIFIC EXPLANATORY REASONING OF LAVOISIER

In the following section Thagard (1989) presents an interesting account of how the competing phlogiston and oxygen theories were evaluated by ECHO.

In the middle of the eighteenth century, the dominant theory in chemistry was the phlogiston theory of Stahl, which provided explanations of important phenomena of combustion, respiration, and calcination (what we would call oxidation). According to the phlogiston theory, combustion takes place when phlogiston in burning bodies is given off. In the 1770's, Lavoisier developed the alternative theory that combustion takes place when burning bodies combine with oxygen from the air (for an outline of the conceptual development of his theory, see Thagard, [1990]). More than ten years after he first suspected the inadequacy of the phlogiston theory, Lavoisier mounted a full-blown attack on it in a paper called "Reflexions sur le Phlogistique" (Lavoisier, 1862).

[Tables 4.1 and 4.2] present the input given to ECHO to represent Lavoisier's argument in his 1783 polemic against phlogiston. [Table 4.1] shows the 8 propositions used to represent the evidence to be explained and the 12 used to represent the competing theories. The evidence concerns different properties of combustion and calcination, while there are two sets of hypotheses representing the oxygen and phlogiston theories, respectively. . . .

[Table 4.2] shows the part of the input that sets up the network used to make a judgement of explanatory coherence. The "explain" statements are based directly on Lavoisier's assertions about what is explained by the phlogiston theory and the oxygen theory. The "contradict" statements reflect my judgement of which of the oxygen hypotheses conflict directly with which of the phlogiston theories. . . . When ECHO runs this network, starting with all hypotheses at activation .01, it quickly favors the oxygen hypotheses, giving them activations greater than 0. In contrast, all of the phlogiston hypotheses become deactivated.

Lavoisier's argument represents a relatively simple application of ECHO, showing two sets of hypotheses competing to explain the evidence. But more complex explanatory relations can also be important. Sometimes a hypothesis that explains the evidence is itself explained by another hypothesis. Depending on the warrant for the higher-level hypothesis, this extra explanatory layer can increase acceptability: A hypothesis gains from being explained as well as by explaining the evidence. The Lavoisier example does not exhibit this kind of coherence, because neither Lavoisier nor the phlogiston theorists attempted to explain their hypotheses using higher-level hypotheses; nor does the example display the role that analogy can play in explanatory coherence. (Thagard, 1989, pp. 445–446)

## ECHO APPLIED TO THE SCIENTIFIC EXPLANATORY REASONING OF DARWIN

The power of ECHO to evaluate competing scientific arguments is demonstrated in the following comparison of evolutionary and creationist theories.

Both these aspects—coherence based on being explained and on analogy—were important in Darwin's argument for his theory of evolution by natural selection (Darwin, 1962). His two most important hypotheses were:

DH2—Organic beings undergo natural selection.

DH3—Species of organic beings have evolved.

These hypotheses together enabled him to explain a host of facts, from the geographical distribution of similar species to existence of vestigial organs. Darwin's argument was explicitly comparative: There are numerous places in the *Origin* where he points to phenomena that his theory explains but that are inexplicable on the generally accepted rival hypothesis that species were separately created by God.

Darwin's two main hypotheses were not simply cohypotheses, however, for he also used DH2 to explain DH3! That is, natural selection explains why species evolve: If populations of animals vary, and natural selection picks out those with features well adapted to particular environments, then new species will arise. Moreover, he offers a Malthusian explanation for why natural selection occurs as the result of the geometrical rate of population growth contrasted with the arithmetical rate of increase in land and food. Thus Malthusian principles explain why evolution occurs, and natural selection and evolution together explain a host of facts better than the competing creation hypothesis does.

The full picture is even more complicated than this, for Darwin frequently cites the analogy between artificial and natural selection as evidence for his theory. He contends that just as farmers are able to develop new breeds of domesticated animals, so natural selection has produced new species. He uses this analogy not simply to defend natural selection, but also to help in the explanations of the evidence: Particular explanations using natural selection incorporate the analogy with artificial selection. Finally, to complete the picture of explanatory coherence that the Darwin example offers, we must consider the alternative theological explanations that were accepted by even the best scientists until Darwin proposed his theory.

Analysis of *On the origin of species* suggests the 15 evidence statements shown in [Table 4.3]. Statements E1–E4 occur in Darwin's discussion of objections to his theory; the others are from the later chapters where he argues for his theory. [Table 4.3] also shows Darwin's main hypotheses. DH2 and DH3 are the core of the theory of evolution by natural selection, providing explanations of its main evidence, E5–E15. DH4–DH6 are auxiliary hypotheses that Darwin uses in resisting objections based on E1–E3. He considers the objections concerning the absence of transitional forms to be particularly serious, but explains it away by saying the geological record is so imperfect that we should not expect to find fossil evidence of the many intermediate species his theory requires. . . . The creationist opposition frequently mentioned by Darwin is represented by the single hypothesis that species were separately created by God.

[Table 4.4] shows the explanation and contradiction statements that ECHO uses to set up its network. . . . [There is a] hierarchy of explanations, with the high rate of population increase explaining the struggle for existence, which explains natural selection, which explains evolution. Natural selection and evolution together explain many pieces of evidence. The final component of Darwin's argument is the analogy between natural and artificial selection. . . . Just as breeders' actions explain the development of domestic varieties, so natural selection explains the evolution of species. At another level, Darwin sees an embryological analogy. The embryos of different domestic varieties are quite similar to each other, which is explained by the fact that breeders do not select for properties of embryos. Similarly, nature does not select for most properties of embryos, which explains the similarities between embryos of different species.

Darwin's discussion of objections suggests that he thought creationism could naturally explain the absence of transitional forms and the existence of complex organs and instincts. Darwin's argument was challenged in many ways, but based on his own view of the relevant explanatory relations, at least, the theory of evolution by natural selection is far more coherent than the creation hypothesis. Creationists, of course, would marshal different arguments. . . . Running ECHO to adjust the network to maximize harmony produces the expected result: Darwin's hypotheses are all activated, whereas the creation hypothesis is de-activated. In particular, the hypothesis DH3—that species evolved—reached an asymptote at .921, while the creation hypothesis, CH1, declines to $-.491$. DH3 accrues activation in three ways. It gains activation from above, from being explained by natural selection, which is derived from the struggle for existence, and from below, by virtue of the many pieces of evidence that it helps to explain. In addition, it receives activation by virtue of the sideways, analogy-based links with explanations using artificial selection. . . .

The Lavoisier and Darwin examples show that ECHO can handle very complex examples of actual scientific reasoning. One might object that in basing ECHO analyses on written texts, I have been modeling the rhetoric of the scientists, not their cognitive processes. Presumably, however, there is some correlation between what we write and what we think. ECHO could be equally well applied to explanatory relations that were asserted in the heat of verbal debate among scientists. Ranney and Thagard (1988) describe ECHO's simulation of naive subjects learning physics, where the inputs to ECHO were based on verbal protocols. (Thagard, 1989, pp. 446–449)

## ECHO AS A PSYCHOLOGICAL MODEL OF BELIEF CHANGE

The psychological validity of ECHO as a model of belief change has been experimentally investigated by Ranney and Thagard (1988). A brief summary of this research is given in the following section.

Ranney and Thagard (1988) describe the use of ECHO to model the inferences made by naive subjects learning elementary physics by using feedback provided on a computer display (Ranney, 1987). Subjects were asked to predict the motion of several projectiles and then explain these predictions. Analysis of verbal protocol data indicate that subjects sometimes underwent dramatic belief revisions while offering predictions or receiving empirical feedback. ECHO was applied to two particularly interesting cases of belief revision with propositions and explanatory relations based on the verbal protocols. The simulations captured well the dynamics of belief change as new evidence was added to shift the explanatory coherence of the set of propositions. (Thagard, 1989, p. 461)

## THE THEORY OF EXPLANATORY COHERENCE: SCOPE AND POWER

Thagard (1989) provides the following summary account of the major strengths of the theory of explanatory coherence and the ECHO system.

I conclude with a brief summary of the chief accomplishments of the theory of explanatory coherence offered here.

First, it fits directly with the actual arguments of scientists such as Lavoisier and Darwin who explicitly discuss what competing theories explain. There is no need to postulate probabilities or contrive deductive relations. The theory and ECHO have engendered a far more detailed analysis of these arguments than is typically given by proponents of other accounts. Using the same principles, it applies to important cases of legal reasoning as well.

Second, unlike most accounts of theory evaluation, this view based on explanatory coherence is inherently comparative. If two hypotheses contradict each other, they incohere, so the subsystems of propositions to which they belong will compete with each other. As ECHO shows, successful subsystems of hypotheses and evidence can emerge gracefully from local judgements of explanatory coherence.

Third, the theory of explanatory coherence permits a smooth integration of diverse criteria such as explanatory breadth, simplicity, and analogy. *ECHO's connectionist algorithm shows the computability of coherence relations. The success of the program is best attributed to the usefulness of the connectionist architectures for achieving parallel constraint satisfaction, and to the fact that the problem inherent in inference to the best explanation is the need to satisfy multiple constraints simultaneously* [italics added]. Not all computational problems are best approached this way, but parallel constraint satisfaction has proven to be very powerful for other problems as well—for example, analogical mapping (Holyoak & Thagard, in press).

Finally, my theory surmounts the problem of holism. The principles of explanatory coherence establish pairwise relations of coherence between propositions in an explanatory system. Thanks to ECHO, we know that there is an efficient algorithm for adjusting a system of propositions to turn coherence relations into judgements of acceptability. The algorithm allows every proposition to influence every other one, because there is typically a path of links between any two units, but the influences are set up systematically to reflect explanatory relations. Theory assessment is done as a whole, but a theory does not have to be rejected or accepted as a whole. Those hypotheses that participate in many explanations will be much more coherent with the evidence, and with each other, and will therefore be harder to reject. More peripheral hypotheses may be deactivated even if the rest of the theory they are linked to wins. We thus get a holistic account of inference that can nevertheless differentiate between strong and weak hypotheses. Although our hypotheses face evidence only as a corporate body, evidence and relations of explanatory coherence suffice to separate good hypotheses from bad. (Thagard, 1989, p. 465)

## COMMENTARY

There are two primary ways in which to establish the significance of the theory of explanatory coherence and the ECHO system. The first regards the adequacy of ECHO as a model of human explanatory reasoning. The second regards its adequacy as a computational approach to explanatory reasoning.

### ECHO as a Model of Human Explanatory Reasoning

Human explanatory reasoning involves both conscience, symbolic, intentional, and serial processing and unconscious, implicit, emergent, and parallel processing periods. ECHO cannot serve as a model of the former set of characteristics, but as a connectionist architecture it may serve as an approximation to the latter set of characteristics.

### ECHO as a Computational Approach to Explanatory Reasoning

ECHO appears to be an important computational approach to establishing the coherence of hypotheses and evidence. ECHO accomplishes its integrated function by means of an algorithm that meets the requirements of parallel constraint satisfaction.

ECHO is a computational mechanism that embodies the basic principles of the theory of explanatory coherence. ECHO and its underlying theory can be evaluated against the criterion of generality of application. Table 4.5 demonstrates generality across the domains of scientific and everyday explanatory reasoning.

**Table 4.5**
**The Generality of Intelligent Explanatory Reasoning: Applications of ECHO**

| Application of ECHO | Reference |
|---|---|
| Evaluation of the oxygen theory versus the phlogiston theory (Lavoisier) | Thagard (1989) |
| Evaluation of evolutionary theory versus creationist theory (Darwin) | Thagard (1989) |
| Evaluation of theories concerning extinction of the dinosaurs | Thagard (1988b) |
| Evaluation of theories concerning continental drift | Thagard & Nowak (1988; 1990) |
| Application of problem solving in physics | Ranney & Thagard (1988) |
| Evaluation of Copernican astronomy versus Ptolemiac astronomy | Nowak & Thagard (1989) |
| Evaluation of legal reasoning | Thagard (1989) |
| Evaluation of text comprehension | Schank & Ranney (1991) |
| Evaluation of belief revision in naive physics | Schank & Ranney (1992) |
| Evaluation of adversarial argumentation | Thagard (1993) |
| Perception of social relationships | Read & Marcus-Newhall (1993) |

# 5

# The Evolution of Scientific Discovery Systems

## *SCIENTIFIC DISCOVERY SYSTEMS AND PHILOSOPHY OF SCIENCE*

### EVOLUTION OF SCIENTIFIC DISCOVERY SYSTEMS: OVERVIEW

Langley and Zytkow (1989) summarize their analysis of the evolution of scientific discovery systems in the following account.

In this paper we trace the development of research in empirical discovery. We focus on four machine discovery systems that share a number of features: the use of data-driven heuristics to constrain the search for numeric laws; a reliance on theoretical terms; and the recursive application of a few general discovery methods. We examine each system in light of the innovations it introduced over its predecessors, providing some insight into the conceptual progress that has occurred in machine discovery. Finally, we reexamine this research from the perspectives of the history and philosophy of science. (Langley & Zytkow, 1989, p. 283)

### EMPIRICAL DISCOVERY: THE INDUCTION OF NUMERIC LAWS

Artificial intelligence research in the area of scientific discovery has been primarily directed toward the achievement of simple physical laws

by data-driven rather than theory-driven methods. Langley and Zytkow
(1989) describe this empirically based computational approach to scientific discovery systems in the following section.

In this paper we trace one evolutionary chain of research on discovery, in particular the development of data-driven methods relating to numeric law induction. We examine four systems—Gerwin's function induction system, Langley,
Bradshaw, and Simon's BACON, Zytkow's FAHRENHEIT, and Nordhausen
and Langley's IDS—and describe how each program introduces abilities lacking
in earlier systems. *The conceptual advances involve three different but interrelated aspects of discovery: the form of laws and theoretical terms discovered;
the ability to determine the scope and context of laws; and the ability to design
experiments.* We evaluate each of the systems, but we focus on their theoretical
contributions rather than on reporting their behavior in specific domains. We
close the paper by reviewing the work on machine discovery from the views of
the history and philosophy of science. . . .
*We can define the task of empirical discovery as*:

• Given. A set of observations or data.
• Find. One or more general laws that summarize those data.

In the domains we will examine, an observation consists of a conjunction of
attribute-value pairs, either numeric or symbolic in nature. For instance, one
might observe a particular combination of values for the temperature (T), volume
(V), and pressure (P) for a contained gas. Laws take the form of relations (usually arithmetic) between these terms (such as $PV/T = k$ in the case of gases)
and the conditions under which these relations hold. *Empirical discovery is the
task of finding such laws that account for a given set of data.*

We have chosen to focus on empirical discovery in this paper for two reasons.
First, most research in machine discovery has dealt with this task, including our
own work. *Second, empirical discovery often occurs in the early stages of a
field's evolution, before scientists have acquired much knowledge of the domain.
As a result, it seems likely that general, domain-independent heuristics play a
more central role in this task than in the process of theory formation and revision.* Nonetheless, empirical discoveries are rare even among trained scientists,
making them eminently worthy of attention. This combination makes a good
starting point for the mechanistic study of discovery. (Langley & Zytkow, 1989,
pp. 283–285, italics added)

## EMPIRICAL DISCOVERY SYSTEMS: A FRAMEWORK
## FOR THEIR ANALYSIS

In the analysis of four discovery systems, Langley and Zytkow (1989)
utilize a generic methodological framework. This framework includes the

interlocking methods of the establishment of theoretical terms, the application of data-driven heuristics, and the systematic use of recursion.

*First, all of the systems define* theoretical terms *that let them state laws in simple forms and that aid in the discovery process.* The concept of momentum, defined as the product of mass and velocity, is one example of such a theoretical term. Using this product, one can state the law of conserved momentum as a simple linear relation. We will see that other types of theoretical terms are also possible. . . .

*Second, the systems all employ* data-driven *heuristics to direct their searches through the space of theoretical terms and numeric laws.* These heuristics match against different possible regularities in the data and take different actions depending on which regularity they detect. Some heuristics propose laws or hypotheses, others define a new theoretical term, and yet others alter the proposed scope of a law. Different data lead to the application of alternative sequences of heuristics, and thus to different sets of empirical laws.

*Finally, all the systems can apply their method* recursively *to the results of previous applications, and they achieve much of their power in this fashion.* Thus, knowledge resulting from the application of one heuristic can later be examined and extended by other heuristics. For instance, once a theoretical term has been defined, it can be used as the basis for defining still other terms. In general, this recursive structure leads to synergistic behaviors that would not otherwise occur. (Langley & Zytkow, 1989, pp. 285–286, italics added)

## GERWIN'S FUNCTION INDUCTION SYSTEM

Gerwin's system is an important starting point in the evolution of computational approaches to scientific discovery. Gerwin's system and, interestingly, his human subjects as well, depended on heuristic methods to attain its discoveries. General characteristics of the Gerwin system are set forth in the following section.

Gerwin [1974] described one of the earliest machine discovery systems. He was concerned with inducing complex functions of one variable in the presence of noisy data. To this end, he collected and analyzed verbal protocols of humans solving a set of function induction tasks, as well as constructing a system that operated on the same class of problems. We will not review his experimental results here, except to note that he observed subjects using heuristic methods in their search for laws. The task itself and the system are more interesting for our purposes.

Gerwin's research on function induction introduced some important ideas that were to influence later work in empirical discovery. For instance, it served to clearly define the task of numeric discovery. At the same time, it also presented evidence that humans invoked heuristic search methods to solve such problems; the use of such methods (rather than algorithmic methods borrowed from statistics) made numeric discovery an interesting task for artificial intelligence.

Although Gerwin focused on functions of only one variable, some of his functions were quite complex. All were defined in terms of one or more primitive functions, taken from the set $e^{x/2}$, $x^2$, $x$, $x^{1/2}$, ln $x$, sin $x$, and cos $x$, and combined using the connectives $+$, $-$, $/$, and x. For instance, one such function is $y = x^2 \sin x - \ln x$; another is $y = x/\cos x$. However, a random component was included in each of the 15 test functions used, so the functions did not describe that data perfectly. *In each case, Gerwin presented his subjects (and his program) with 10 $\times$ values and their associated y values. From these data, the subjects and program were to infer the function best fitting the observations.* (Langley & Zytkow, 1989, pp. 287–288, italics added)

## GERWIN'S SYSTEM: METHODS AND RESULTS

Gerwin's function induction system achieved its results by the methods of detecting patterns and computing residuals. These methods are described in the following section.

Gerwin's system included a number of condition-action rules for detecting regularities in the data. For instance, it looked for patterns having periodic trends with increasing (or decreasing) amplitudes; it also noted monotonic increasing (or decreasing) trends when they occurred. Each such pattern suggested an associated class of functions (or combination of functions) that could lead to its production. Thus, when the program noted a trend, it hypothesized that some member of the associated class was an additive component of the overall function.

Having identified a set of likely components, the system selected one of those functions and used it to generate predicted $y$ values for each $x$ value. It then subtracted the predicted data from the actual values, checking to see whether the *residuals* had less variance than the original observations. If not, the system tried some other function from the same class and repeated the process. If none of these were successful, it looked for some other pattern in the data.

Upon finding a useful component function, Gerwin's system applied the same induction method to the residual data. It looked for patterns in these data, proposed component functions, tested their effect, and either rejected them or included them as another component in the developing overall function. This process continued until the system could no longer detect any patterns in the residual data. Since no regularity remained, the program would halt at this point, assuming it had found the best description of the original data. Using this approach, Gerwin's program was able to discover many of the functions used in his experiment, some of them quite complex. (Langley & Zytkow, 1989, pp. 288–289)

## GERWIN'S SYSTEM: STRENGTHS AND LIMITATIONS

Langley and Zytkow (1989) provide the following evaluation of Gerwin's system.

The particular system that Gerwin implemented relied on three important notions that we have already discussed. The first was the use of data-driven heuristics— his pattern-detecting condition-action rules—to direct the discovery process. The second was the notion of adding component functions, which can be viewed as computing the values of those new terms. The final idea involved the recursive application of the original heuristics to these residuals, leading to new residuals and new data until a satisfactory function had been obtained. Taken together, these three features led to a simple yet powerful method for empirical discovery.

Despite its innovations, Gerwin's system was simplistic along a number of dimensions. It could discover only functions in one variable; it could define only one form of theoretical term; and its data-driven heuristics were specific to particular classes of functions. Moreover, the system was tested only on a set of artificially generated functions, so its implications for real-world discovery tasks was not clear. Later work in machine discovery would address all of these issues. (Langley & Zytkow, 1989, p. 289)

## THE BACON SCIENTIFIC DISCOVERY SYSTEM: GENERAL BACKGROUND

Langley and Zytkow (1989) provide a concise history of the development of the BACON system in the following passage.

Although Gerwin's early work had many limitations, it provided an initial definition of the numeric discovery task and it suggested that this problem was amenable to the same heuristic search methods that had been used to explain other forms of intelligent behavior. These insights led directly to the BACON project (Langley [1978, 1981]; Bradshaw, Langley and Simon [1980], Langley, Bradshaw, and Simon [1983]), an attempt to construct a more general and more comprehensive model of empirical discovery.

BACON is actually a sequence of discovery systems that were developed over a number of years. In this paper, we will focus on BACON.4, since that program incorporates the main ideas and tells the most coherent story. (Langley & Zytkow, 1989, p. 289)

## THE BACON SYSTEM: GENERAL METHODS

In the following section, Langley and Zytkow (1989) describe BA-CON's methods for representing data and laws.

As input, the system accepts a set of independent terms and requests the corresponding values of the dependent terms. As an example, BACON might be given three independent terms—the pressure P on a gas, the temperature T of the gas, and the quantity N of the gas—and the single dependent term V, the resulting volume of the gas. Independent terms may take on either numeric or nominal (symbolic) values, whereas dependent terms are always numeric.

As output, BACON.4 generates three interrelated structures that constitute its empirical discoveries:

(1) a set of numeric laws stated as simple constancies or linear relations, such as X = 8.32, and U = 1.57V + 4.6, along with some simple conditions under which each law holds;

(2) a set of definitions that relate theoretical terms to directly observable variables, such as X = Y/T and Y = PV; it is these definitions that let BACON state its laws in such a simple form;

(3) a set of intrinsic properties, such as *mass* and *specific heat*, that take on numeric values; these values are associated with the symbolic values of nominal terms; thus, the *mass* of *object* A may be 1.43 while the *mass* of *object* B is 2.61.

*Although each structure has a simple form, taken together they provide BA-CON with considerable representational power. Using these three knowledge types, the system has rediscovered a wide range of laws from the history of physics and chemistry, including forms of the ideal gas law, Coulomb's law, Snell's law of refraction, Black's law of specific heat, Gay-Lussac's law of combining volumes, and Canizzaro's determination of relative atomic weights.* (Langley & Zytkow, 1989, pp. 289–290, italics added)

## THE BACON SYSTEM: PROCEDURES FOR PHYSICAL LAW DISCOVERY

BACON contains elementary processes for the discovery of simple physical laws. These laws typically involve the establishment of a relationship between two variables. In the following section, BACON's discovery heuristics are stated in general terms and then applied to Galileo's law that relates time elapsed and distanced traversed by a falling object.

BACON's most basic operation involves discovering a functional relation between two numeric terms. This is the direct analog to Gerwin's function induc-

**Table 5.1**
**Data Obeying the Law of Uniform Acceleration**

| Time (T) | Distance (D) | D/T | D/T² |
|---|---|---|---|
| 0.1 | 0.098 | 0.98 | 9.80 |
| 0.2 | 0.390 | 1.95 | 9.75 |
| 0.3 | 0.880 | 2.93 | 9.78 |
| 0.4 | 1.572 | 3.93 | 9.83 |
| 0.5 | 2.450 | 4.90 | 9.80 |
| 0.6 | 3.534 | 5.89 | 9.82 |

*Source:* Langley, P., and Zytkow, J. (1989). Data-driven approaches to empirical discovery. *Artificial Intelligence, 40*, p. 291.

tion task. For example, Galileo's law of falling bodies relates the distance D from which an object is dropped to the time T it takes to reach the ground. This law can be stated as $D/T^2 = k$, where $k$ is a constant. To discover laws relating two numeric variables, BACON employs three simple heuristics:

INCREASING
IF the values of X increase as the values of Y increase, THEN define the ratio X/Y and examine its values.

DECREASING
IF the values of X increase as the values of Y decrease, THEN define the product XY and examine its values.

CONSTANT
IF the values of X are nearly constant for a number of values, THEN hypothesize that X always has this value.

[Table 5.1] presents some idealized data that obey the law of falling bodies. Given the co-occurring values of D and T shown in the table, BACON notices that one term increases as the other increases. This leads the INCREASING rule to apply, defining the ratio D/T and computing its values. Since the resulting values increase as those of D decrease, they lead the system to apply the DECREASING heuristic, which defines the product $D^2/T$. When it computes the values for this new term, BACON notes that all the values are very near the mean of 9.795. This causes the rule CONSTANT to apply, hypothesizing that

$D^2/T$ always has this value; the system has rediscovered a form of Galileo's law. From this example, one can see that BACON makes no distinction between directly observable terms and those it has defined itself. The system can also discover other complex relations in this way, such as Kepler's third law of planetary motion: $d^3/p^2 = k$, where $d$ is the planet's distance from the sun, $p$ its period, and $k$ is a constant. (Langley & Zytkow, 1989, pp. 290–291)

## THE BACON SYSTEM: ADVANCED DISCOVERY PROCEDURES

In the previous section, BACON discovered simple scientific laws that involve only two variables. In the following section, BACON's advanced procedures for discovering complex physical laws that involve more than two variables are described and exemplified.

In order to see how BACON discovers more complex laws involving a number of independent terms, let us consider a simple form of Black's heat law. This relates the initial temperatures of two substances ($T_1$ and $T_2$) with their temperature after they have been combined ($T_f$). The law can be stated as: $(c_1 M_1 + c_2 M_2) T_f = c_1 M_1 T_1 + c_2 M_2 T_2$, where $M_1$ and $M_2$ are the two initial masses and $c_1$ and $c_2$ are constants associated with the particular substances used in the experiment. For now we will assume the same substance is used in both cases; this makes $c_1 = c_2$ and lets us cancel them out from the equation. This gives the simpler law $T_f = (M_1/(M_1 + M_2)) T_1 + (M_2/(M_1 + M_2)) T_2$.

Given a set of independent terms such as $M_1$, $M_2$, $T_2$, BACON constructs a simple factoral design experiment involving all combinations of independent values, and proceeds to collect data. In this case, the system begins by holding $M_1$, $M_2$, and $T_1$ constant and varying the values of $T_2$, examining the effect on the final temperature $T_f$ in each situation. In this way, the program collects the co-occurring independent and dependent values it requires to discover a simple law. In this case it finds the linear relation $T_f = aT_2 + b$, where $a$ is the slope of the line and $b$ its intercept. However, the system follows a conservative strategy upon discovering such a law, stating only that it holds when the other independent terms ($M_1$, $M_2$, and $T_1$) take on their observed values.

Nevertheless, BACON's ultimate goal is to discover a more general relation that incorporates all the independent variables. Thus, the system runs the same experiment again, but this time with different values for $T_1$, the temperature of the other substance. The result is a number of specific laws that hold for different values of $T_1$, but which all have the form $T_f = aT_2 + b$. At this point, the program shifts perspectives and begins to treat $a$ and $b$ as higher-level dependent terms, the values of which it has determined from the earlier experiments.

BACON then uses its methods for finding simple laws to uncover a relation

**Table 5.2**
**Relations Discovered at Different Levels for Black's Law**

| Level | Term varied | Laws found | Laws implied |
|-------|-------------|------------|--------------|
| 1 | $T_2$ | $T_f = aT_2 + b$ | $T_f = aT_2 + b$ |
| 2 | $T_1$ | $a = c$ | $T_f = cT_2 + dT_1$ |
|   |   | $b = dT_1$ |   |
| 3 | $M_2$ | $M_2 = e(M_2/c) + f$ | $T_f = eM_2T_2/(M_2 - f)$ |
|   |   | $dM_2 = gd + h$ | $\quad + hT_1/(M_2 - g)$ |
| 4 | $M_1$ | $f = jM_1, \ g = kM_1$ | $T_f = M_2T_2/(M_2 - jM_1)$ |
|   |   | $h = lM_1, \ e = 1.0$ | $\quad + lM_1T_1/(M_2 - kM_1)$ |
| 5 | Substance$_2$ | $j = pc_2, \ k = qc_2$ | $T_f = M_2T_2/(M_2 - pc_2M_1)$ |
|   |   | $l = rc_2$ | $\quad + rc_2M_1T_1/(M_2 - gc_2M_1)$ |
| 6 | Substance$_1$ | $pc_1 = -1.0$ | $T_f = M_2T_2/(M_2 + (c_2/c_1)M_1)$ |
|   |   | $qc_1 = -1.0$ | $\quad + (c_2/c_1)M_1T_1/(M_2 + (c_2/c_1)M_1)$ |

*Source:* Langley, P., and Zytkow, J. (1989). Data-driven approaches to empirical discovery. *Artificial Intelligence, 40,* p. 293.

between the values of $T_1$ and these two terms. In this example, the system finds that the slope $a$ is unaffected by $T_1$, which it states as the second-level law $a = c$. It also discovers a linear relation between temperature and the intercept that can be stated as $b = dT_1$; since the intercept of this line is zero, it is omitted.

Having established two second-level laws, BACON now proceeds to vary $M_2$, the mass of the second substance, and to observe its effects on the parameters in these laws. This involves running additional experiments by varying $T_1$ and $T_2$, but once this has been done the system has a set of values for the parameters $c$ and $d$, each pair associated with a different value of $M_2$. Upon examining these values, BACON does not find any simple laws but it notes that $c$ and $M_2$ increase together; as a result, it defines the ratio term $M_2/c$. This new term is linearly related to $M_2$, giving the third-level law $M_2 = e \ (M_2/c) \ + f$. Similar regularities lead the program to define the product $dM_2$ and to find the linear relation $dM_2 = gd + h$.

Now that it has incorporated the independent terms $T_1$, $T_2$, and $M_2$ into its laws, BACON turns to the final variable, $M_1$. Varying this leads to a set of additional experiments in which the other terms are varied, and from these the system estimates values for the parameters $e, f, g,$ and $h$ for each value of $M_1$. The slope term $e$ has the constant value 1.0 in all cases, but the remaining terms vary. Closer inspection reveals that $f, g,$ and $h$ are all linearly related to $M_1$ and that each line has a zero intercept, with slopes respectively $j, k,$ and $l$.

At this point, BACON has rediscovered the simplest version of Black's law presented above, though not in the form we specified. [Table 5.2] traces the steps followed by the system, listing the laws formulated at each level of the discovery process; at this point of the discussion we are at level 4. We should note that, as it finds laws at each level, the program places conditions on these laws corresponding to the values of the terms that it has not yet varied. As it incorporates these terms into higher-level laws, the conditions are generalized. *Thus, BACON gradually expands the scope of its laws as it moves to higher levels of description.* (Langley & Zytkow, 1989, pp. 291–293, italics added)

## THE BACON SYSTEM: THE PROCEDURE OF INTRINSIC PROPERTIES

In addition to discovering physical laws composed of numeric terms, the BACON system can also discover physical laws that involve symbolic terms. For the latter type of discovery, the procedure of intrinsic properties is deployed. In the following section, BACON's procedure of intrinsic properties is described and exemplified.

The above methods suffice to discover laws that relate numeric terms, such as occur in the ideal gas law. However, there are many historical cases in which scientists were also confronted with nominal or symbolic attributes. For instance, the two substances in Black's law are best described in this manner; one can combine water with water, water with mercury, and so forth. Upon varying the substances in this manner, one finds that the values of parameters in the various laws also change. However, one cannot incorporate such symbolic terms directly into its numeric laws; some other step is required.

BACON's response in such cases is to *postulate* numeric terms that are associated with the observable nominal ones; we call these *intrinsic properties*. In the Black's law example, one can introduce such a property (called *specific heat*), the values of which are associated with different substances. Thus, if we let the specific heat $c$ for *water* be 1.0, then the specific heat for *mercury* is 0.0332 and the specific heat for *ethyl alcohol* is 0.456. Once BACON has established these values, it can relate the values of $c$ to parameters from its various laws, giving a higher-level law that effectively incorporates the two substances.

Let us continue with the Black's law example where we left off. BACON had incorporated the numeric terms $M_1$, $M_2$, $T_1$, and $T_2$ into a coherent set of laws, all ultimately related to the final temperature $T_f$. The system had also arrived at values for four parameters at the fourth level of description. One of these (call it $i$) involved a simple constancy; the others, $j$, $k$, and $l$, were the slopes of linear relations. The values for these parameters were conditional on the particular pair of substances used in the experiment, in this case two containers of water.

BACON's next step is to vary the second substance, using different materials such as mercury and ethyl alcohol with the first substance (still held constant as water). Upon doing this, the system notes that the values of $j$, $k$, and $l$ all vary, though the value of $i$ remains unchanged. In order to incorporate these terms into a higher-level law, the program requires some numeric independent variable associated with the second substance; we will call this $c_2$. BACON must assign values for this term, one for each nominal value of the substance, and it bases these values on those for the parameter $j$ (though $k$ or $l$ would have served equally well). The term $c_2$ is an intrinsic property, and the numeric values assigned to it are intrinsic values. These are initially stored with the condition that the first substance be water.

At this point BACON notes a linear relation between $c_2$ and $j$, but this is tautological, since it had defined the intrinsic property using the values of the latter term. However, the system also discovers linear relations between $c_2$ and $k$ and between $c_2$ and $l$; these are not guaranteed to hold and so have empirical content. The program has moved beyond tautologies and into laws capable of making predictions. Even more interesting events occur when the program varies the first substance in the experiment.

Upon placing mercury in contact with water, with mercury, and with ethyl alcohol, BACON finds that the values of the slope $j$ differ from when the first substance was water. But more important, they are linearly related to the earlier values of $j$. This tells BACON that the values of its intrinsic property should be useful regardless of the first substance; the condition that the first substance be water is dropped and the intrinsic values are stored with only the values of the second substance as a condition for retrieval. Thus, one value of $c_2$ is associated with water, another with mercury, and a third with ethyl alcohol. This lets the system retrieve the values of $c_2$ that it identified earlier and to note a linear relation between $c_2$ and the parameter $j$. Moreover, this law is nontautological; the values of $c_2$ were based on earlier values of $j$, not the current ones.

This generalization of the conditions on the intrinsic values also proves useful at the next (and highest) level of description. Different linear relations occur when different substances are placed in the first container, and the slopes of these lines provide the dependent terms for BACON to relate to the first substance. Since this is a nominal term, one could define a new intrinsic property, but there is no need; the conditions on the property $c$ have been sufficiently generalized to let its values be used in this case as well. Thus, BACON infers the values of $c_1$ and relates these to the various slope terms. *The final set of relations correspond to Black's heat law, and the terms $c_1$ and $c_2$ correspond to the specific heats of the first and second substance, respectively. [Table 5.2] summarizes the forms of the final laws.* (Langley & Zytkow, 1989, pp. 293–294, italics added)

## THE BACON SYSTEM: STRENGTHS AND LIMITATIONS

Langley and Zytkow (1989) evaluate the concepts and procedures of BACON as a scientific discovery system in the following terms.

Now that we have examined BACON's representation and heuristics, we can evaluate its behavior in terms of some general issues relating to empirical discovery. *Basically, we will conclude that on two dimensions—the forms of laws it can handle and the types of new terms it can define—the system performs quite well. However, the program's ability to determine the scope of laws and its ability to design experiments leave much to be desired* [italics added].

Recall that BACON states all laws as either simple constancies or linear relations between two variables. However, when combined with the ability to define new ratio/product terms and to introduce intrinsic properties, this is sufficient to state a wide range of laws. For instance, the system can formulate laws involving exponents; one example is Kepler's law ($d^3/p^2 = k$) and another is Coulomb's law ($FD^2/q_1q_2 = k$). Another is Ohm's law for electric circuits, which in its most general form can be stated as $TD^2/(LI - rI) = b$. BACON can also discover a general version of the ideal gas law that does not rely on the absolute temperature scale: $PV = aNT + bN$. *These suggest that the system can discover a respectable variety of empirical laws.*

*BACON also fares well in its ability to define new terms, and as we have stated, much of its overall power resides in this capability* [italics added]. The method of defining products and ratios may seem very weak at first glance, but recall that once a new term has been defined, the system does not distinguish it from observable terms. Thus, the program can define products of ratios, ratios of products of products, and so forth. *Also, upon discovering a linear relation at one level of description, the system treats the slope and intercept as new dependent terms at the next level. This means that slopes and intercepts can themselves be incorporated in complex relations, as we saw in the general version of the ideal gas law above. The ability to introduce intrinsic properties provides power of an entirely different type, letting BACON effectively transform nominal variables into numeric ones, which can then be incorporated into numeric laws.*

*However, the system is less robust in representing and discovering the scope of laws* [italics added]. We have seen that BACON places conditions—in the form of the values of unvaried terms—on both its laws and its intrinsic values, and that it cautiously drops these conditions if the data merit such action. But one can imagine alternatives that BACON ignores. For instance, Black's law holds across a broad range of temperatures, but not across the phase boundaries at which substances change from liquid to solid. Similarly, the ideal gas law is an excellent approximation for normal temperatures, but it breaks down at high levels. *Ideally, an empirical discovery system should be able to detect and represent such constraints on the laws it formulates.*

*BACON's ability to generate experiments is also quite limited. The system is presented with independent terms and their suggested values, and from this it algorithmically produces a combinatorial design. There is no sense in which the system gathers data adaptively in response to the observations it makes.*

*Such intelligent experiment generation is an important component of scientific discovery, and a robust empirical discovery system should have this capacity.* (Langley & Zytkow, 1989, pp. 295–296, italics added)

## THE FAHRENHEIT SYSTEM: GENERAL BACKGROUND

Langley and Zytkow (1989) describe general developmental features of the FAHRENHEIT system in the following passage.

We have seen that BACON constituted a significant step beyond Gerwin's early discovery work, but that it still had a number of limitations. The most pressing of these revolved around identifying the scope of the discovered laws and generating experiments in an intelligent manner. In this section, we describe FAHRENHEIT (Zytkow [1987], Koehn and Zytkow [1986]), a successor to BACON that responds to these issues.

The FAHRENHEIT system borrows heavily from the earlier work by Langley, Simon, and Bradshaw, including a BACON-like routine as one of its basic components. This component is similar enough to BACON.4 that we will ignore the differences and focus instead on its interaction with the remainder of the system. In other words, Zytkow's work does not question the basic validity of the earlier system; rather, it argues that BACON told only part of the story. The form of FAHRENHEIT's input is identical to that given in BACON: a set of independent and dependent attributes that take on numeric or symbolic values. Zytkow's program interacts with a separate simulated environment that eases the running of experiments, but this difference is not theoretically significant.

The system's output is also very similar: a set of numeric laws that summarize the data, stated through a set of theoretical terms defined using observables. The existing version does not incorporate intrinsic properties, but these could be easily added. (Langley & Zytkow, 1989, p. 296)

## THE FAHRENHEIT SYSTEM: REPRESENTING LAWS AND THEIR SCOPE

FAHRENHEIT possesses the capacity to determine the scope or limits of numeric laws. The means for achieving this determination is explained in the following section.

Rather than stating the scope of the law as a simplistic set of independent values, FAHRENHEIT specifies these limits as another set of numeric laws. It accomplishes this feat through a familiar ploy—defining new theoretical terms.

Let us consider a simple form of Black's specific heat law, in which one combines the substances water and mercury and in which one holds their masses constant at 0.1 kg and 5.0 kg, respectively. The simplified law can be stated as $T_f = jT_m + kT_w$, where $T_m$ and $T_w$ are the initial temperatures for mercury and water, and $T_f$ is the final temperature of both. The terms $j$ and $k$ are constants that hold for this particular pair of substances and the given masses. In fact, this relationship holds only for limited values of the temperature $T_m$ and $T_w$, and it is with representing this limitation that we are concerned.

Like its laws, FAHRENHEIT represents limits on laws at varying levels of description. For instance, suppose the system has formulated the first-level law $T_f = aT_m + b$, where $a$ and $b$ are constants for a given temperature $T_w$. Along with these parameters, FAHRENHEIT also defines two *limit* terms, one representing the maximum value of $T_m$ for which the law holds and another for the minimum value. We will call these $T_{m\ min}$ and $T_{m\ max}$, respectively.

These limit terms may have different values for different settings of $T_w$, and these values are carried to the second level of description along with $a$ and $b$. At this level, the limit terms themselves may enter into relations with the independent variable. In this case, simple laws exist for both boundary terms: $T_{m\ max} = -0.6T_w + 160$ and $T_{m\ min} = -0.6T_w$. Of course, the system also states laws involving the slope and intercept parameters from the first level; in this case, $a$ is constant and $b = dT_m$.

In addition, FAHRENHEIT also specifies limits on all four of these higher-level laws, defining versions of $T_{w\ max}$ and $T_{w\ min}$, the maximum and minimum temperatures for which each law is valid. *This means that the system not only has the ability to place limits on its basic laws; it can also state the boundary conditions under which its boundary laws hold. This is another instance of the recursive theme underlying the class of discovery systems we have been considering.* (Langley & Zytkow, 1989, pp. 296–297, italics added)

## THE FAHRENHEIT SYSTEM: ITS DISCOVERY METHODS

Langley and Zytkow (1989) describe FAHRENHEIT's methods for the discovery of scientific laws in the following section.

Now that we have examined FAHRENHEIT's representation of empirical laws, let us turn to the method by which it discovers them. The system's basic organization is very similar to that used in BACON, and it begins in exactly the same manner—by varying the values of one independent term and examining the effect on the dependent variables. Returning to the Black's law example, suppose FAHRENHEIT varies $T_m$ and observes the resulting values of $T_f$. Using the same heuristics as BACON.4, the program notes a linear relationship between the two terms and formulates the law that $T_f = aT_m + b$, where the slope $a = 0.624$ and the intercept $b = 11.28$.

At this point, BACON would assume that the only conditions on the new law are the values of the independent terms that have not yet been varied; i.e., that the substances are mercury and water, that $T_w = 30°$, that $M_m = 5$ kg, and that $M_w = 0.1$ kg. It would proceed to vary these terms in order to determine their effect on the parameters $a$ and $b$. FAHRENHEIT does not make this assumption, realizing that the law relating $T_m$ and $T_f$ may hold for only *some* values of $T_w$. To check this possibility, the system selectively gathers additional data, varying the value of $T_w$ in an attempt to determine upper and lower boundaries on the law.

FAHRENHEIT first increments the independent term by the same user-specified amount used in its earlier data-gathering steps. If the law still holds, it increments by double this amount and checks again. This doubling continues until the system arrives at some value of the variable for which the law is violated, or until it reaches values beyond the range of the measuring instrument. In the latter case, the program assumes the law has no upper limit; in the former case, it attempts to find the exact point at which the law ceases to hold. For this the system uses a successive approximation method, halving the distance between the highest known value that obeys the law and the lowest known value that violates the law. This process continues until it has determined the upper limit within the desired (user-specified) degree of precision. FAHRENHEIT employs the same method to determine the lower limit on the law.

Returning to our example, after discovering the law $T_f = aT_m + b$ when $T_w = 30°$, the system would determine the upper and lower bounds on this law. For this situation, the law holds only between $T_m = 142°$ and $T_m = -18°$; for values outside this range, the linear relation cannot be used to predict the dependent term. Other limits hold for other values of $T_w$, and this leads to the next stage in FAHRENHEIT's discovery process. (Langley & Zytkow, 1989, pp. 298–299)

## THE FAHRENHEIT SYSTEM: ESTABLISHING THE LIMITS OF COMPLEX LAWS

Langley and Zytkow (1989) set forth FAHRENHEIT's procedures for the discovery of complex laws and their limits in the following account.

Recall that once BACON has induced a law relating one independent term to a dependent term (say $T_f$ and $T_m$), it recourses to a higher level. The program varies another independent term (say $T_w$) and, for each value of that term, repeats the experimentation that led to the original law. In each case, the system finds the same form of the law, but the parameters (say $a$ and $b$) in that law may take on different values. These become dependent values at the next higher level of description and are associated with the independent values under which they occurred. Once it has collected enough higher-level data, BA-CON applies its heuristics to induce a higher-level law (say $a = c$ and $b = dT_w$).

BACON's successor follows the same basic strategy, but as we have seen, it defines two additional theoretical terms for each law discovered at the lower level. The system treats these terms as dependent variables at the next higher level and attempts to relate their values to those of the varied independent term. In our Black's law example, the limit terms are $T_{m\ max}$ and $T_{m\ min}$, whereas the second independent term (to which they must be related) is $T_w$. In this case, FAHRENHEIT discovers the two linear relations described above, one between $T_{m\ max}$ and $T_w$ $(T_{m\ max} = -0.6T_w + 160)$ and the other between $T_{m\ max}$ and $T_w$ $(T_{m\ max} = -0.6T_w)$. They state that, as the temperature of mercury increases, there is a decrease in both the maximum and minimum temperatures of water for which the law holds.

FAHRENHEIT's next step follows from its inherently recursive nature—it attempts to establish limits on these limit laws. It uses the same scheme it employed at the lower level, exploring values of the independent term (this time $T_w$) until it finds the upper and lower limits on each law.

However, recall that FAHRENHEIT has also discovered another law at the current level; this is $b = dT_w$, which relates the intercept of the lower-level law to the temperature of water. Naturally, the program also searches for the limits on this law in terms of $T_w$. The lower limit for this law (zero) corresponds to the lower limit for both the maximum and minimum laws, and the upper limit (100) corresponds to the upper limit for the maximum law. However, the latter differs from the upper limit (64.2) for the minimum law, indicating a range of the basic law $(a = cT_w)$ for which the lower limit is unknown. . . . The current version of FAHRENHEIT leaves this range unspecified, but future versions should attempt to determine its functional form as well.

In summary, the new system employs the same recursive structure as BA-CON, which lets it discover the same higher-level laws (relating multiple variables) as did the earlier system. However, FAHRENHEIT's inclusion of theoretical terms for the scope of a law also lets it discover:

1) upper and lower limits on the higher-level laws;

2) laws that express upper and lower limits as functions of other terms; and

3) limits on these limit-based laws themselves.

The example we have considered is relatively simple in that it involved only two independent terms and thus generated only two levels of description. But FAHRENHEIT's discovery strategy applies equally well to more complex situations involving many variables and levels, and the system will recursively apply its heuristics until it can discover no further regularities. (Langley & Zytkow, 1989, pp. 299–300)

## THE FAHRENHEIT SYSTEM: SEQUENCES OF INDEPENDENT TERMS

An important feature of the FAHRENHEIT system is its ability to modify the order in which independent terms are varied. Langley and Zytkow (1989) describe this ability in the following section.

Another of BACON's limitations involved the order in which terms were varied. Although in many cases the system was insensitive to the order, this did not hold for some of the more complex laws. Let us return to Black's law for an example. In its full form, this law relates the final temperature $T_f$ not only to the initial temperatures $T_1$ and $T_2$ of the combined substances, but also to the masses $M_1$ and $M_2$ of those substances. In the reported runs on Black's law (Langley, Bradshaw, and Simon, 1983; Langley, Simon, Bradshaw, and Zytkow, 1987), the temperatures were always varied first, but let us examine the result when the masses are used instead.

Suppose we place two containers of water into contact, with $T_1 = 20°$, $T_2 = 40°$, and $M_1 = 1$. Upon varying the mass of the second container $M_2$ and observing the resulting values of $T_f$, we obtain data that obey the law $T_f = 20 (1 + 2M_2)/(1 + M_2)$. However, BACON's heuristics are not powerful enough to discover this law. When we tell the system to vary the independent terms in this order, it will fail to recognize any regularity in the resulting data. One response would be to replace BACON's law-finding rules with more powerful curve-fitting methods, but this is sidestepping the real issue. Any law-finding method will have some limits, and these limits will eventually emerge when encountering the right order of variation.

*FAHRENHEIT responds to this possibility by considering different orders of varying the independent terms. The system operates in normal Baconian mode until it encounters some term that appears relevant, but for which it cannot find any regular law. In such cases, the program sidesteps the variable and places it at the end of the queue to ensure that it will be reconsidered later. It then varies the next independent term in the queue and attempts to incorporate this variable into some law. If this also fails, FAHRENHEIT considers the next term, and so forth. If it cannot find laws for any of the remaining independent terms, the system halts with only a partial law* [italics added].

Although this strategy is more robust than BACON's method and can handle the Black's law example given above, it does not consider all possible orders and thus is not guaranteed to find the maximal laws. FAHRENHEIT's authors have experimented with a variant on the above algorithm that, upon failing to find laws for any of the remaining terms, backtracks to consider different orders of variables that have already been successfully related. This scheme is more complete, but it is also more expensive. In the worst case, the simpler method has a computational complexity of $\frac{1}{2} N (N + 1)$, where $N$ is the number of independent terms. In contrast, the backtracking method has a worst-case complexity of $N!$, though we doubt this would occur very often. (Langley & Zytkow, 1989, pp. 301–302, italics added)

## THE FAHRENHEIT SYSTEM: STRENGTHS AND LIMITATIONS

Langley and Zytkow (1989) provide the following summary evaluation of the FAHRENHEIT system.

*We have seen that FAHRENHEIT introduced a number of improvements over BACON. The system's ability to consider alternative orders of varying independent variables lets it discover laws under conditions in which BACON would have failed.* The program also handles irrelevant terms in a more sensible way than its precursor, leading to savings in both time and in the amount of data required.

*Most important, FAHRENHEIT represents the scope of laws in a more robust manner than did BACON, and it incorporates heuristics to discover such limits in scope. This requires a more intelligent data-gathering strategy than was present in the earlier program, involving the selective generation of experiments that depend on the results of earlier experiments.* Moreover, FAHRENHEIT does not halt on finding the upper and lower limits on the law; it defines theoretical terms for these limits and carries them to the next level of description, along with the parameters for its basic laws. Using its recursive structure, the system then searches for laws relating these limit terms to new independent variables, and searches for limits on these laws in turn.

The resulting limits and limit-related laws establish a clear context in which FAHRENHEIT believes its basic laws to hold. But this context is still based largely on "number games," and it tells one little about the qualitative structure of situations in which the laws are valid. (Langley & Zytkow, 1989, p. 302, italics added)

## THE IDS SYSTEM: GENERAL BACKGROUND

The integrated discovery system (IDS) is distinguished from the BACON and FAHRENHEIT systems by its ability to discover both qualitative and numeric laws. General characteristics of IDS are described in the following section.

Langley and Nordhausen (1986) have described IDS, an integrated discovery system that formulates both qualitative laws and discovers numeric relationships.

Although this program is superficially responding to the same task as the other systems we have examined, it differs significantly in both its representation of laws and in its discovery process. . . .

Like FAHRENHEIT, the IDS system interacts with a simulated world in which it can gather data. But this environment differs from Zytkow's simulation in two important ways: (1) all attribute-value pairs are associated with specific objects; and (2) the values of these attributes change over time. Thus, IDS has available to it a more realistic environment than earlier systems, and this is reflected in its representation of laws. (Langley & Zytkow, 1989, pp. 302–303)

## THE IDS SYSTEM: REPRESENTATION OF LAWS

The representation of laws in IDS is described, exemplified, and compared with the BACON and FAHRENHEIT systems in the following account.

This representation is best explained through an example, and since we have used Black's law earlier in the paper, let us consider it again. The previous versions of this law, as represented by BACON and FAHRENHEIT, related the masses ($M_1$ and $M_2$), specific heats ($c_1$ and $c_2$), and initial temperatures ($T_1$ and $T_2$) of two substances to their final temperature ($T_f$) after they had been in contact for some time. However, Black's law actually involves much more than this single equation. Let us walk through what actually transpires in such an experiment.

We begin with two substances, having known masses and stable temperatures, which are then placed in contact. If we measure the temperatures over time, we will observe that the higher one gradually decreases and the lower one gradually increases. This process continues until the two temperatures become equal, at which point both remain constant. *Note that much of the interesting detail in the example is lost in the BACON/FAHRENHEIT representation. Some might be regained by including separate final temperatures for each object, but there would still be no sense of two quantities gradually moving towards equilibrium.* (Langley & Zytkow, 1989, p. 303, italics added)

## THE IDS SYSTEM: QUALITATIVE SCHEMAS

In IDS, knowledge concerning changes in conditions is represented in the form of qualitative schemas.

IDS is able to represent [changes] knowledge by using *qualitative schemas* that summarize changes over time in the values of one or more objects. A schema consists of a finite state diagram in which successive states represent succeeding intervals of time. For instance, the schema for Black's law contains three such states: the first describes temperatures before contact; the second describes temperatures after contact but before equilibrium is reached; and the last describes temperatures after the physical system achieves equilibrium. . . .

Each state in the schema has an associated description of the observed attributes. These descriptions state whether a given attribute's values are increasing, decreasing, or constant during that state. In fact, these "qualitative derivatives" define the boundaries of each state. In matching the schema against a new instance of Black's law, IDS knows when the physical system has moved into the next state by noting when the signs of the various derivatives change. For instance, the . . . state . . . applies only to those time steps in which the first object's temperature is increasing (the qualitative derivative is positive) and the . . . object's temperature is decreasing (the derivative is negative).

This knowledge representation is very similar to that suggested by Forbus [1984] in his qualitative process (QP) theory, and we have been strongly influenced by this work. Given a set of physical processes and some initial description of the environment, QP theory describes how one can generate an *envisionment* of the states the physical system will enter as those processes operate. The qualitative schemas of IDS are nearly identical to Forbus' envisionments. We have used a different term because IDS induces its schemas directly from observations, whereas in qualitative process theory, envisionments are deduced from process descriptions. *We do not have the space to describe the generality of this approach to representing physical systems, but it can be used to provide qualitative descriptions for a substantial range of phenomena from both physics and chemistry. For this reason, we believe it provides an excellent basis for machine discovery.* (Langley & Zytkow, 1989, pp. 303–304, italics added)

## THE IDS SYSTEM: INDUCING QUALITATIVE SCHEMAS

The processes by which IDS develops its qualitative schemas is described in the following section.

In its initial state, IDS contains a simple set of qualitative schemas. For instance, the initial schema for heating includes two states: one in which a heater near an object is turned off (and in which the object's temperature is constant); and another in which the heater is turned on (and in which the object's temperature is increasing). The initial schema for placing objects in contact is even simpler; IDS expects that the only effect of placing one object adjacent to another is to change its location.

However, experiments with objects having different temperatures lead to violated expectations, and these in turn cause IDS to modify the qualitative structure of this second schema. *We do not have the space to detail the processes used in acquiring qualitative schemas, but we can list the three basic methods*:

- *If IDS encounters entirely new behavior, it creates a new state and adds this to the current schema.*
- *If the system recognizes itself in a known state that was not predicted, it adds a connection between this state and the previous one.*
- *Upon finding evidence that a state's description is overly general, IDS makes that description more specific.*

*Taken together, these methods let the program incrementally improve its qualitative schemas as it gains more experience with its environment. . . .* (Langley & Zytkow, 1989, pp. 304–305, italics added)

## THE IDS SYSTEM: QUALITATIVE SCHEMAS AND NUMERIC LAWS

IDS represents numeric laws within a context of its qualitative schemas and thereby augments its discovery powers.

*We have focused on representing qualitative knowledge in IDS, but the system can also state numeric laws. The form of these laws is intimately related to the structure of the schemas, which are both object-oriented and time-oriented.* As a result, numeric terms are specified using two subscripts, one for the object involved and another for the state. In the Black's law schema, the temperature of the first object ($A$) in the second state would be $T_{A,2}$, whereas the temperature of the second object ($B$) in the third (final) state would be $T_{B,3}$. Thus IDS would state the numeric aspects of Black's law as

$$T_{A,3} = \frac{C_A M_A T_{A,2} + C_B M_B T_{B,2}}{C_A M_A + C_B M_B} \text{ and } T_{V,3} = T_{A,3}.$$

*Qualitative schemas serve two main purposes with respect to numeric laws. First, they provide a context within which the law has meaning* [italics added]. Clearly, if one places two objects into contact and they do not obey the qualitative structure of the schema . . . , then one would not expect their quantitative relations to obey Black's law. For example, some substances might be so well insulated that their temperature loss is negligible. This approach also lets one qualitatively handle phase shifts, which FAHRENHEIT modeled in a purely quantitative fashion.

*Second, qualitative schemas constrain the search for numeric laws* [italics added]. Different instances of the Black's law schema provide IDS with data that differ in terms of the masses, temperatures, and substances involved. However, these data are much more structured than those available to BACON or FAHRENHEIT, simplifying the law discovery process.

IDS applies data-driven heuristics to these numeric data in hopes of finding constant terms and simple linear relations. In the Black's law example, it follows a path much like that taken by BACON, though the terms involved are slightly different. One important difference is that *all* terms that are constant throughout the schema can be viewed as intrinsic properties of the objects used in the experiment. Moreover, when IDS encounters the same qualitative situation involving different objects, different substances, or different classes of substances, it may discover the same values for these terms. In such cases, it raises the retrieval conditions for the intrinsic value *t* the appropriate level of generality. In this framework, intrinsic values are associated directly with objects or classes of objects, not with nominal values themselves.

*In addition, new types of intrinsic properties arise within the IDS schema that do not appear within earlier approaches. The system may note that the schema shifts from one state to its successor whenever the value of a particular term reaches a certain value. The introduction of such* limit conditions *lets one represent and discover concepts like melting points and boiling points, which signal changes in qualitative state. IDS may also note that the* duration *of a state is constant or that it is related to some other term. This leads to concepts such as heat of fusion and heat of vaporization. All of these concepts are types of intrinsic property, with different values associated with different substances. Thus, the use of qualitative schemas provides representational support for intrinsic terms that could not be handled in earlier frameworks.* (Langley & Zytkow, 1989, pp. 305–306, italics added)

## THE IDS SYSTEM: STRENGTHS AND LIMITATIONS

In the following section, Langley and Zytkow (1989) evaluate the performance of IDS and compare it with the BACON and FAHRENHEIT systems.

Our research on IDS is still in its early stages, though we have a running system that we have tested on a variety of heat-related laws. The representational power of the system seems considerably greater than that of BACON, and it provides more context for its numeric laws than does FAHRENHEIT. That does not mean that one system is superior to the other. The current version of IDS does not include the methods for determining scope that Zytkow's system introduced, and these should definitely be considered for future versions. Nor does the system consider different orders of independent variables, though the use of qualitative schemas significantly simplifies the search for numeric relations.

*We would argue that IDS's greatest significance lies in its attempt to integrate the discovery of qualitative and quantitative laws. Earlier work has focused on one or the other, but has not considered their combination. One ultimate goal of research in machine discovery is the construction of an integrated discovery system that covers many aspects of scientific reasoning, and we believe IDS is an important step in that direction.* (Langley & Zytkow, 1989, p. 306, italics added)

## DISCOVERY SYSTEMS AND THE HISTORY OF SCIENCE

As discussed earlier, the BACON system has rediscovered a number of physical laws such as those of Galileo and Kepler. The BACON system, however, did not make its discoveries by duplicating the experimental and cognitive processes of the scientists. Whereas the BACON program met a sufficiency criterion by its rediscoveries, the KEKADA program [Kulkarni and Simon, 1988] duplicated, in detail, the experimental discovery processes of the biochemist Hans Krebs. In the following section, Langley and Zytkow (1989) discuss discovery systems and the history of science.

The history of science studies the actual path followed by scientists over the years, attempting to understand the steps taken towards a particular scientific advance, along with the reasons for those steps. Traditionally, historians of science have been content with verbal descriptions of scientific behavior, but the advent of machine discovery systems suggests an alternative: one can view AI discovery systems as computational models of the historical discovery process.

Whether or not they provide *adequate* models is partly a matter of one's goals. In their early work on computational models of human problem solving, Newell and Simon (1972) argued for the usefulness of *sufficient* models of behavior. Such models do not account for the details of human behavior on a task, but they do have roughly the same capabilities. Once such models have been developed, they may be replaced by more careful simulations. We would argue that BACON and its successors provide such sufficient models of empirical discovery. On close inspection, we find that the detailed behavior of early scientists like Ohm, Coulomb, Black, and others diverges from that followed by the programs. Nevertheless, these systems have shown themselves capable of discovering the same laws as the scientists, and this provides an excellent starting point for more detailed computational models.

Within both frameworks, one can take two approaches to testing the adequacy of discovery models. The most common technique involves arguing for the model's generality by showing it can discover a wide range of laws with a variety of forms. This is the approach taken in BACON, and Falkenhainer and Michalski (1986) have evaluated their ABACUS system along similar lines. The other approach involves running the model on an extended example that consists of a lengthy sequence of discoveries. This is the approach taken by Lenat (1977) with his AM system, and Kulkarni and Simon (1988) have used a similar strategy in testing their KEKADA system. *To the extent that the system's steps followed the same path that was taken historically, one can argue that it constitutes a plausible model of historical discovery.*

*Although none of the systems that we have described give an acceptable detailed account of historical discoveries, we believe they provide an excellent framework for future work in this direction. Whether such efforts should have high priority is an open question. Clearly, much more remains to be done in developing sufficient models of the discovery process, but this does not exclude the development of detailed models by other researchers. In many ways the latter is more difficult, since it requires intimate familiarity with historical developments. However, this road must ultimately be taken if we hope to formulate complete descriptive theories of scientific discovery.* (Langley & Zytkow, 1989, pp. 307–308, italics added)

## DISCOVERY SYSTEMS AND THE PHILOSOPHY OF SCIENCE: BACKGROUND

The development of scientific discovery systems has implications for traditional problems of validity and verification in the philosophy of science. In the following section, general implications are considered and in later sections more specific implications are discussed.

Historically, the nature of induction and discovery have played an important role in the philosophy of science. Early contributors such as Sir Francis Bacon (1620) [1960] and John Stuart Mill (1843) [1974] proposed "logics of induction" as methods for uncovering scientific laws. However, with the advent of the 20th century this interest passed, and most philosophers turned their attention to the *validation* of scientific laws and theories. Indeed, some researchers even argued that a "logic of discovery" was impossible (Popper, 1961). Recently, some have regained interest in the topic of discovery (Nickles, 1978), but the mainstream has retained its skepticism about the normative study of discovery.

Let us consider more closely what is meant by a normative or prescriptive theory of discovery [Zytkow and Simon, 1988]. Obviously, it suggests a set of methods that one *should* follow in formulating scientific laws. For those with a logical bent, this may translate as "a deductively valid set of methods," and we agree that no such methods are possible; inductive inference is clearly not deductively valid. However, this definition seems overly constraining. We cannot expect inductive techniques to give us *correct* laws, but we might legitimately require them to provide *useful* laws. Let us see what this might mean; the philosophy of science itself provides several responses, as we will discuss in the following sections. (Langley & Zytkow, 1989, p. 308)

## DISCOVERY SYSTEMS AND THE PHILOSOPHY OF SCIENCE: THEORETICAL TERMS

Langley and Zytkow (1989) discuss the function of theoretical terms from the point of view of the philosophy of science and as they operate in the BACON, FAHRENHEIT, and IDS systems.

The nature of theoretical terms has occupied a central role in recent philosophy of science. One important result involves the notion of *eliminability*. A theoretical term is said to be *eliminable* if one can replace all of its occurrences in a theory with directly observable terms. A theory containing only eliminable terms can be tested in a straightforward manner, by simply replacing these terms with observables and comparing its predictions against the data. In contrast, theories that contain noneliminable terms cannot always be tested, giving them questionable status.

Given this view, one might want a discovery method that introduces noneliminable terms into its law and theories only as a last resort. We have seen the role played by theoretical terms in BACON, FAHRENHEIT, and IDS. Some of these terms, such as the product *PV* in the ideal gas law, are defined directly using observable variables. Others, such as the intrinsic property of specific heat in Black's law and FAHRENHEIT's limit terms, are defined in a more roundabout manner. However, all such terms can be eliminated from the law and replaced with direct observables. *In this sense, the systems we have examined employ normative discovery methods.* (Langley & Zytkow, 1989, pp. 308–309, italics added)

## DISCOVERY SYSTEMS AND THE PHILOSOPHY OF SCIENCE: LAWS AND DEFINITIONS

In the following section, Langley and Zytkow (1989) draw parallels between the concept of intrinsic properties, discovery systems, and the concepts of law and definition in the philosophy of science.

Another issue involves Glymour's (1980) criterion of *bootstrap confirmation*. Many philosophers have made a strong distinction between *definitions* and *laws*, with only the latter having an empirical content. Glymour argues against this dichotomy, claiming that it is the combination of laws and definitions that have empirical content, and that these combinations can be tested against the same type of data used in generating them.

This is exactly the situation that occurs when BACON postulates an intrinsic property. In the Black's law example, we saw that when the system initially proposed the property of specific heat, the assigned numeric values were tautologically defined. At this point, the law involving the new term has no empirical content; it was guaranteed to hold. However, as new data were gathered, there was no (deductive) reason to expect it to apply in these cases. Had it failed to describe the new observations, the law would have been disconfirmed. In this case, it successfully covered the data and so was retained, but that is not the issue. *Rather, the point is that what begins as a definition with no empirical content can be tested as additional data become available. This is the essence of Glymour's bootstrapping criterion, and to the extent that BACON's methods incorporate this criterion, it can be viewed as a normative theory of discovery.* (Langley & Zytkow, 1989, p. 309, italics added)

## DISCOVERY SYSTEMS AND THE PHILOSOPHY OF SCIENCE: OPTIMAL LAWS

In the following section, Langley and Zytkow (1989) contend that although the philosophy of science can construe optimal scientific laws, artificial intelligence discovery systems aim not at optimization but at usefulness.

The notations of eliminability and bootstrapping place constraints on laws and theories, but they do not specify which laws are optimal for a given set of data. Some proposals have been made for such criteria. For instance, Popper (1961) has suggested that more falsifiable theories should be preferred to less easily rejected ones. Other suggestions have invoked the notions of simplicity and fertility. We feel that stating such criteria is a useful task for both machine discovery and philosophy of science, but even if we could agree on such criteria, we would not insist that a normative theory be able to achieve such optimal laws.

*One of the central insights of AI is that intelligence involves search through combinatorial spaces, and that one can seldom afford to search these spaces exhaustively. Instead, one must employ heuristic methods that cannot guarantee optimal solutions, but which are reasonably efficient* [italics added]. As Simon (1956) has argued, one must often be content with solutions that *suffice* for a given problem. *This means that realistic discovery methods cannot guarantee the generation of optimal laws and theories, even if the criteria for such optimality are clearly defined. Instead, a normative theory of discovery should generate laws that approximate these criteria* [italics added].

Progress can occur in prescriptive fields just as it can in descriptive ones. The fact that BACON and its successors constitute normative theories of discovery does not mean they are the best such theories. For example, Kokar (1986) has argued that his COPER method is superior to the BACON approach along a number of dimensions, and Falkenhainer and Michalski (1986) have made similar claims about their ABACUS system. *Future work in machine discovery and the philosophy of science may produce improved logics of discovery. Such improvements should be measured by the degree to which a normative theory produces laws that account for existing data and correctly predict new observations.* (Langley & Zytkow, 1989, pp. 309–310, italics added)

## DISCOVERY SYSTEMS AND THE SCIENTIFIC ENTERPRISE

The scientific enterprise has both theoretical and empirical aspects. The BACON, FAHRENHEIT, and IDS systems are empirical discovery systems. Theory formation systems and theory revision systems constitute important aspects of the general artificial intelligence approach to scientific discovery.

As we stated at the outset, empirical discovery is only one part of the complex phenomenon that we call science. But we feel that it is an important part, and that the systems we have described constitute a significant step towards understanding the nature of scientific discovery. *Recent work has started to address other aspects of the scientific process, including theory formation (Falkenhainer, 1987), theory revision (Rose and Langley, 1986; Shrager, 1987; Rajamoney, 1989), and experimentation (Kulkarni and Simon, 1988).* We expect future work to extend these promising efforts on isolated aspects of science. *However, we also expect researchers to develop* integrated *models that combine many aspects of the discovery process, and we would be surprised if they did not incorporate at least some ideas from the work that we have examined here.* (Langley & Zytkow, 1989, p. 311, italics added)

## COMMENTARY

The field of artificial intelligence has been neither a theoretical science nor a mathematical science (Simon, 1979), but rather an applied inductive science. This is especially clear in the case of BACON.3, in which heuristics are used to carry out inductive experiments that may lead to the establishment of regularities among independent and dependent variables. The regularities established are data driven rather than theory driven. The discoveries take the form of empirical functional relationships among variables. The laws discovered by BACON.3 are expressed as equations, but having been derived by inductive logic alone, the explanation of the laws, their possible embodiment in a wider net of theories is completely absent. BACON.3 is mechanism, not mind (Boden, 1988, 1990; Newell, 1990; Rychlak, 1990; Simon, 1990; Wagman, 1991a, 1991b). Even the human mind, when relying solely on inductive logic, cannot develop theoretical science:

There is no inductive method which could lead to the fundamental concepts of physics . . . in error are those theorists who believe that theory comes inductively from experience. (Einstein, 1933)

In the scientific era following Einstein, the technologies of computers and artificial intelligence developed with applications ramifying throughout the natural sciences. These ramifications include theoretical physics, as enthusiastically specified by Stephen Hawking, one of the most eminent theoretical physicists of the last quarter of the twentieth century.

At present computers are a useful aid in research but they have to be directed by human minds. However, if one extrapolates their recent rapid rate of development, it would seem quite possible that they would take over altogether in theoretical physics. So maybe the end is in sight for theoretical physicists and not for theoretical physics. (Hawking, in Davis & Hersh, 1986, p. 158)

# 6

# Artificial Intelligence Discovery in Chemistry

## DISCOVERY IN CHEMISTRY AND THE MECHEM SYSTEM

### THE MECHEM SYSTEM: BACKGROUND

The original expert system in chemistry was the DENDRAL program that made scientific discoveries subsequently published in prestigious journals. The more recent MECHEM program continues the DENDRAL tradition by contributing new computational and architectural strategies in machine chemistry that yield valuable applications within industrial chemistry and that have advanced developments in the theory of artificial intelligence approaches to scientific discovery in general.

### THE MECHEM SYSTEM: OVERVIEW

Valdés-Pérez (1995a) describes theory, results, and implications of the MECHEM program in the following summary account:

Earlier we proposed an idea conjecturing unseen entities in science, and described its application within MECHEM to the chemistry task of inferring the mechanism of a chemical reaction based on experimental evidence. However, the program was a prototype, and lacked several capabilities that rendered it incompetent on current science.

We now describe extensions that enable reasoning about the molecular structural transformations that are the focus of modern chemistry. We also report successful applications of MECHEM to chemical problems of current interest, and point out subsequent machine discovery work that the MECHEM project has strongly influenced. These new results demonstrate the efficacy and generality of the original idea for machine discovery, and vindicate the research strategy of emphasizing specific task competence and deferring concerns with generality. (Valdés-Pérez, 1995a, p. 191)

## THE MECHEM SYSTEM: DEVELOPMENTS

In the following section, Valdés-Pérez (1995a) presents the major steps in the development of the MECHEM program.

The original motivation for MECHEM was to select some challenging discovery task from current scientific practice and to demonstrate its automation by a logical analysis of hypothesis generation and of the relation between evidence and hypothesis (Valdés-Pérez, 1990). We began by searching within chemistry for circumstantial reasons, and then settled on the task of elucidating the multi-step character (or *mechanism*) of a chemical reaction on the basis of experimental evidence. . . . Elucidating reaction mechanisms has been a nearly universal task of experimental chemists since it was first proposed by van 't Hoff in the late 1800s that many chemical reactions do not occur as a single act, but instead involve a number of consecutive or parallel steps. The fact that the mechanism elucidation task is of a long scientific tradition adds an extra interest to its successful automation, since it enhances the credibility of the overall machine discovery enterprise.

The task of mechanism elucidation had been first addressed within AI by the Ph.D. Thesis of V. W. Soo at Rutgers (Soo et al., 1987; Soo et al., 1988), although his work focused on enzymatic reactions. One important drawback to that work was its dependence on a small catalogue of candidate mechanisms, which were discriminated by applying known experiment-analysis rules from enzymology. Outside of AI, chemists and engineers have also addressed task automation. Typically, chemical engineering work has assumed complete knowledge of all reaction intermediates and products, an untenable assumption in practice. Virtually all the chemistry work has followed a schema based on searching a space of chemical-reaction operators (e.g., Wipke, Ouchi, and Krishnan, 1978); we will not contrast that work here, but this difference is discussed in the chemical papers cited throughout this note.

*A main obstacle to formulating mechanistic hypotheses competently, here and in many other scientific tasks, is finding some means to conjecture unseen entities, e.g., unseen reaction intermediates and products. Typically, one knows the starting materials of a reaction and has identified some of the products or even intermediates, but others remain undetected because of practical limitations of experimental technique.*

*The obstacle of conjecturing unseen entities is overcome in MECHEM by a simple and seemingly naive method: conjecture "wild cards" such as X, Y, Z, etc., use these wild cards together with the seen entities to formulate hypotheses, and then use the domain laws of a science to constrain these variables sufficiently (within the context of a specific hypothesis) to entail a small set of possible identities for the variables* [italics added]. For example, using the conservation constraint of reaction balance, the unknown $X$ in the following single-step hypothesis

$$CH_3 + MCH_2OOH \rightarrow X + CH_3OH$$

is inferred to consist of 1 $M$, 1 carbon, 2 hydrogen, and 1 oxygen atoms. In more complex cases involving multiple steps and unknowns, and possibly more than one unknown per step, a generalized linear equation solver is used to infer the chemical composition of the wild cards.

The previous idea was combined with a number of other methods in order to implement a working prototype. For example, a constrained-generation algorithm (Valdés-Pérez, 1991, 1992) generated hypotheses non-redundantly under a bias for simplicity (fewer reaction steps and conjectured entities), which was needed if a systematic search was to have any hope against the powerful combinatorial increase in the hypothesis space with increments in steps and conjectured entities. MECHEM's canonical generator of mechanisms evokes the earlier DENDRAL (Lindsay et al., 1993) generator CONGEN (Lederburg, 1965), although the issue of simplicity did not arise there in the same way, since CONGEN was not required to conjecture unseen entities (also, CONGEN generated structures, not mechanisms). Returning to the MECHEM prototype, there were also a number of other program components that tested hypotheses against various given experimental evidence, such as overall stoichiometry.

The above was the state of MECHEM as described in an earlier paper in this journal (Valdés-Pérez, 1994c). Enough machinery was in place to enable the program to systematically find, from historical data, the simplest reaction pathways for urea synthesis in biochemistry, whose discovery in 1932 by Hans Krebs (Holmes, 1991) had been modeled by Kulkarni and Simon in their KEKADA program (Kulkarni and Simon, 1988).

However, despite the novelty and promise of MECHEM, as demonstrated on the urea pathway, the program could not reason *structurally* about chemical substances and reactions. That is, the graph-like nature of chemical molecules was ignored, since substances were represented as molecular formulas (simple vectors). For example, methanol (whose molecular structure is depicted in Figure [6.1]) was represented as consisting of 1 carbon, 4 hydrogens, and 1 oxygen, which obscured the known structural connectivity among these atoms. Although

**Figure 6.1**
**The Molecular Structure of Methanol**

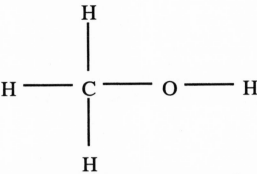

*Source:* Valdés-Pérez, R. E. (1995a). Machine discovery in chemistry: New results. *Artificial Intelligence, 74*, p. 193.

Krebs's (and MECHEM's) discovery of the urea pathway did not involve much structural reasoning (historically speaking) (Holmes, 1980), the graph-like structure of molecules is nevertheless at the heart of modern chemistry.

This gap in MECHEM was problematic for two reasons. Firstly, it suggested that the program's basic hypothesis-formation method of conjecturing hidden entities was naive and not really up to the task of current science, which usually involves reasoning more complex than the simple balancing of accounts. Secondly, the program would have no impact on practicing experimentalists, since it would report mechanistic hypotheses that were obviously implausible for structural reasons that the program did not know about, hence an experimentalist would quickly lose interest (we speak from experience). Our goal for MECHEM had become to complete transition from theory to practical impact, hence the problem. (Valdés-Pérez, 1995a, pp. 192–194)

## THE MECHEM SYSTEM: CONCEPTS AND ALGORITHMS

In the following section, Valdés-Pérez (1995a) describes the interesting concepts and algorithms of the MECHEM system.

. . . we designed a heuristic graph algorithm to test whether a given, single reaction step *reactants* → *products* was structurally plausible (Valdés-Pérez, 1993). The criterion of plausibility is that at most a small number $N$ of bonds could be broken or formed during the conversion of the reactants into products; $N$ is adjustable, but is set to 3 by default, which covers almost all elementary

**Figure 6.2**
**An Example of Six Conjectured Wild Cards**

| | | | |
|---|---|---|---|
| 1. | $H_2 + M_2$ | $\rightarrow$ | $2u$ |
| 2. | $M_2$ + ethane | $\rightarrow$ | $u + v$ |
| 3. | $M_2 + v$ | $\rightarrow$ | $CH_2M\text{-}CH_2M + u$ |
| 4. | $M + CH_2M\text{-}CH_2M$ | $\rightarrow$ | $u + w$ |
| 5. | $2w$ | $\rightarrow$ | $CH_2M\text{-}CH_2M + CHM\text{-}CHM$ |
| 6. | $CHM\text{-}CHM$ | $\rightarrow$ | $2x$ |
| 7. | $u + x$ | $\rightarrow$ | $M + y$ |
| 8. | $2y$ | $\rightarrow$ | $x + z$ |
| 9. | $u + z$ | $\rightarrow$ | $M_2$ + methane |

*Source:* Valdés-Pérez, R. E. (1995a). Machine discovery in chemistry: New results. *Artificial Intelligence, 74,* p. 195.

chemical structural fragments through the use of tables that store all the fragments derivable from a given molecule. With this new algorithm, if the reactants and products of a step are known, then MECHEM never reports that step if it is structurally implausible.

However, this graph-algorithmic test could not be applied to any step that contained a wild card, even if a formula has already been inferred for it, since the structural information is missing from wild cards. There seemed little chance of overcoming this last problem, hence it appeared that MECHEM would remain an AI research program that fails to have an impact outside of AI. Finally, we realized that it must be possible to *infer* the molecular structure of any wild cards, given their already-inferred formulas, and given the overall multi-step context in which they appeared. For example, Figure [6.2] shows a nine-step mechanism in which there appear the six wild cards *U, V, W, X, Y,* and *Z* (M is not a wild card, but a catalyst reaction site). Later, Figure [6.3] shows the same mechanism but with the wild cards replaced by the molecular structures that are inferred for them.

In short, the same general idea for conjecturing hidden entities could work for structures as well as formulas, although the algorithm in the newer case would be considerably more complex. The details of this algorithm are given elsewhere (Valdés-Pérez, 1994b); here we merely state its feasibility and remark that the algorithm relies on a case-by-case breakdown of the various schematic ways that structures and formulas can appear within a single reaction step, together with the previous assumption of at most *N* bond changes per step.

Together, these two new algorithms ensured that MECHEM would no longer report mechanisms that contained obviously wrong steps. A final problem was the combinatorial increase in run time due to increments in the number of wild

**Figure 6.3**
**MECHEM's Reaction Mechanism for Catalytic Hydrogenolysis of Ethane**

| | | | |
|---|---|---|---|
| 1. | $H_2 + M_2$ | $\rightarrow$ | $2\langle HM \rangle$ |
| 2. | $M_2$ + ethane | $\rightarrow$ | $\langle HM \rangle + \langle CH_3\text{-}CH_2M \rangle$ |
| 3. | $M_2 + \langle CH_3\text{-}CH_2M \rangle$ | $\rightarrow$ | $CH_2M\text{-}CH_2M + \langle HM \rangle$ |
| 4. | $M + CH_2M\text{-}CH_2M$ | $\rightarrow$ | $\langle HM \rangle + \langle CH_2M\text{-}CHM \rangle$ |
| 5. | $2 \langle CH_2M\text{-}CHM \rangle$ | $\rightarrow$ | $CH_2M\text{-}CH_2M + CHM\text{-}CHM$ |
| 6. | $CHM\text{-}CHM$ | $\rightarrow$ | $2\langle CHM \rangle$ |
| 7. | $\langle HM \rangle + \langle CHM \rangle$ | $\rightarrow$ | $M + \langle CH_2M \rangle$ |
| 8. | $2 \langle CH_2M \rangle$ | $\rightarrow$ | $\langle CHM \rangle + \langle CH_3M \rangle$ |
| 9. | $\langle HM \rangle + \langle CH_3M \rangle$ | $\rightarrow$ | $M_2$ + methane |

*Source:* Valdés-Pérez, R. E. (1995a). Machine discovery in chemistry: New results. *Artificial Intelligence, 74,* p. 196.

cards that were conjectured. Under MECHEM's systematic search regimen, the program could not handle any problem for which more than four unseen entities had to be conjectured. Hence, the program was limited to relatively easy problems, thus narrowing its scope and potential impact. This final problem was solved by the invention of a divide-and-conquer heuristic (Valdés-Pérez, 1994d) that partitions the given products and intermediates into two or more sets according to various chemical criteria. This heuristic, together with others of more modest power reported in the cited paper, enlarged tremendously the class of practical problems to which MECHEM could be applied. (Valdés-Pérez, 1995a, pp. 193–195)

## THE MECHEM SYSTEM: APPLICATIONS

The performance of MECHEM in highly competent computer-human collaborative chemical analyses with both simple and more complex problems is elucidated in the following section.

Surprisingly, one of MECHEM's mechanisms differed significantly from the others. Figure [6.3] shows this mechanism, in which the intermediates conjectured by MECHEM appear within angle brackets to distinguish them from the given substances. We reported this mechanism, together with an analysis of how well it explains various qualitative evidences reported in the chemical literature, to *Catalysis Letters* as a successful example of a human-computer collaboration (Valdés-Pérez, 1994e). In turn, the latter is proposed within that paper as a fruitful new technique in studies of catalytic reaction mechanisms.

**Figure 6.4**
**Constraints on Ethane Hydrogenolysis Reaction**

| | |
|---|---|
| 1. | The overall stoichiometry is 1 (ethane) + 1 ($H_2$) → 2 (methane). |
| 2. | A catalyst reaction site (modeled as M) forms one bond. |
| 3. | Two catalyst reaction sites are modeled as M |
| | (this notion does not by itself imply a bond across the two sites). |
| 4. | $CH_2M$-$CH_2M$ and CHM-CHM are required intermediates |
| | (these do form "bridges" over two reaction sites on the catalyst). |
| 5. | $H_2$ is not a product of a step (except as the reverse of initial dissociation). |
| 6. | Every reaction intermediate is adsorbed on the catalyst, |
| | i.e., every intermediate contains M. |
| 7. | No species contains three carbons nor spans three catalyst reaction sites. |
| 8. | There is a maximum of three bond changes (cleavage or formation) per step. |
| 9. | $CH_2M$-$CH_2M$ is a precursor (not necessarily single-step) of CHM-CHM. |

*Source:* Valdés-Pérez, R. E. (1995a). Machine discovery in chemistry: New results. *Artificial Intelligence, 74*, p. 195.

We have also applied MECHEM to more complex reactions involving a dozen or more steps, such as the potentially lucrative catalytic conversion of alkanes (e.g., natural gas, or methane) by partial oxidation (Haggin, 1992). We have not yet found any specific mechanism of clear chemical interest, for lack of close involvement with experimentalists who are active in that type of chemistry. However, we have illustrated MECHEM's capabilities on representative input constraints at the 1994 Spring National Meeting of the American Chemical Society, during a symposium on alkane conversion (Valdés-Pérez, [1995c]).

. . . From a chemist's viewpoint, MECHEM is an interactive program. First, the experimentalist/user states the starting materials, what species have been observed experimentally, and other constraints on the reaction. The program then reports the simplest mechanisms, which typically prompt the user to object to various aspects of these, which may lead to rejecting all of the proposed mechanisms. The user then articulates his objections by formulating new constraints, and the program is re-run by adding these constraints to the earlier ones. This interactive process continues until the user is satisfied that none of the reported mechanisms is objectionable, or until the problem becomes too complex for the current program to handle. This interaction lasted two or three cycles on the above ethane reaction, resulting finally in the constraints shown in Figure [6.4].

In general, MECHEM will report several plausible reaction mechanisms. Knowledge of these (whether generated by human or machine) can prompt the chemist to try a different catalyst, design an experiment, carry out a kinetic analysis, and so on. However, such steps are outside the current scope of this research, and are left to the expert or to other techniques. (Valdés-Pérez, 1995a, pp. 196–197)

## THE MECHEM SYSTEM: COMPLEX CONSTRAINT SATISFACTION

The problem of developing coherence between theoretical chemical constraints and computational algorithmic constraints is addressed in the following section.

It is accurate to view MECHEM as carrying out a heuristic breadth-first tree search with complicated node generators and node evaluators. It is also fruitful to view it as a complex constraint-satisfaction program (Simon [1983] analyzes the relation between the heuristic search and constraint satisfaction problem-solving metaphors). A major project effort has been to identify new chemical constraints—arising from background theory or as typical experimental evidence—and to design algorithms that test whether a given, partially-built reaction mechanism is consistent with a given constraint.

A possible approach to this and other constraint-satisfaction problems of scientific inference is to draw on parallel work in constraint satisfaction, e.g., constraint logic programming (CLP) (Hentenryck, Simonis, and Dincbas, 1992). We have previously experimented with the CLP language Prolog III (Colmerauer, 1990) in the context of MECHEM's pathway generator (Jourdan and Valdés-Pérez, 1990), but returned to programming from scratch in Lisp because of the complicated algorithmic nature of the further constraints that were needed to make MECHEM into a competent program. With current constraint-satisfaction tools, it seems awkward to implement the constraint that every individual reaction be realizable in at most $N$ bond changes, not to mention the preliminary step of inferring the molecular structure of wild cards. Another problem with typical CLP-based search engines is that they carry out a depth-first search, whereas in scientific model-building applications a breadth-first search is preferable, since the shallower nodes correspond to simpler models.

Nevertheless, a CLP or generic constraint-satisfaction approach may be promising when addressing scientific tasks that involve mostly simple constraints, or when building demonstration prototypes for tasks that are potentially quite complicated. (Valdés-Pérez, 1995a, p. 198)

## THE MECHEM SYSTEM: FUTURE DEVELOPMENTS

In the following section, Valdés-Pérez (1995a) discusses the possibility that the future development of chemistry in general cannot proceed without computational aid such as provided by MECHEM and then describes plans for augmenting the capacity of the MECHEM system.

If there were a theory to predict reliably the exact course of a complex chemical reaction based on starting materials and initial conditions, then the experimentalist's task of elucidating reaction mechanisms on the basis of evidence would be superceded. However, no such theory is yet available, and the study of reaction mechanisms continues to be dominated by experimentation. From our readings of papers in catalytic chemistry, we know of no computer tools that can assist experimenters in devising reaction mechanism hypotheses.

Up to now, MECHEM has been applied only a few times to evidences gathered by others, for reasons already discussed. *We will attempt to make chemists aware of the benefits that can accrue from making use of the program early in mechanistic studies, so that the program's outputs can help guide experimental decision-making. We believe that the program can increase the speed with which mechanistic conclusions are reached, as well as improve their accuracy. As evidence for this belief, we recall that the program has already turned up new simple hypotheses on the first reaction (ethane hydrogenolysis) of current interest to which it was applied. Given our observations of the density of plausible hypotheses of equal simplicity, as reflected in MECHEM's outputs, we can predict frequent such occurrences. If these predictions hold true, they will raise the question of whether complicated reaction mechanisms can be elucidated at all reliably without computerized hypothesis-generation tools.*

Our immediate plans are to implement a course-grain parallel version of MECHEM, perhaps using PVM (Sunderam, 1990), but keeping Lisp as the main implementation language. MECHEM's tree search is "embarrassingly parallel" so that a distribute version should be possible with relatively minor changes. In addition, this author is currently serving both as programmer and as "user interface," and the latter role will need to change before MECHEM becomes available for autonomous use by chemists. (Valdés-Pérez, 1995a, pp. 198–199, italics added)

## MECHEM: RELATION TO OTHER SCIENTIFIC DISCOVERY SYSTEMS

In the following interesting account, Valdés-Pérez (1995a) discusses the involvement of MECHEM in other scientific discovery systems and its place in a general matrix of space search.

The work on MECHEM has strongly influenced several subsequent results, which one may interpret as evidence for the generality of the idea. *Perhaps more significantly, these results vindicate the research strategy of selecting a*

*specific problem in science and providing an automation of it, while postponing*
*much consideration of generality until a successful automation is near at hand.*
During a sabbatical visit by J. Zytkow to Carnegie Mellon, the two of us
together with H. A. Simon sought generalizations among several discovery systems, including MECHEM, that had been developed separately. *The result was*
*the new concept of search in matrix spaces (Valdés-Pérez, Zyktow, and Simon,*
*1993), which expresses the idea that the top-level search space of many scientific*
*model-building tasks can be fruitfully viewed as a matrix-algebraic equation*
*whose unknown entries are filled in subject to a variety of domain constraints.*

*We have since used this concept (Valdés-Pérez, submitted for publication) to*
*re-design (with some advantages) the GELL-MANN program (Fischer and Zyk-*
*tow, 1990) that postulates quark models in particle physics. Also, concurrently*
*with the work on matrix-space search, we used some of the representational*
*and algorithmic techniques in MECHEM to re-design (Valdés-Pérez, 1994a) the*
*BR-3 program (Kocabas, 1991), which finds phenomenological quantum prop-*
*erties in particle physics. The latter effort resulted in the PAULI program, which*
*carries out simplicity-guided search with a linear optimization in its inner loop.*
*The work on PAULI has led [to] a novel theorem in particle physics (Valdés-*
*Pérez, 1994f) which space prevents discussion of here.* (Valdés-Pérez, 1995a, p.
199, italics added)

## THE MECHEM SYSTEM: CONCLUSION

Valdés-Pérez (1995a) concludes the description of work on the
MECHEM system with the following succinct and informative account.

The original idea for conjecturing hidden entities in chemistry (Valdés-Pérez,
1994d) was seemingly naive in the sense that the modern focus on molecular
structure was not accommodated. This note reports the extension of the idea to
conjecturing molecular structures, which are in essence topological graphs,
hence are more complex objects than the molecular formulas which constituted
the representational scope of MECHEM previously. We also report the first
convincing evidence that MECHEM has reached competence on a significant
class of chemical reactions of current interest. Finally, MECHEM has strongly
influenced some of our subsequent research in machine discovery, which is
evidence for the general applicability of ideas underlying the program, and is a
vindication of the research strategy of deferring considerations of generality in
favor of specific task competence. (Valdés-Pérez, 1995a, pp. 199–200)

# 7

# Artificial Intelligence Discoveries in Particle Physics

## ARTIFICIAL INTELLIGENCE DISCOVERY OF A NEW THEOREM IN PARTICLE PHYSICS

### THE PAULI SYSTEM AND DISCOVERY IN PARTICLE PHYSICS: OVERVIEW

In the following section, Valdés-Pérez (1996b) summarizes (a) criticism of discovery systems, (b) the counterexample of the PAULI system that enabled discovery of a novel theorem in particle physics, and (c) the ensuing complications in particle physics research and theory related to PAULI's discovery of the theorem that specified a single conservation law.

A widespread objection to research on scientific discovery is that there has been a noticeable dearth of significant novel findings in domain sciences contributed by machine discovery programs. The implication is that the essential parts of the discovery process are not captured by these programs. The aim of this note is to document for the AI audience a novel finding in particle physics that was enabled by the machine discovery program PAULI reported previously. This finding consists of a theorem that expresses the minimum number of conservation laws that are needed, mathematically speaking, to account for any consistent experimental data on particle reactions. This note also reports how a puzzle raised by a theorem—its conflict with physics practice—is resolved.

A widespread objection to research on computational scientific discovery is that there has been a noticeable dearth of significant novel findings in domain science contributed by discovery programs. The implication is that the essential parts of the discovery process are not captured by these programs. If this implication is true, then the whole automated scientific discovery enterprise is so far of doubtful soundness. Of even wider consequence is that the theory of heuristic search is seriously incomplete, since it fails to account for a salient aspect of human reasoning: discovery in science. Therefore, it becomes critical to record instances of novel machine discovery in order to falsify the premise that underlies this serious implication; i.e., the premise that discovery programs have enabled no significant new discoveries.

The aim of this note is to document for the AI audience a novel finding in particle physics that was enabled by the machine discovery program PAULI reported previously (Valdés-Pérez, 1994a). This finding consists of a theorem that expresses the minimum number of conservation laws that are needed, mathematically speaking, to account for any consistent experimental data on particle reactions.

I proceed by describing briefly the discovery task and summarizing prior work on it. Then I present the novel finding and the circumstances that led to it, and explore some of the implications of this finding within particle physics domain. Since our research on scientific discovery emphasizes generality within science, I examine briefly the generic character of this task in science generally. This note closes by summarizing the lessons for machine discovery. (Valdés-Pérez, 1996b, pp. 331–332)

## CONSERVATION LAWS IN PARTICLE PHYSICS

Valdés-Pérez (1996b) discusses a postulation of conservation laws in particle physics in the following section.

The task of postulating conservation laws from observational data on particle reactions was apparently first mentioned in the scientific discovery literature by Langley, Simon, Bradshaw, and Zytkow (1987). I illustrate the task by a simple example.

Let us suppose that experiments have shown that the following reaction among particles is observed to occur:

$$\bar{\pi} + p \rightarrow \pi^0 + n.$$

Furthermore, this second reaction

$$p \nrightarrow \pi + \pi^0$$

has *never* been observed (this is implied by the symbol $\nrightarrow$), despite much experimental effort, and despite the fact that the reaction is not ruled out by existing theory. These circumstances raise a quandary which calls out for resolution.

An adequate resolution lies in postulating a new conserved property that has the value of unity for the particles *p* and *n* and zero for the other particles. This property is conserved by the *observed* reaction and violated by the *unobserved* one, which explains why the unobserved reaction never occurs. Historically, particle physicists have faced similar puzzles involving more numerous reactions and have resolved them in such a partially data-driven manner by postulating conserved particle properties (Ne'eman and Kirsh, 1986).

We can generalize the previous simple example into some general concepts of particle physics. First, a *conservation law* states that some aggregate quantity is conserved by a stated physical process. A *phenomenological conservation law* is one that is not discovered or justified on theoretical grounds, but instead serves as a rather ad-hoc explanation of observations; phenomenological reasoning in physics corresponds roughly to the data-driven reasoning of AI terminology. Conservation laws in particle physics are examples of *selection rules*: they select which hypothetical reactions cannot occur because they violate conservation; not all selection rules need be conservation laws. Finally, the quantities that these conservation laws conserve are *quantum numbers*: simple, small numbers that characterize particles and which are not necessarily integers. (Valdés-Pérez, 1996b, pp. 332–333)

## DISCOVERY SYSTEMS AND CONSERVATION LAWS

Discovery system research concerned with the postulation of conservation laws in particle physics is discussed in the following section.

Langley, Simon, Bradshaw, and Zytkow (1987) were apparently the first in the AI literature to mention the discovery task of postulating phenomenological conservation laws. These authors pointed out the task's resemblance to the task carried out by their DALTON program in chemistry, implying that the former task was possibly amenable to the heuristic search methods that DALTON used, although no specific approach was given.

Kocabas (1991) was the first to describe a program BR-3 capable of performing the task; his BR-3 used some algebraic manipulation to reduce the initial search space, followed by generating specific quantum numbers for particles, testing for contradictions, and backtracking. Given historical data on particle reactions, BR-3 was able to re-discover laws such as the conservation of baryon quantum number, lepton quantum number, and electron and muon numbers. However, Kocobas reported that BR-3 did not find the accepted strangeness

**Table 7.1**
**Reactions Giving Rise to the Baryon and Lepton Conservation Laws**

| Observed reactions | Unobserved reactions |
| --- | --- |
| $p + p \rightarrow p + p + \pi^0$ | $p \rightarrow \bar{e} + \gamma$ |
| $p + p \rightarrow p + \pi + n$ | $p \rightarrow \pi + \pi^0$ |
| $p + \pi \rightarrow \pi + p$ | $p \rightarrow \pi + \gamma$ |
| $\bar{\pi} + p \rightarrow \bar{\pi} + p$ | $p \rightarrow \pi + \pi + \bar{\pi} + \pi^0 + \pi^0$ |
| $\bar{\pi} + p \rightarrow \pi^0 + n$ | $p + p \rightarrow \Lambda + \bar{\Lambda}$ |
| $\bar{\pi} + p \rightarrow p + \pi + \bar{\pi} + \pi$ | |
| $\gamma + e \rightarrow \gamma + e$ | |
| $e + p \rightarrow e + p$ | |
| $\pi^0 \rightarrow \gamma + \gamma$ | |
| $\bar{\pi} \rightarrow \mu + \bar{\nu}_\mu$ | |
| $\pi \rightarrow \bar{\mu} + \nu_\mu$ | |
| $\mu \rightarrow e + \nu_\mu + \bar{\nu}_e$ | |
| $n \rightarrow p + e + \bar{\nu}_e$ | |
| $\bar{\pi} + p \rightarrow \Lambda + K^0$ | |

*Source:* Valdés-Pérez, R. E. (1996b). A new theorem in particle physics enabled by machine discovery. *Artificial Intelligence, 82*, p. 334.

quantum numbers when given the reactions that led historically to the discovery of strangeness.

Valdés-Pérez (1994a) then described the PAULI program which uses a combination of linear programming and backtrack search. PAULI's approach is based on re-representing the particle reactions as two sets of linear algebraic expressions, making use of a well-known technique in chemistry (Valdés-Pérez, 1994b) for reasoning about multi-step reaction pathways. PAULI was able to re-discover the strangeness quantum numbers using the historical assumptions and data available to Murray Gell-Mann, the co-discoverer of strangeness (Ne'eman and Kirsh, 1986). (Valdés-Pérez, 1996b, p. 333)

## COMPARISON OF THE BR-3 AND PAULI SYSTEMS

Theoretical implications of discrepancies between the BR-3 and the PAULI systems in the postulation of conservation laws are discussed in the following section.

Kocabas' paper showed how, given the reactions in [Table 7.1], BR-3 postulates the two accepted conservation laws of baryon and lepton number shown in [Table 7.2]. Every observed reaction in [Table 7.1] conserves the sum of baryon

**Table 7.2**
**Quantum Numbers for the Particles**

| Particle | Baryon number | Lepton number | PAULI's number | Particle | Baryon number | Lepton number | PAULI's number |
|---|---|---|---|---|---|---|---|
| $p$ | 1 | 0 | 1 | $\bar{\nu}$ | 0 | -1 | 0 |
| $n$ | 1 | 0 | 1 | $\mu$ | 0 | 1 | 0 |
| $e$ | 0 | 1 | 0 | $\bar{\mu}$ | 0 | -1 | 0 |
| $\bar{e}$ | 0 | -1 | 0 | $\gamma$ | 0 | 0 | 0 |
| $\Lambda$ | 1 | 0 | 0 | $\pi$ | 0 | 0 | 0 |
| $\bar{\Lambda}$ | -1 | 0 | 0 | $\bar{\pi}$ | 0 | 0 | 0 |
| $K^0$ | 0 | 0 | 1 | $\pi^0$ | 0 | 0 | 0 |
| $\nu$ | 0 | 1 | 0 | | | | |

*Source:* Valdés-Pérez, R. E. (1996b). A new theorem in particle physics enabled by machine discovery. *Artificial Intelligence, 82,* p. 334.

numbers; that is, the summed baryon numbers of the reactants equals the corresponding products sum. The same conservation condition holds in the case of lepton numbers. On the other hand, each unobserved reaction in [Table 7.1] violates at least one of the two laws. For example, the reaction $p \rightarrow \pi + \gamma$ violates baryon number conservation, but not lepton conservation.

On the same reactions data from [Table 7.1], PAULI finds that one conservation law is enough to account for the observations; its quantum numbers also appear in [Table 7.2]. Only the three particles $p$, $n$, and $K^0$ receive unit quantum numbers, whereas the other particles are assigned zero. As is required of any solution, the observed reactions conserve PAULI's quantum number, whereas the unobserved ones violate it. Note that the program's quantum number is not a simple sum of the baryon and lepton numbers found by BR-3.

To explain its input data, PAULI prefers fewer conservation laws, ideally a single law (unless there are no unobserved reactions, in which case no "selection rules" are needed, since there is nothing to select *against*). This is the primary criterion of simplicity in the program. Given competing explanations of the same data, e.g. two alternative conservation laws, PAULI prefers the law that involves the smaller sum of the absolute values of quantum numbers; this preference expresses the program's secondary simplicity criterion. (Valdés-Pérez, 1996b, pp. 333–334)

## POSTULATING QUANTUM NUMBERS

In the following section, Valdés-Pérez (1996b) discusses puzzles in the postulation of quantum numbers afforded by discrepancies among theoretical physicists, the authors, and PAULI.

On the same input data, PAULI consistently found simpler (one-conservation-law) solutions than did BR-3, which was puzzling, since BR-3's achievements were re-discoveries of accepted results in particle physics. Our previous explanation for this puzzle (Valdés-Pérez, 1994a) consisted of three alternatives:

(1) Physicists erred by proposing unnecessarily complex assignments of quantum numbers.

(2) Physicists used further constraints to postulate the new quantum numbers.

(3) PAULI's simplicity criteria (inductive bias) are different from (and inferior to) the criteria used by physicists.

The second of these alternatives was correct in the case of PAULI's surprising conclusions about strangeness. That is, on the same strangeness input data as were used historically, consisting of (1) observed particle reactions, and (2) unobserved particle reactions, PAULI's solution was at first simpler than the solution accepted in physics. However, Ne'eman and Kirsh (1986) mention a further constraint (the nucleon and pion families possess zero strangeness) that was not mentioned in the textbook (Omnès, 1971) cited by Kocabas, but was assumed by Murray Gell-Mann for his discovery of the strangeness conservation law in 1953. When this constraint was incorporated into PAULI for the strangeness case, the program did not find the accepted values of strangeness for the particles involved in the input reactions. This solution to the puzzle *in the case of strangeness* involved the second alternative above (i.e., physicists had used additional constraints), and suggested that perhaps the entire puzzle of why PAULI persisted in finding simpler solutions could be solved by recourse to the same explanation, of an omission of analogous constraints. Surprisingly, this suggestion turned out to be wrong in the general case.

To gain further insight into this mystery, Kocabas and this author each ran his program on other inputs besides those in Kocabas' original paper; PAULI invariably found that the simplest solution involved only one conservation law, despite the fact that BR-3 would find multiple ones, and despite the fact that particle physicists had also postulated several conservation laws. From these observations of PAULI's invariant behavior, I conjectured that, on *any* consistent reaction data *whatsoever*, one conservation law was probably sufficient to rule out the unobserved particle reactions and rule in the observed reactions. I turned to a colleague (Michael Erdmann) for help in proving this theorem, which he carried out by building on the matrix algebraic representations used to design PAULI.

**Theorem.** *For any set O of observed reactions and set U of unobserved reactions, at most one quantum number conservation law suffices to rule out U and rule in O. That is, there exists a numerical assignment to each particle appearing in the reactions such that every reaction in O conserves this number via summation, and every reaction in U fails to conserve it.*

We then reported these results to a physics audience (Valdés-Pérez and Erdmann, 1994) as three contributions: (1) an automation of the discovery task based on simple principles; (2) a systematic derivation of the strangeness quantum numbers using historically accurate data and assumptions; and (3) the cited theorem on the parsimony of phenomenological conservation laws (i.e., one law is enough for all conceivable, consistent experimental data). . . .

I now proceed to explore some of the implications of this theorem, which is not without interest for those concerned with the philosophy and practice of induction in scientific inference. (Valdés-Pérez, 1996b, pp. 335–336)

## THE THEORY OF A SINGLE CONSERVATION LAW

Valdés-Pérez (1996b) discusses, in the following section, the differential implications of a single law versus multiple laws for predictions in particle physics.

For any given input data, the single all-encompassing conservation law found by PAULI is not in general logically equivalent to the alternative multiple conservation laws. That is, although both theories explain the reactions data, they make discrepant predictions about *unseen* data. In general, each theory prohibits some reactions that the other theory allows, although one expects that the multiple conservation laws will be more restrictive, since each law serves as an independent constraint on the possible reactions.

For example, [Table 7.2] above showed two theories for the reactions of [Table 7.1]: the baryon/lepton numbers accepted by physicists and PAULI's numbers. As an experiment, I formed all 1575 possible reactions of the form $A \rightarrow B + C$ that involve the given particles. Of these reactions, the baryon/lepton theory prohibits 1325 reactions and accepts 250, while PAULI's theory prohibits 675 and allows 900 (as expected, the dual-conservation-law theory is more stringent). There are 168 reactions that are allowed by both theories, 593 reactions that are prohibited by both, and 814 reactions (more than half) on which the two theories disagree. Two examples of these 814 discordant reactions are: $p \rightarrow e + n$ is prohibited by the baryon/lepton theory, but not by PAULI's theory, and $K^0 \rightarrow \gamma + \pi$ is provided by PAULI, but not by baryon/lepton.

In brief, one law and multiple law theories can make conflicting predictions on unseen data; they are not generally equivalent. (Valdés-Pérez, 1996b, p. 336)

## IMPLICATIONS OF THE DISCOVERY THEOREM

Enabled by the mathematical foundation of the PAULI system, a discovery of a new theorem in particle physics led to some interesting consequences as described in the following account.

[Earlier I mentioned] one puzzle: PAULI consistently yielded single-conservation-law solutions where BR-3 and particle physics practice yielded solutions based on multiple conservation laws. This puzzle was resolved by discovering that single law solutions were to be expected *mathematically*, so that PAULI, which is based on a systematic, mathematical formulation of the search space, should not find anything other than single laws.

However, this mathematical resolution of the puzzle immediately raised a second puzzle which the closing statement in our physics article (Valdés-Pérez and Erdmann, 1994) expressed thus: "It might be worthwhile to reconcile this theorem with the multiplicity of phenomenological quantum properties." In other words, what criteria could lead, under a purely data-driven regime, to a *justification* of the multiple conservation laws found in particle physics phenomenology?

This latter question motivated a follow-up article (Valdés-Pérez, 1996b) that examined and rejected two such criteria: *optimism* (all unseen reactions can occur) and *pessimism* (all unseen reactions are impossible) because they are easily shown to fail to provide the needed justification. A third, *minimax*, criterion, according to which one seeks to *minimize* the *maximum* quantum number, does lead to a theoretical justification, since a single conservation law might involve, for example, a maximum number of 3, whereas multiple laws might lead to a maximum number of 2. However, even though minimax is a powerful concept in optimization, a justification of physics laws based on it seems somewhat esoteric and *ad hoc*.

The fourth and final justification examined in the cited follow-up article leads to the seemingly most satisfactory resolution, and is based on the following preliminary observation: If the number of observed, linearly independent reactions equals or exceeds the number of particles, then elementary matrix algebra indicates that *no* conservation law can exist, that is, no law can rule in the observed reactions and rule out the unobserved ones. In such a case, one must either seek alternative selection rules not based on conservation of a quantum number, or perform *divide-and-conquer*.

The divide-and-conquer approach implied dividing all the observed reactions into two or more groups which need not be disjoint, such that within each group, the number of observed reactions is less than the number of particles. One then finds a conservation law for each group separately. Since no single law will cover all reactions, the result is that every group's conservation law will find exceptions among some reactions outside that group. This is precisely the situation in particle physics practice, in which some reactions fail to conserve one quantum number while conserving all the others.

The resolution of this second puzzle, then, is that one can show, via our machine discovery aided theorem and some further analysis, that the multiple conservation laws of particle physics phenomenology are *mathematically necessary* whenever the observed reactions become numerous relative to the number of particles. Curiously, this constitutes a top-down justification of the state reached in a partly bottom-up manner by physics phenomenology. (Valdés-Pérez, 1996b, pp. 336–337)

## GENERIC RESEARCH IN DISCOVERY SYSTEMS

Valdés-Pérez (1996b) asserts, in the following section, that progress in discovery systems can be facilitated by marking off scientific problem solving from problem solving in general.

Most research on scientific discovery has been concerned with the relation of discovery processes to *general* problem solving (Langley, Simon, Bradshaw, and Zytkow, 1987). Our recent research, in contrast, has been overtly preoccupied with the relation of a given discovery task to problem solving in *science*. That is, we seek generalization *not* within general problem solving, *but within science* (Valdés-Pérez, [1996c]). We proceed thus not from lack of ambition, but in a belief that a body of computationally oriented theory about science will yield different, and perhaps crisper, results than will an analogous theory about much broader phenomena. These research goals are explicated elsewhere under the organizing concept of *generic task of scientific discovery* (Valdés-Pérez, 1995b). Previously, Valdés-Pérez, Zytkow, and Simon (1993) showed that the current discovery task lies within a formally defined generic category that they called *scientific model building as search in matrix spaces*. Here I will analyze briefly some broader, but less formal, generic aspects of the discovery task.

PAULI addresses the task of providing a theoretical basis to distinguish the possible reactions that particles undergo from the impossible reactions. In an abstract sense, this task is common throughout science: to find or postulate a feature that distinguishes two classes of objects. For example, a developmental biologist searches for developmental characteristics that distinguish a mutant organism from the wild-type (normal) organism. A psychiatrist looks for eye-movement patterns that discriminate between psychotics and normal subjects. A physiologist seeks features to classify diseased and healthy cells. All of these tasks are somewhat analogous to the concept learning task in machine learning. However, all these scientific tasks emphasize *finding* or *postulating* discriminatory features rather than selecting from a known list.

As in concept learning, a correct but uninteresting theoretical explanation of the observed and unobserved reactions consists of a trivial disjunction of the observed reactions, meaning that all other reactions are prohibited. A more interesting and useful partial explanation was attempted by the physicist Abraham Pais, who pointed out that, for the reactions that led to the discovery of strangeness, particles are generally produced in pairs and never as single particles (Ne'eman and Kirsh, 1986). This observational pattern of *associated production* could serve as a partial discriminating feature between possible and impossible reactions. However, particle physicists eventually followed a more theoretical and complete approach by postulating unseen, conserved properties (quantum numbers) such that any hypothetical reaction that violated conservation was deemed impossible. This approach is, of course, the one followed by BR-3 and PAULI.

So, although the task of inventing features to discriminate between two classes is broadly generic throughout science, the detailed solution strategies may be highly particular, as in the approach followed by particle physics in this case. (Valdés-Pérez, 1996b, pp. 337–338)

## PAULI AND THE DISCOVERY OF THE CONSERVATION THEOREM: CONCLUSION

In the following account, Valdés-Pérez (1996b) draws the concluding implications of his research.

The lesson of this paper for artificial intelligence is that machine discovery based on heuristic search does lead to new findings in science, even in sciences of such celebrity and theory density as particle physics. In this instance, the new finding is a theorem which *was enabled by machine discovery* in the sense that observations of the invariant behavior of a machine discovery program directly led to the theorem's conjecture; its proof used representational techniques borrowed from the design of the program itself. Follow-up work then addressed— and resolved—the question of why physics practice seemingly conflicts with the theorem.

It is important to document such results for AI audiences, in order to falsify the premise of an otherwise powerful argument: a dearth of machine discoveries implies that machine discovery research is not addressing the essential parts of the discovery process in science. (Valdés-Pérez, 1996b, p. 338)

# PART III

# HUMAN AND COMPUTER SCIENTIFIC DISCOVERY PROCESSES

# 8

## General Processes of Scientific Discovery

### *SCIENTIFIC DISCOVERY AND ARTIFICIAL INTELLIGENCE*

#### THE GENERAL LOGIC OF BACON.3

The process of scientific discovery depends on the detection of patterns in data and the summary representation of these patterns in theoretical terms. BACON.3 uses general heuristics and production system methodology to accomplish pattern detection and the discovery of scientific laws. Among the classical laws rediscovered by BACON.3 is Kepler's third law of planetary motion. It must be emphasized that BACON.3's discoveries of scientific laws do not entail an explanation of the data; the laws only provide a summary of the data in the form of equations. In this section, BACON.3, developed by Langley (1981), is described with respect to its major characteristics, a summary and analysis of BACON.3's discoveries are presented, and a commentary on BACON.3's strengths and limitations is offered.

#### CHARACTERISTICS OF BACON.3

In order to discover scientific laws, BACON.3 relies on a set of general heuristics that recast data and theoretical terms at increasingly abstract levels of description. The first set of these heuristics operates at the level of data collection.

In order to recast the collected data, BACON.3 applies a set of heuristics that discerns patterns or regularities and leads to higher levels of description.

A third set of heuristics is devoted to the calculation of values of theoretical terms at a given level of description.

A fourth set of productions is devoted to the detection of redundancies of new theoretical terms with existing theoretical terms.

A fifth set of productions controls an abstraction process whereby differences in theoretical terms can be ignored.

A sixth set of productions is devoted to the process of combining clusters that have identical conditions.

A seventh set of productions is directed toward the detection of irrelevant variables and to dropping their values from consideration.

A detailed description of BACON'S heuristics can be found in Wagman (1995, p. 118).

The BACON.3 system depends on these seven sets of productions (86 productions in all) for the discovery of physical laws.

## SCIENTIFIC DISCOVERIES OF BACON.3

In addition to the discovery of a version of Kepler's third law, BACON.3 discovered a number of other empirical laws. In this section, the empirical laws, their diversity, and their relative complexity will be discussed. The generality of BACON.3's methodology will be considered in two ways: the extent to which each of its seven sets of heuristics was involved in the discoveries and the effect of changing the order of the experiments that led to the discoveries.

BACON.3 discovered five scientific laws: the ideal gas laws, Kepler's third law, Coulomb's law, Galileo's laws, and Ohm's law (a detailed description of these equations is given in Wagman, 1995, p. 124).

The empirical laws discovered by BACON.3 exhibit diversity in subject matter and in algebraic expression: from the laws of the solar system to the physics of motion, gases, and electricity; from the squaring of a ratio (Kepler's law) to simple ratios and products (ideal gas laws) to the ratio of squared variables (Galileo's laws).

The algebraic complexity of Ohm's law suggests computational complexity in its discovery. As compared with the other laws, the discovery of Ohm's law required a larger number of productions, a larger size of working memory, more levels of description, and more theoretical terms.

BACON.3's heuristics appear to be general across the set of five empirical laws. This generality held in the case of five sets of productions: factorial experimental design in the collection of data, discovering the regularities, calculating theoretical values, noting redundant theoretical terms, and collapsing clusters. The heuristics involved in the development of abstractions by ignoring differences were used in the discovery of four of the laws (the discovery of Galileo's laws was the exception). The productions involved in the handling of irrelevant variables were used only for the discovery of Galileo's laws.

The generality of the BACON.3 system is indicated by its ability to arrive at the empirical laws by various orders or sequences of experimental observations. Variations in order could lengthen or shorten the time required to discover a law, but the identical law was still discovered. Computational complexity (for example, number of productions used, size of working memory) was an experimental order effect, but the attainment of the empirical law was not an experimental order effect.

## COMMENTARY ON BACON.3

BACON.3 embodies a set of heuristics that perform, in machine fashion, intellective functions of induction, abstraction, generalization, factorial experimentation, and calculation. The machine executes these intellective functions under the guidance of its symbolic language.

The heuristic codes are, as indicated in the previous section, general in the sense that they can execute different content, but the heuristic codes are indifferent to and uncomprehending of the content. The comprehension lies with the human user of BACON.3. BACON.3 did not independently discover or rediscover any laws; it merely executed heuristic codes designed and interpreted by its developer.

BACON.3 produced equations that are descriptive and empirical. Its heuristics can, no doubt, be extended to other descriptive laws in physics and other domains (Langley et al., 1987). However, its heuristics are inadequate for theoretical conceptualization of the complex explanatory laws that constitute contemporary knowledge in such areas as nuclear physics.

In conclusion, BACON.3 is a machine representation of the inductive and Baconian (Francis Bacon, 1561–1626, a British philosopher of science) method of descriptive science. It remains to be seen whether artificial intelligence research (Caudill and Butler, 1990; Partridge and Wilkes, 1990) can develop machine representation (Boden, 1996; Kulkarni and Simon, 1988) of discovery in theoretical science (Wagman, 1998).

## EXPERIMENTAL REDISCOVERY OF KEPLER'S THIRD LAW

### GENERAL LOGIC OF THE LABORATORY REPLICATION

As discussed in the previous section of this chapter, the BACON.3 program employed systematic heuristics to rediscover by inductive or data driven procedures a number of physical science laws, including Kepler's third law of planetary motion. Qin and Simon (1990) conducted a laboratory experiment whose objective was to compare BACON's discovery heuristics with the heuristics of university students given the task of discovering the functional relationship between two sets of data that, unknown to the subjects, was equivalent to the data available to Kepler: for each of five planets (Mercury, Venus, Earth, Mars, Jupiter), its distance from and period of revolution around the sun. The function discovered by Kepler and rediscovered by BACON.3 and possibly to be discovered in a laboratory experiment by university students states that the ratio of planetary distance cubed to planetary period squared is a constant. Qin and Simon (1990), in two experiments, obtained the protocols of successful and unsuccessful university students and related their problem-solving heuristics to heuristics embodied in the BACON program. Qin and Simon's interesting research will be described, and the implications of their results will be discussed in a commentary section.

### THE FIRST EXPERIMENT: METHOD, MATERIALS, AND SUBJECTS

Subjects were given two sets of data, simply labeled as $s$ and $q$. The data under $s$ and $q$ consisted of five rows of 2-, 3-, or 4-digit numbers. The meaning of $s$ and $q$ was not revealed to subjects, but, in fact, they referred to distances ($s$) and periods ($q$) of five planets.

Qin and Simon (1990) began their experiment by informing the participants that their task was to construct a mathematical formula summarizing the relationship between two sets of experimental data. Subjects were asked to think aloud as they worked on the task.

To discover the scientific formula, subjects (unlike Kepler, who discovered the planetary law in 1620) were permitted to use a modern calculator that computed mathematical functions including multiplication, division, exponents, and logarithms.

Qin and Simon (1990) indicate that of the nine subjects who participated in the first experiment, seven were taking or have taken university-level science or mathematics courses.

## RESULTS

Qin and Simon (1990) indicate that because of a number of difficulties in solving the problem only two of the nine experimental subjects succeeded. The correct relationship between $q$ and $s$ is non-linear, or the subjects tried only linear relationships. Two subjects failed to detect that the relationship between $q$ and $s$ involves a non-integral exponent. Finally, two subjects assumed incorrectly that the relationship between $q$ and $s$ did not involve a constant.

Qin and Simon (1990) found that, across all subjects, simple linear functions were used more often than complex quadratic or logarithmic functions.

Qin and Simon (1990) compare successful and unsuccessful subjects in a use of BACON's heuristics or finding laws. Unsuccessful subjects were less systematic in applying the results of feedback to their hypotheses concerning possible formulas relating to $s$. Thus, although unsuccessful subjects might use BACON's heuristics 4 and 5 (listed in the section Subjects' Heuristics and BACON's Heuristics, below), they did so in a relatively haphazard way.

## THE SECOND EXPERIMENT

The second experiment introduced one change. Subjects were not provided with a calculator to compute exponential and logarithmic functions, thereby more nearly matching Kepler's computational resources. The expected result was that subjects took longer than subjects in the first experiment to discover Kepler's third law of planetary motion. Of the five subjects in the second experiment, two succeeded.

Qin and Simon (1990) indicate that the general outcome of the second experiment was similar to the findings of the first experiment in that linear and simple functions were used more often than complex functions as subjects searched for the correct formula.

Qin and Simon (1990) report that the problem-solving behavior of successful subjects is quite similar to that of the successful subjects in the first experiment. Successful, as compared to unsuccessful subjects, searched systematically and provided feedback to modify their hypotheses.

## SUBJECTS' HEURISTICS AND BACON'S HEURISTICS

BACON rediscovered Kepler's third planetary law by systematic application of recursive heuristics. BACON's program moves with relentless efficiency.

Qin and Simon (1990) found that BACON'S mechanical recursive heuristics are only approached by the heuristics of the human subjects (see Wagman, 1995, p. 132, for a detailed description of BACON's five heuristics).

Heuristic 1 seeks to find laws by reiterating through the values of the independent variable and then calculating the pre-integers values in the dependent variable until a law is found. Heuristic 2 discovers the constants in a law by noting the invariant value that appears in all manipulations of all the data clusters. Heuristic 3 determines the presence of a linear function of a law when the values of variable $x$ and the values of variable $y$ have slope $m$ and intercept $b$. Heuristic 4 asserts that under the condition that the absolute values of $X$ increase as the absolute values of $Y$ increase, the law can be expressed as the ratio of $X$ and $Y$. Heuristic 5 asserts that under the condition that the absolute values of X increase as the absolute values of Y decrease and provided that these values cannot be characterized as linearly related, the law can be expressed as the product of X and Y.

Qin and Simon (1990) report that all subjects used heuristics 1, 2, and 3. In using heuristics 4 and 5, successful and unsuccessful subjects are distinguished in that successful subjects were systematic and perceptive in their use, whereas unsuccessful subjects used the heuristics 4 and 5 sporadically and inappropriately. BACON searched sufficiently and recursively and systematically using only linear functions and simple operations such as ratios and products.

## COMMENTARY

It is important to recognize that scientific or philosophical theory played no role in the discovery of Kepler's third law of planetary motion by the BACON program and by the university students. The discovery was an exercise in mathematical computation. Kepler, on the other hand, was motivated not only by the need for a descriptive mathematical law but also by an overwhelming need to find an explanation for the relationship between the variables of planetary period and planetary distance. Had he not been absorbed in theoretical and cosmological speculations for a period of two decades, he would have, more quickly and with less personal frustration, found and accepted the mathematical function that so elegantly captures the planetary data. The need to know why is a human need, and many great scientists following Kepler sought explanations for descriptive mathematical laws.

Maxwell formulated a theory of electromagnetism, but electrical fields are fictions, and the knowledge we have of electromagnetism is embodied in Maxwell's partial differential equations. As Helmholtz said, "In Maxwell's theory an electric charge is but the recipient of a symbol" (quoted in Kline, 1985, p. 146). Indeed, much of current theoretical science consists of no more than mathematical symbols and mathematical equations.

The implication is that further development of intelligent systems, of which BACON is a primitive example, may accelerate the pace with which the knowledge of nature is captured by and represented in expanding sets of mathematical functions that yet fail, somehow, to satisfy the human need to know why.

It is important to recognize that it was by means of inductive reasoning that the relationship between a planet's distance from the sun and its period of rotation was computed by university students in the Qin and Simon experiment, the BACON program, and Johannes Kepler. The discovered equation was, in each case, data driven. A mathematical derivation of the equation provides the certainty characteristic of deductive reasoning. This derivation can be accomplished from Newtonian laws of motion and gravitation. The challenge to cognitive science is to go beyond data-driven procedures such as those in the BACON program to theory-based procedures that would emulate mathematical derivation of Kepler's third law. The EUREKA program (Elio and Scharf, 1990) can use its stock of equations to solve problems in elementary kinematics and, as discussed elsewhere, may be capable of deriving Kepler's third law from its equations.

## *SCIENTIFIC DISCOVERY AND HUMAN INTELLECT*

### THE TRANSFORMATION OF SCIENTIFIC CONCEPTS

The processes of scientific discovery are complex and dependent upon the achievement of a resolution of empirical and theoretical stringencies. The transformation and dissolution of conflicting stringencies depend on restructuring the configuration of the problem and its conflicting elements. There is, perhaps, no clearer example of this process of scientific discovery than that of the astronomer Johannes Kepler, who transformed the concept of circular planetary motion (Hanson, 1958). An additional reason for selecting Johannes Kepler is to permit a comparison of the intellectual processes involved in his astronomical discoveries with the machine processes involved in BACON.3's rediscovery of Kepler's third law (see the section on scientific discovery and artificial intelligence in this chapter). The comparison of scientific discovery processes in Kepler and BACON.3 will be presented later in this chapter (see the section on discovery and a general theory of intelligence).

### KEPLER'S TRANSFORMATION OF THE CONCEPT OF CIRCULAR PLANETARY MOTION

During the two millennia preceding the scientific discoveries of Johannes Kepler (1571–1630), the Platonic analogy between the perfection of geometry and the perfection of the heavens commanded the absolute and universal allegiance of astronomers, philosophers, and theologians. The doctrine of circular planetary orbits operated as a conceptual ligature in Kepler's scientific investigations. Thus, as will be detailed later, Kepler developed a sound method (equal areas in equal times) and sound reasoning concerning the orbit of the planet Mars but came to mistrust and abandon, for a time, both his method and reasoning when they led to the conclusion that the orbit of Mars could not be circular.

In a treatise of more than 300 pages, entitled *De Motibus Stellae Martis* (1937), Kepler presented a detailed account of his investigations concerning the orbit of Mars and the nature of the solar system. *De Motibus Stellae Martis* contains Kepler's complex reasoning, his perplexities, his attempts to reconcile theory and data, his many hypotheses, misconceptions, and errors, and, after years of work, his culminating discoveries elegantly set forth in three laws of the solar system.

## FROM GEOCENTRISM TO HELIOCENTRISM

In the early chapters of *De Motibus Stellae Martis*, Kepler presents an account of his discussions with his fellow astronomer Tycho Brahe. These discussions were held in Prague in 1600 and concerned Brahe's theory of the orbit of Mars. The theory included the postulates of geocentrism and of circular planetary motion. Kepler could not accept Brahe's theory, which, under the postulate of geocentrism, led to discrepancies of as much as five degrees of arc with observations. Kepler replaced the geocentrism postulate with a heliocentrism hypothesis on the basis that the Sun's huge magnitude compared with any of the planets and its centrist location in the planetary system probably determine the character of planetary motion.

Whereas Brahe's geocentrism postulate led him to study first the orbit of Mars (in his theory, there is no terrestrial orbit), Kepler's heliocentrism hypothesis led him to study first the orbit of the Earth.

## FROM CIRCULAR ORBIT TO NONCIRCULAR ORBIT

Kepler applied the method of equal angles in equal times (or equal areas in equal times) to his studies of the orbit of Mars. However, as detailed in *De Motibus Stellae Martis*, under the postulate that the orbit of Mars was circular (see earlier discussion of the two-millennia belief in the doctrine of circular planetary motion), the method of equal areas in equal times produced errors of plus or minus eight minutes of arc deviation from observations. Kepler responded to these stringencies among the observations, the postulate of circular orbit, and the method of equal areas by protracted self-debate as to which would have to be given up—the circular orbit postulate or the equal areas method: "From which it is shown what I promise to do in chapters XX, XXII . . . that the planet's orbit is not a circle but has the figure of an oval" (Kepler, quoted in Hanson, 1958, p. 75).

As indicated in *De Motibus Stellae Martis*, Kepler then proceeds to reject his own conclusion that the orbit is not circular and reaches, instead, the conclusion that his method of areas is incorrect:

"Given that the orbit is circular, and supposing my reasoning to be correct, then the observations α, β, γ, are directly predicted; but α, β, γ do not occur; *therefore my reasoning was not correct*." After failing to reconcile the circular orbit with the equations given by the method of areas, [Kepler] actually abandoned *the latter*. Different considerations were required to convince him that it was the circular orbit hypothesis that was ruining his theory. Only when the distances given to him by the circle were repeatedly inconsistent with those observed by Tycho, did Kepler begin systematically to doubt the circular orbit hypothesis. Even then he headed the next chapter "De Causis Naturalibus Hujus Deflexionis Planetae a Circulo." (Hanson, 1958, p. 76)

## FROM OVOID ORBIT TO ELLIPTICAL ORBIT

After Kepler had finally and resolutely decided that the orbit of Mars was not circular, his next self-debate turned on the question of the specific nature of the noncircular orbital curve:

Whichever of these ways is used to describe the line on which the planet moves, it follows that this path, indicated by the following points, β, μ, α, δ, π, ρ, λ), is ovular, and not elliptical; to the latter, Mechanicians wrongly give the name derived from ovo. The egg (ovum) can be spun on two vertices, one flatter (obtuse), one sharper (acute). Further it is bound by inclined sides. This is the figure I have created.

All of this conspires to show that the resegmentum of our eccentric circle is much larger below than above, in equal recession from the apsides. Anyone can establish this either by numerical calculation or by mechanical drawing—some eccentricity being assumed. (Kepler, quoted in Hall, 1955, p. 295)

Kepler now became concerned with creating a physical explanation for the physical oviform motion of Mars. He arrived at the explanatory hypothesis that the oviform orbit was the resultant of two attractive physical forces, one emanating from the Sun and one emanating from Mars.

However, the peculiar geometric properties of the oviform presented computational problems to Kepler, and he began to entertain the possibility that the orbit was a perfect ellipse. Once more, conceptual and empirical stringencies resulted in difficulties for Kepler. On the one hand, the oviform (as in the case of the circle) has but one focus. On the other hand, the geometric difficulties of the oviform could be relaxed if it were made to approximate an ellipse, but an ellipse has two foci. The required restructuring of his geometric model and reasoning preoccupied Kepler for some time. Ultimately, he was able to fit his physical data concerning the orbital motion of Mars to the mathematical properties of a perfect ellipse, with the Sun in one of the foci.

**Table 8.1**
**Kepler's Scientific Discoveries**

---

1.   Planetary orbits are elliptical with the sun in their common focus (1609).

2.   They describe around the sun areas proportional to their times of passage (1609).

3.   The squares of the time of their revolutions are proportional to the cubes of their
     greater axes, or their mean distances from the sun (1619).

---

*Source:* Hanson, N. R. (1958). *Patterns of discovery: An inquiry into the conceptual foundations of science.* Cambridge, MA: Cambridge University Press, p. 84.

The enormous heap of calculations, velocities, positions and distances which had set Kepler his problem now pulled together into a geometrically intelligible pattern. The elliptical areas were seen to be equivalent; similarly, equations following from the ellipse were general expressions of Tycho's original data. All this made it clear that Mars revolved around the sun in an ellipse, describing around the sun areas proportional to its times of passage. (Hanson, 1958, p. 83)

## THE LAWS OF THE SOLAR SYSTEM

Kepler then reasoned that, because the physical forces controlling the motion of the planet Mars operated throughout the solar system, the orbits of the other planets would also fit the mathematical model of the ellipse, obey the principle of equal areas in equal times, and have periods of revolution about the Sun and distances from the Sun in the ratio of $p^2/d^3$. These laws are presented in more detail in Table 8.1. The extraordinary astronomical discoveries of Johannes Kepler required two decades to completely revolutionize astronomical paradigms and dogma that had dominated conceptions of the solar system for two millennia.

## *DISCOVERY AND A GENERAL THEORY OF INTELLIGENCE*

The previous sections of this chapter have presented two approaches to scientific and mathematical discovery. The artificial intelligence approach was illustrated by the BACON.3 program. The human intellect approach was exemplified by Kepler's astronomical work. The purpose of the present section is to identify commonalities and differences in the two approaches.

## DISCOVERY AND INDUCTIVE LOGIC

Inductive logic is well represented in artificial intelligence research (Osherson and Smith, 1982) concerned with discovery and learning (Larkin et al., 1988). The LEX program (Mitchell, Utgoff, & Banerji, 1983) learns symbolic integration by generalizing and specializing among examples in a version space. The AM program (Lenat, 1976) uses inductive logic in generalizing and specializing numerical examples and relationships in order to discover conjectures and concepts in elementary number theory. The BACON.3 program (see the section on scientific discovery and artificial intelligence in this chapter) uses inductive logic in its data-driven detection of regularities and abstractions to discover or rediscover empirical laws in astronomy and physics.

The discovery of the laws of the solar system by Johannes Kepler and their rediscovery (Kepler's third law, in particular) by BACON.3 demonstrate essential identity as products in the form of equations. However, the processes of discovery are essentially disparate. BACON.3 obeyed its rules, performed its calculations, developed its abstractions, detected its regularities, and determined invariants in the ratios of variables, all in mechanical accordance with general heuristics (applicable to other domains of physical science as well) and generally followed a rigid inductive logic. In contrast, Kepler struggled to resolve theoretical and empirical constraints, to surmount his deep belief in the circularity of planetary motion, to reconcile conflicts involving his method of equal areas in equal times with the proper mathematical curve, to propose and reject numerous hypotheses, and to create an integrated theory that unified physical explanation and mathematical description of the motion of the planets and of the solar system.

## THEORETICAL SCIENCE AND INDUCTIVE LOGIC

The field of artificial intelligence has been neither a theoretical science nor a mathematical science (Simon, 1979) but, rather, an applied inductive science. This is especially clear in the case of BACON.3, in which heuristics are used to carry out inductive experiments that may lead to the establishment of regularities among independent and dependent variables. The regularities established are data driven rather than theory driven. The discoveries take the form of empirical functional relationships among variables. The laws discovered by BACON.3 are expressed as equations; but as the laws have been derived by inductive logic alone, their explanation—that is, their possible embodiment in a wider net of theory—is completely absent. BACON.3 is mechanism, not mind (Boden, 1988, 1990; Newell, 1990; Rychlak, 1990; Simon, 1990; Wagman, 1991b). Even the human mind, when relying solely on inductive logic, cannot develop theoretical science: "there is no inductive method which could lead to the fundamental concepts of physics. . . . In error are those theorists who believe that theory comes inductively from experience" (Einstein, 1933).

In the scientific era following Einstein, the technology of computers and artificial intelligence developed with applications ramifying throughout the natural sciences. These ramifications include theoretical physics as enthusiastically specified by Stephen Hawking, one of the most eminent theoretical physicists of the last quarter of the twentieth century:

At present computers are a useful aid in research but they have to be directed by human minds. However, if one extrapolates their recent rapid rate of development, it would seem quite possible that they will take over altogether in theoretical physics. So maybe the end is in sight for theoretical physicists if not for theoretical physics. (Hawking, quoted in Davis and Hersh, 1986, p. 158)

The nature of human intellect is discoverable, the mathematics of human intellect is describable, and the computational representation of human intellect is constructible. A general unified theory of human and artificial intelligence can evolve (Wagman, 1997a).

# 9

## Computational Simulation of Scientific Discovery Processes

### ARTIFICIAL INTELLIGENCE AND THE PROCESSES OF SCIENTIFIC DISCOVERY

#### THE GENERAL LOGIC OF COMPUTATIONAL THEORIES OF SCIENTIFIC DISCOVERY

The general logic of computational theories of scientific discovery includes the assumption that the creative processes of scientific discovery are knowable and definable, the assumption that they represent subsets of general strategies of problem solving, the assumption that they can be modeled by the standard heuristics of problem-solving computational systems, and the assumption that scientific discovery systems cannot only replicate discovery processes and products but also make independent and original discoveries. Each of these assumptions is now briefly discussed.

The assumption that creative and discovery processes are not unknowable or undefinable is in conflict with the prevalent and ancient belief that human creativity is mysterious and beyond the ken of science. Creativity, whether artistic, literary, musical, philosophical, mathematical, or scientific, was a gift from capricious muses; a special blessing from God; the crystallization of unconscious dynamics in a neurotic personality; an inexplicable and sudden inspiration (literally, spirit); or the intuitive insight that illumines, as if by magic, the nature of the solution to a puzzle, problem, or paradox.

The assumption that the inductive and deductive logics of scientific discovery can be mapped as sets of mechanistic problem-solving heuristics may be unacceptable, as it appears to deny or foreshorten the significance of the human qualities of curiosity about a problem, interest in a phenomenon, disappointment in an experimental outcome, surprise in the face of an unexpected scientific result, frustration over failure, and elation in response to minor successes that give encouragement to the continuation of a difficult and challenging scientific enterprise. The assumption that a mechanism is necessary and sufficient appears to be unacceptable because it denies exclusivity of intellect to humans and denies the necessity of nonintellective processes.

The assumption that computer programs can replicate scientific and mathematical discoveries has received some justification. Lenat's Automatic Mathematician (AM) program (Davis & Lenat, 1982) discovered the fundamental theorem of arithmetic and the concept of prime numbers. Langley's BACON.3 program (Langley et al., 1987) rediscovered Kepler's laws of planetary motion, Galileo's laws of acceleration, Georg Ohm's laws of electricity, and the ideal gas law. The assumption that computer programs can make independent and original scientific discoveries has received some support. The Meta-DENDRAL program (Buchanan & Feigenbaum, 1978) has made discoveries in chemistry that were considered sufficiently significant to be published in a prestigious scientific journal.

These programs demonstrate the power of mechanistic problem solving. However, they were not designed to illumine or precisely model the nature of the scientist's creative processes. For example, BACON.3 rediscovered Kepler's laws of the solar system by applying general heuristics for relating variables to data presented to it; but unlike Johannes Kepler, BACON.3 did not construct and reconstruct hypotheses, explanations, and theories. Similarly, BACON.3 was provided with data from which it constructed the equations for Coulomb's laws; but unlike Charles Coulomb, it did not conduct the complex experimentation and theorizing that culminated in the collected data.

In order to advance the computational theory of scientific discovery, it is necessary to develop programs that can model the scientist's experimental concepts and procedures. The KEKADA program (Kulkarni & Simon, 1988) was developed to model the creative processes of Hans Krebs, who made important discoveries in biochemistry.

## KREBS' DISCOVERY OF THE ORNITHINE EFFECT

In 1932, by means of systematic experimentation, Hans Krebs discovered the metabolic cycle and biochemical events involved in the liver's synthesis of urea. The discovery was highly significant in its own right, and as a model of biochemical metabolic theory it has been characterized by J. S. Fruton as "a new stage in the development of biochemical thought" (1972, p. 95). A highly detailed reconstruction of the experimental and conceptual steps by which Krebs made his discovery was achieved by F. L. Holmes (1980) on the basis of interviews with Krebs and the examination of Krebs' meticulous laboratory logs of his ongoing experiments. Holmes' description of the processes of Krebs' scientific discovery was used by D. Kulkarni and H. A. Simon (1988) to develop KEKADA, a program that would duplicate those processes and contribute to a computational theory of scientific discovery.

## GENERAL CHARACTERISTICS OF THE KEKADA PROGRAM

Intended to simulate Krebs' processes of discovery, as described by Holmes (1980), KEKADA's discovery processes followed the conceptual structure of general problem solving as developed by Simon and Lea (1974).

The two-space model of learning (Simon and Lea, 1974) provided the conceptual framework for the KEKADA system. The model contains an instance space and a rule space. KEKADA performs experiments in order to search the instance space. The rule space is searched for hypotheses, expectations, and confidences that guide the selection of experiments to be carried out. Experimental results, in turn, modify the hypotheses, and cycles of search in the two spaces continue.

Search in the instance spaces is carried out by heuristic operators that include operators that propose experiments and operators that execute the experiments.

Rule space search is conducted by heuristic operators that include operators that propose strategy and hypotheses to be tested, operators for the generation of problems and their sequencing, operators that generate hypotheses to interpret hidden mechanisms or poorly understood observations, and operators that adapt hypotheses and confidence in hypotheses according to feedback evidence.

KEKADA possesses decision-maker heuristics that determine which of the operator heuristics are applicable at a given point in the discovery process.

As KEKADA searches its problem spaces and seeks to make its discoveries, its heuristics interact appropriately.

Problem-chooser heuristics determine what tasks the person should focus on. Hypothesis-generator heuristics together with confidence heuristics appear in working memory. Strategy proposers select a strategy, and experiments are suggested by the experiment proposers. Decision-maker heuristics come into operation. Experimenters execute experiments that include expectations as generated by the expectation-setter heuristics. Experimental outcomes are reviewed by confidence and hypothesis-modifier heuristics.

A computer program like KEKADA, which attempts to simulate the discovery processes of the human scientist, must be alert to unexpected turns and results in the course of experimentation. KEKADA has mechanisms that simulate the cognitive (if not affective) aspects of surprise that are present in the discovery process.

KEKADA contains surprise-detector heuristics and an operating code that adds a surprising experimental outcome as a set of results to the gender of problems to be worked on by the system. The surprise-detector heuristics note violations of expectations that were set prior to the experiment concerning what substances, in what amounts, and with what limits can be produced as the outcome by chemical experiment.

KEKADA must not only be able to recognize surprising and puzzling events occurring in the experimental process, but it must also be able to advance hypotheses that guide the continuation of exploration.

KEKADA responds to surprising experimental outcomes by applying hypothesis-generating heuristics. For example, when a reaction contains A, a class of substances containing A may be hypothesized to result in the same reaction. In a case where the surprising result contains several sub-processes, the heuristics direct a strategy of exploring the sub-processes, one by one, to locate the cause of the experimental outcome. Where a one-step chemical transformation is impossible from input to output, the hypothesis heuristic postulates an intermediate.

## KEKADA'S SIMULATION OF KREBS' DISCOVERIES

Krebs began his work with a certain technical knowledge. During the course of his work, he acquired additional knowledge from scientific journals and from professional colleagues. All this knowledge influenced the choice and course of his experimentation. In order to simulate the onset and course of Krebs' experiments and discoveries, KEKADA was provided with the same knowledge.

Kulkarni and Simon (1988) conclude that not only does KEKADA succeed in its simulation but that it also "constitutes a theory of Krebs' style of experimentation."

According to Kulkarni and Simon (1988), the KEKADA system, using its knowledge and heuristics, not only made the discovery of the ornithine effect but did so in a manner of experimentation and with reasons for experimentation that closely matched, if they did not duplicate, the scientific creativity of Hans Krebs.

## KEKADA AS A GENERAL SIMULATOR OF THE SCIENTIFIC DISCOVERY PROCESS

From the point of view of Kulkarni and Simon (1988), the processes of scientific discovery, whether those of Krebs or those of any other scientist, can be represented as a goal-directed series of problem-solving steps guided by domain-directed knowledge and heuristic operators that are both domain-specific and domain-general. The KEKADA system simulates this theory of the nature of the scientific discovery process.

## COMMENTARY

At the beginning of this section, it is stated that the general logic of computational theories of scientific discovery includes a set of general assumptions. The research of Kulkarni and Simon (1988) on the KEKADA system is now used to examine these assumptions and, to that extent, to evaluate the logic of computational theories of scientific discovery.

The assumption that the processes of creativity in scientific discovery have a knowable character can be supported once it is granted that some degree of confidence can be placed in Holmes' (1980) account and that Krebs' logs and recollections of the onset, course, and outcome of his experimentation possess an acceptable level of completeness and reliability. The assumption that the creative processes of scientific discovery are definable can be supported given KEKADA's definitional heuristics, which include the capacity for planning and executing experiments, the recognition of surprising experimental results, and the consequent revision of hypotheses and continuation of the control strategies of systematic experimentation.

The assumption that scientific discovery processes represent subsets of general problem-solving strategies is supported by the two-space (instance space and rule space) model of problem solving (Simon & Lea, 1974), which provided the general superstructure for the development of the control logic in the KEKADA system. KEKADA's success in replicating Hans Krebs' scientific discoveries appears to support the understanding of scientific discovery as a special case of the two-space problem-solving theory.

The assumption that scientific discovery processes can be modeled by the standard heuristics of computational problem-solving systems is supported by the use in KEKADA of the familiar artificial intelligence methodology of the production system. In addition, KEKADA's possession of a large set of general heuristics, potentially applicable to scientific discovery problems beyond those of Krebs, lends credence to the assumption that a computational system such as KEKADA can model general aspects of the process of scientific discovery.

The assumption that a computational system such as KEKADA can make original and independent discoveries is difficult to evaluate. To KEKADA, as to Krebs, the discoveries were new. To the scientific world, KEKADA's discoveries were replications and rediscoveries. The metabolic processes of the ornithine cycle were disclosed by Krebs, and that disclosure was repeated by KEKADA. The developers (Kulkarni & Simon, 1988) cannot claim for KEKADA the status of making an original contribution to contemporary knowledge in the field of biochemistry.

The general logic of computational theory of scientific discovery processes should be contrasted with theories of human scientific discovery that characterize or require the existence of intrinsic motivation. Theories of the nature of human creativity (Sternberg, 1988) are in general agreement that the conditions for creativity require inherent interest in the subject and love for the creative task:

Guiding our investigations is what we have termed the *intrinsic motivation principle of creativity*:

People will be most creative when they feel motivated primarily by the interest, enjoyment, satisfaction, and challenge of the work itself—not the external pressures.

In essence, we are saying that the love people feel for their work has a great deal to do with the creativity of their performance. This proposition is clearly supported by accounts of the phenomenology of creativity. Most reports from and about creative individuals are filled with notions of an intense involvement in and unrivaled love for their work. Thomas Mann, for example, described in one of his letters his passion for writing (John-Steiner, 1985), and physicists who were close to Albert Einstein saw in him a similar kind of intensity. In the words of the Nobel Prize–winning inventor Dennis Gabor, "no one has ever enjoyed science as much as Einstein" (John-Steiner, 1985, p. 67). (Hennessey & Amabile, 1988, p. 11)

I want to know how God created this world. I am not interested in this or that phenomenon, in the spectrum of this or that element. I want to know His thoughts, the rest are details. . . . Once the validity of this mode of thought has been recognized, the final results appear almost simple; any intelligent under-graduate can understand them without much trouble. But the years of searching in the dark for a truth that one feels, but cannot express; the intense desire and the alternations of confidence and misgiving, until one breaks through to charity and understanding, are only known to him who has himself experienced them. (Einstein, quoted in Ferris, 1988, p. 177)

Clearly, computational theories of discovery do not require that the computational system possess intrinsic motivation as a necessary condition for creativity. The heuristic mechanisms of computational systems are sufficient.

Finally, it is not clear that the use of a scientist's laboratory logs and recollections is adequate for areas of science that, unlike the rather applied bench experimentation of Krebs, depend upon complex reflection, deep theory, and thought experimentation, as exemplified in the creative processes of Albert Einstein. It remains to be seen whether the intellectual levels of advanced theoretical science can be encompassed by computational theories of scientific discovery.

There is no inductive method which could lead to the fundamental concepts of physics . . . in error are those theorists who believe that theory comes inductively from experience. (Einstein, 1933)

The unconscious processes (Feldman, 1988; Hadamard, 1949; Langley & Jones, 1988; Torrance, 1988) that lead to great insights of scientific discovery in astronomy, mathematics, biology, and molecular genetics remain a scientific enigma whose decipherment may depend on advances in the neural sciences in conjunction with psychological and computational approaches.

Just as the mind in its many facets stands as the major "general" target for current neurobiological work, creative efforts are among the most important "specifics" in need of elucidation. Numerous electrophysiological and neuroradiological tools now make feasible studies of individual differences. . . .

One other point worth stressing is that neurobiologists can now expect to receive aid from researchers working at the other side of the cognitive-scientific interface. Many psychologists and artificial intelligence researchers working at the level of "domain" or "intelligence" are now probing cognitive processes in great detail; an account in terms of underlying neurophysiological or neurochemical processes is no longer remote. And when it comes to the study of particular human faculties, ranging from language to vision, there is again a cadre of workers prepared to see their work analyzed in terms of underlying biological systems. (Gardner, 1988, p. 318)

A complete science of the nature of scientific discovery processes cannot beg the question of the heart of the discovery process by using different terminologies equivalently limited to only a descriptive function, but must possess a theory capable of predicting, under specified conditions, the emergence of new creative insights. The possibility of such a theory remains a beckoning and honorable destiny.

# PART IV

## CONCLUSIONS

# 10

# Scientific Problem Types and Computational Discovery Systems

Scientific research involves an intricate set of interrelated problems. The problems range from data and observation to technique and experimentation to theory formation and revision. A schematic analysis of these problem types, developed by Root-Bernstein (1989), is presented in Table 10.1.

To what extent have artificial intelligence approaches (Boden, 1996) to the problems of scientific discovery encountered and solved the types of problems described by Root-Bernstein (1989)? I have constructed Table 10.2, "Scientific Problem Types and Computational Discovery Systems," as a parallel to Root-Bernstein's table. Table 10.2 suggests that computational discovery systems have made considerable progress in dealing with the types of problems encountered in standard scientific research.

**Table 10.1**
**Problem Types**

| Type | Examples | Method of Solution |
|------|----------|--------------------|
| Definition | What is energy? What species is this? | Invention of concept or taxonomy |
| Theory | How do we explain the distribution of the species? What causes objects to fall? | Invention of theory |
| Data | What information is needed to test or build a theory? | Observation, experiment |
| Technique | How can we obtain data? How do we analyze it? How may the phenomenon best be displayed? | Invention of instruments and methods of analysis and display |
| Evaluation | How adequate is a definition, theory, observation, or technique? Is something a true anomaly or an artifact? | Invention of criteria for evaluation |
| Integration | Can two disparate theories or sets of data be integrated? Does Mendel contradict Darwin? | Reinterpretation and rethinking of existing concepts and ideas |
| Extension | How many cases does a theory explain? What are the boundary conditions for applying a technique or theory? | Prediction and testing |
| Comparison | Which theory or data set is more useful? | Invention of criteria for comparison |
| Application | How can this observation, theory, or technique be used? | Knowledge of related unsolved problems |
| Artifact | Do these data disprove a theory? Is the technique for data collection appropriate? | Recognition that problem is insoluble as stated |

*Source:* Root-Bernstein, R. S. (1989). *Discovering: Inventing and solving problems at the frontiers of scientific knowledge.* Cambridge, MA: Harvard University Press, p. 61.

**Table 10.2**
**Scientific Problem Types and Computational Discovery Systems**

| Type | Examples | System and Reference |
|------|----------|----------------------|
| Definition | How can taxonomies be constructed from primitive observations? How can hierarchies of concepts be formed from primitive taxonomies? | AM (Lenat, 1979); BACON (Langley & Zytkow, 1989); GLAUBER (Langley et al., 1983); ARE (Shen, 1990) |
| Theory | How can qualitative and quantitative theory formation be achieved? | PHINEAS (Falkenhainer, 1990); PAULI (Valdés-Pérez, 1996b); SHUNYATA (Ammon, 1993) |
| Data | How can data required for theory formation and revision be systematically collected? | IDS (Nordhausen & Langley, 1990); DENDRAL (Lindsey et al., 1993); MATHEMATICA (Wolfram, 1997) |
| Technique | How can data be analyzed and conceptualized? | ABACUS (Falkenhainer & Michalski, 1986) |
| Evaluation | How can the validity of theories and experimental findings (including anomalies) be determined? | KEKADA (Kulkarni & Simon, 1988) |
| Integration | Can conflicting theories be resolved? | ECHO (Thagard, 1989) |
| Extension | How can the limits of a theory be determined? | FAHRENHEIT (Langley & Zytkow, 1989) |
| Comparison | How can the relative merits of two theories be ascertained? | ECHO (Thagard & Nowak, 1988) |
| Application | How can established theory be applied to exploration of novel problems? | PHINEAS (Falkenhainer, 1990); EURISKO (Lenat and Brown, 1984; MECHUM (Valdés-Pérez, 1995a) |
| Artifact | How does surprising experimental data modify current theory? | KEKADA (Kulkarni & Simon, 1988) |

# Bibliography

Ammon, K. (1993). An automatic proof of Godel's incompleteness theorem. *Artificial Intelligence, 61 (2)*, 291–306.

Anderson, A., and Belnap, N. (1975). *Entailment*. Princeton, NJ: Princeton University Press.

Backus, J. (1978). Can programming be liberated from the von Neumann style? *Communications of the ACM, 21*, 613–671.

Bacon, F. (1960). *The new organon and related writings*. New York: Liberal Arts Press.

Baldwin, E. (1947). *Dynamic aspects of biochemistry*. New York: Macmillan.

Boden, M. A. (1988). *Computer models of mind*. Cambridge: Cambridge University Press.

Boden, M. A. (1990). *The philosophy of artificial intelligence*. Oxford: Oxford University Press.

Boden, M. A. (1996). Creativity. In M. A. Boden (Ed.), *Artificial intelligence*, pp. 267–291. San Diego, CA: Academic Press.

Bonjour, L. (1985). *The structure of empirical knowledge*. Cambridge, MA: Harvard University Press.

Bradshaw, G. L., Langley, P., and Simon, H. A. (1980). BACON.4: The discovery of intrinsic properties. In *Proceedings, third biennial conference of the Canadian Society for Computational Studies of Intelligence*, pp. 19–25. Victoria, BC, Canada.

Brewer, W. F., and Samarapungavan, A. (1991). Child theories versus scientific theories: Differences in reasoning or difference in knowledge? In R. R. Hoffman and D. S. Palermo (Eds.), *Cognition and the symbolic processes: Applied and ecological perspectives*. Hillsdale, NJ: Erlbaum.

Bruner, J. S., Goodnow, J. J., and Austin, G. A. (1956). *A study of thinking*. New York: Science Editions.

Buchanan, B. G., and Feigenbaum, E. A. (1978). DENDRAL and Meta-DENDRAL: Their application dimension. *Artificial Intelligence, 11*, 5–24.

Carey, S. (1985). *Conceptual change in childhood.* Cambridge, MA: MIT Press.

Case, R. (1974). Structures and strictures: Some functional limitations on the course of cognitive growth. *Cognitive Psychology, 6*, 544–573.

Caudill, M., and Butler, C. (1990). *Naturally intelligent systems.* Cambridge, MA: MIT Press.

Cheng, P. W., and Holyoak, K. J. (1985). Pragmatic reasoning schemas. *Cognitive Psychology, 17*, 391–416.

Cohen, P., and Feigenbaum, E. (1982). *The handbook of artificial intelligence, 3.* Los Altos, CA: William Kaufmann.

Colmerauer, A. (1990). An introduction to Prolog III. *Communications of the ACM, 33* *(7)*, 69–90.

Darwin, C. (1962). *On the origin of species* (text of sixth edition of 1872). New York: Macmillan.

Davis, M. D., and Weyuker, E. J. (1983). *Computability, complexity, and languages.* New York: Academic Press.

Davis, P. J., and Hersh, R. (1986). *Descartes' dream: The world according to mathematics.* San Diego, CA: Harcourt Brace Jovanovich.

Davis, R., and Lenat, D. (1982). *Knowledge-based systems in artificial intelligence.* New York: McGraw-Hill.

Duhem, P. (1954). *The aim and structure of physical theory* (P. Wiener, Trans.). Princeton, NJ: Princeton University Press. (Original work published 1914).

Dunbar, K. (1992, November). *Evidence evaluation and planning heuristics in molecular biology laboratories.* Paper presented at the annual meeting of the Judgement and Decision Making Society, St. Louis, MO.

Dunbar, K. (1993). Concept discovery in a scientific domain. *Cognitive Science, 17*, 397–434.

Dunbar, K., and Klahr, D. (1989). Developmental differences in scientific discovery strategies. In D. Klahr and K. Kotovsky (Eds.), *Complex information processing: The impact of Herbert A. Simon.* Hillsdale, NJ: Erlbaum.

Dunbar, K., and Schunn, C. D. (1990). The temporal nature of scientific discovery: The roles of priming and analogy. In *Proceedings of the twelfth annual conference of the Cognitive Science Society,* pp. 93–100. Hillsdale, NJ: Erlbaum.

Einhorn, H. J., and Hogarth, R. J. (1986). Judging probable cause. *Psychological Bulletin, 99*, 3–19.

Einstein, A. (1933). *The method of theoretical physics.* Oxford: Oxford University Press.

Einstein, A. (1952). On the electrodynamics of moving bodies. In H. A. Lorentz, A. Einstein, H. Minkowski, and H. Wehl (Eds.), *The principle of relativity.* Dover (originally published in 1905).

Elio, R., and Scharf, P. B. (1990). Modeling novice-to-expert shifts in problem-solving strategy and knowledge organization. *Cognitive Science, 14*, 579–639.

Ericsson, K. A. (1975). Instruction to verbalize as a means to study problem-solving processes with the Eight puzzle: A preliminary study. Technical Report No. 458. Stockholm: University of Stockholm, Department of Psychology.

Ericsson, K. A. and Simon, H. (1984). *Protocol analysis: Verbal reports as data.* Cambridge, MA: MIT Press.

Falkenhainer, B. (1987). Scientific theory formation through analogical inference. In *Proceedings of the fourth international workshop on machine learning*, pp. 218–229. Irvine, CA: Morgan Kaufmann.

Falkenhainer, B. (1990). A unified approach to explanation and theory formation. In J. Shrager and P. Langley (Eds.), *Computational models of scientific discovery and theory formation*, pp. 157–196. San Mateo, CA: Morgan Kaufmann.

Falkenhainer, B., and Michalski, R. S. (1986). Integrating quantitative and qualitative discovery: The ABACUS system. *Machine Learning, 1*, 367–402.

Fay, A. L., Klahr, D., and Dunbar, K. (1990). Are there developmental milestones in scientific reasoning? In *Proceedings of the twelfth annual conference of the Cognitive Science Society*, pp. 333–339. Hillsdale, NJ: Erlbaum.

Feldman, D. H. (1988). Creativity: Dreams, insights, and transformations. In R. J. Sternberg (Ed.), *The nature of creativity*, pp. 271–297. Cambridge: Cambridge University Press.

Ferris, T. (1988). *Coming of age in the Milky Way*. New York: William Morrow and Company.

Fischer, P., and Zytkow, J. M. (1990). Discovering quarks and hidden structure. In Z. Ras, M. Zemankova, and M. Emrich (Eds.), *Proceedings, Fifth International Symposium on Methodologies for Intelligent Systems*, pp. 362–370. Amsterdam: North-Holland.

Forbus, K. D. (1984). Qualitative process theory. *Artificial Intelligence, 24*, 85–168.

Foster, M., and Martin, M. (Eds.) (1966). *Probability, confirmation, and simplicity*. Odyssey Press.

Fruton, J. S. (1972). *Molecules and life*. New York: Wiley-Interscience.

Gardner, H. (1988). Creative lives and creative works: A synthetic scientific approach. In R. J. Sternberg (Ed.), *The nature of creativity*, pp. 288–324. Cambridge: Cambridge University Press.

Gentner, D. (1983). Structure-mapping: A theoretical framework for analogy. *Cognitive Science, 7*, 155–170.

Gentner, D. (1989). The mechanisms of analogical learning. In S. Vosniadou and A. Ortony (Eds.), *Similarity and analogical reasoning*, pp. 194–241. Cambridge: Cambridge University Press.

Gerwin, D. G. (1974). Information processing, data inferences, and scientific generalization. *Behavioral Science, 19*, pp. 314–325.

Gholson, B., Levine, M., and Phillips, S. (1972). Hypotheses, strategies, and stereotypes in discrimination learning. *Journal of Experimental Child Psychology, 13*, 423–446.

Gick, M. L., and Holyoak, K. J. (1983). Schema induction and analogic transfer. *Cognitive Psychology, 15*, 1–38.

Glymour, C. (1980). *Theory and evidence*. Princeton, NJ: Princeton University Press.

Gooding, D. (1992). The procedural turn. In R. N. Giere (Ed.), *Minnesota studies in the philosophy of science: Vol. 15. Cognitive models of science*. Minneapolis: University of Minnesota Press.

Gorman, M. E. (1986). How the possibility of error affects falsification on a task that models scientific problem solving. *British Journal of Psychology, 77*, 85–96.

Hadamard, J. (1949). *The Psychology of invention in the mathematical field*. Princeton, NJ: Princeton University Press.

Haggin, J. (1992). Direct conversion of methane to fuels, chemicals still intensely sought, *Chem. Engineering News, 70(17)*, 33–35.

Hall, A. R. (1955). *The scientific revolution*. London.

Hanson, N. R. (1958). *Patterns of discovery: An inquiry into the conceptual foundations of science*. Cambridge: Cambridge University Press.

Harman, G., Ranney, M., Salem, K., Doring, F., Epstein, J., and Jaworksa, A. (1988). A theory of simplicity. In *Proceedings of the tenth annual conference of the Cognitive Science Society*, pp. 42–45. Hillsdale, NJ: Erlbaum.

Hennessey, B. A., and Amabile, T. M. (1988). The conditions of creativity. In R. J. Sternberg (Ed.), *The nature of creativity*, pp. 11–38. Cambridge: Cambridge University Press.

Hentenryck, P. V., Simonis, H., and Dincbas, M. (1992). Constraint satisfaction using constraint logic programming, *Artificial Intelligence, 58*, 113–159.

Hergenrather, J. R., and Rabinowitz, M. (1991). Age-related differences in the organization of children's knowledge of illness. *Developmental Psychology, 27*, 952–959.

Holland, J., Holyoak, K., Nisbett, R. E., and Thagard, P. (1986). *Induction: Processes of inference, learning, and discovery*. Cambridge: Cambridge University Press.

Holmes, F. L. (1980). Hans Krebs and the discovery of the ornithine cycle. In *Proceedings 63rd annual meeting of the Federation of American Societies for Experimental Biology, 39*, pp. 216–225. Symposium on Aspects of the History of Biochemistry.

Holmes, F. L. (1985). *Lavoisier and the chemistry of life: An exploration of scientific creativity*. Madison: University of Wisconsin Press.

Holmes, F. L. (1991). *Hans Krebs*. New York: Oxford University Press.

Holyoak, K. J., and Thagard, P. (1989). Analogical mapping by constraint satisfaction. *Cognitive Science, 13*, 295–355.

Jacob, F. (1988). *The statue within*. New York: Basic Books.

Jacob, F., and Monod, J. (1961). Genetic regulatory mechanisms in the synthesis of proteins. *Journal of Molecular Biology, 3*, 318–356.

John-Steiner, V. (1985). *Notebooks of the mind*. Albuquerque, NM: University of New Mexico Press.

Jourdan, J., and R. E. Valdés-Pérez. (1990). Constraint logic programming applied to hypothetical reasoning in chemistry. In *Logic programming: Proceedings 1990 North American Conference*, pp. 154–172. Cambridge, MA.

Judson, H. F. (1979). *The eighth day of creation*. New York: Simon and Schuster.

Kaplan, C. A., and Simon, H. A. (1990). In search of insight. *Cognitive Psychology, 22*, 374–419.

Karmiloff-Smith, A. (1988). A child is a theoretician, not an inductivist. *Mind and Language, 3*, 183–195.

Keil, F. C. (1981). Constraints on knowledge and cognitive development. *Psychological Review, 88*, 197–227.

Kepler, J. (1937). De Motibus Stellae Martis. In *Johannes Kepler gesammelte Werks*. München: Ch Beck.

Kern, L. H. (1983). The effect of data error in inducing confirmatory inference strategies in scientific hypotheses testing. Paper presented at the meeting of the Society of the Social Studies of Science, Blacksburg, VA.

Kern, L. H., Mirels, H. L., and Hinshaw, V. G. (1983). Scientists' understanding of propositional logic: An experimental investigation. *Social Studies of Science, 13,* 131–146.

Klahr, D. (1985). Solving problems with ambiguous subgoal ordering: Preschoolers' performance. *Child Development, 56,* 940–952.

Klahr, D., and Dunbar, K. (1988). Dual space search during scientific reasoning. *Cognitive Science, 12,* 1–55.

Klahr, D., Dunbar, K., and Fay, A. L. (1989). Designing good experiments to test "bad" hypotheses. In J. Shrager and P. Langley (Eds.), *Computational models of scientific discovery and theory formation.* San Mateo, CA: Morgan Kaufmann.

Klahr, D., Fay, A. L., and Dunbar, K. (1993). Heuristics for scientific experimentation: A developmental study. *Cognitive Psychology, 25,* 111–146.

Klahr, D., and Robinson, M. (1981). Formal assessment of problem solving and planning processes in preschool children. *Cognitive Psychology, 13,* 113–148.

Klayman, J., and Ha, Y. (1987). Confirmation, disconfirmation and information in hypothesis testing. *Psychological Review, 94,* 211–228.

Kline, M. (1985). *Mathematics and the search for knowledge.* New York: Oxford University Press.

Kocabas, S. (1991). Conflict resolution as discovery in particle physics. *Machine Learning, 6 (3),* 277–309.

Koehn, B. W., and Zytkow, J. M. (1986). Experimenting and theorizing in theory formation. In *Proceedings ACM SIGART international symposium of methodologies for intelligent systems,* pp. 296–307. Knoxville, TN.

Kokar, M. M. (1986). Determining arguments of invariant functional descriptions. *Machine Learning, 1,* 403–422.

Kuhn, D., Amsel, E., and O'Loughlin, M. (1988). *The development of scientific thinking skills.* New York: Academic Press.

Kulkarni, D., and Simon, H. A. (1988). The processes of scientific discovery: The strategy of experimentation. *Cognitive Science, 12,* 139–175.

Lakatos, I. (1970). Falsification and the methodology of scientific research programmes. In I. Lakatos and A. Musgrave (Eds.), *Criticism and the growth of knowledge.* Cambridge: Cambridge University Press.

Langley, P. (1978). BACON.1: A general discovery system. In *Proceedings of the second biennial conference of the Canadian Society for Computational Studies of Intelligence.* pp. 173–180. Toronto, Canada.

Langley, P. (1981). Data-driven discovery of physical laws. *Cognitive Science, 5,* 31–54.

Langley, P., Bradshaw, G. L., and Simon, H. A. (1983). Rediscovering chemistry with the BACON system. In R. S. Michalski, J. G. Carbonell, and T. M. Mitchell (Eds.), *Machine learning: An artificial intelligence approach,* pp. 307–330. Palo Alto, CA: Tioga.

Langley, P., and Jones, R. (1988). A computational model of scientific insight. In R. J. Sternberg (Ed.), *The nature of creativity,* pp. 177–201. Cambridge: Cambridge University Press.

Langley, P., and Nordhausen, B. (1986). A framework for empirical discovery. In *Proceedings, international meeting on advances in learning.* Les Arcs, France.

Langley, P., Simon, H. A., Bradshaw, G. L., and Zytkow, J. M. (1987). *Scientific discovery: Computational explorations of the creative processes.* Cambridge, MA: MIT Press.

Langley, P., and Zytkow, J. (1989). Data-driven approaches to empirical discovery. *Artificial Intelligence, 40,* 283–312.

Langley, P., Zytkow, J., Bradshaw, G., and Simon, H. A. (1983). Three facets of scientific discovery. In *Proceedings of the eighth international joint conference on artificial intelligence,* pp. 465–468. Karlsruhe, Federal Republic of Germany: Morgan Kaufmann.

Larkin, J. H., Reif, F., Carbonell, J., and Gugliotta, A. (1988). FERMI: A flexible expert reasoner with multi-domain inferencing. *Cognitive Science, 12,* 101–138.

Lavoisier, A. (1862). *Oeuvres* (6 vols.). Paris: Imprimerie Impèriale.

Lederberg, J. (1965). Topological mapping of organic molecules, *Proceedings of the National Academy of Science, 53 (1),* pp. 134–139.

Lenat, D. B. (1976). AM: An artificial intelligence approach to discovery in mathematics as heuristic search. Ph.D. dissertation, Computer Science Department, Stanford University.

Lenat, D. B. (1977). Automated theory formation in mathematics. *Proceedings IJCAI-77,* pp. 833–842. Cambridge, MA.

Lenat, D. B. (1979). On automated scientific theory formation: A case study using the AM program. In J. Hayes, D. Michie, and L. I. Mikulich (Eds.), *Machine Intelligence, Vol. 9.* New York: Halstead Press.

Lenat, D. B. (1982). The nature of heuristics. *Artificial Intelligence, 19,* 189–249.

Lenat, D. B. (1983a). Theory formation by heuristic search. The nature of heuristics II: Background and examples. *Artificial Intelligence, 21,* 31–59.

Lenat, D. B. (1983b). EURISKO: A program that learns new heuristics and domain concepts. The nature of heuristics III: Program design and results. *Artificial Intelligence, 21,* 61–98.

Lenat, D. B. and Brown, J. S. (1984). Why AM and EURISKO appear to work. *Artificial Intelligence, 23,* 269–294.

Lindsay, R., Buchanan, B., Feigenbaum, E., and Lederberg, J. (1993). DENDRAL: A case study of the first expert system for scientific hypothesis formation. *Artificial Intelligence, 61 (2),* 209–261.

Luck, J. M. (1932). *Annual review of biochemistry.* Stanford, CA: Stanford University Press.

Markman, E. M. (1979). Realizing that you don't understand: Elementary school children's awareness of inconsistencies. *Child Development, 50,* 643–655.

Michalski, R., Carbonell, J. G., and Mitchell, T. M. (Eds.). (1983). *Machine learning: An artificial intelligence approach.* Palo, Alto, CA: Tioga.

Mill, J. S. (1974). *Philosophy of scientific method.* New York: Hafner Press.

Minsky, M. (1975). A framework for representing knowledge. In P. Winston (Ed.), *The psychology of computer vision,* pp. 211–277. New York: McGraw-Hill.

Mitchell, T. M., Utgoff, P. E., and Banerji, R. (1983). Learning by experimentation: Acquiring and refining problem-solving heuristics. In R. Michalski, J. G. Carbonell, and T. M. Mitchell (Eds.), *Machine learning: An artificial intelligence approach*, pp. 163–190. Palo Alto, CA: Tioga.

Mitroff, I. I. (1974). *The subjective side of science*. New York: Elsevier.

Mynatt, C. R., Doherty, M. E., and Tweney, R. D. (1977). Confirmation bias in a simulated research environment: An experimental study of scientific inference. *Quarterly Journal of Experimental Psychology, 29*, 85–95.

Mynatt, C. R., Doherty, M. E., and Tweney, R. D. (1978). Consequences of confirmation and dis-confirmation in a simulated research environment. *Quarterly Journal of Experimental Psychology, 30*, 395–406.

Ne'eman, Y., and Y. Kirsh (1986). *The particle hunters*. New York: Cambridge University Press.

Nersessian, N. (1992). How do scientists think? Capturing the dynamics of conceptual change in science. In R. N. Giere (Ed.), *Minnesota studies in the philosophy of science: Vol. 15, Cognitive models of science*. Minneapolis: University of Minnesota Press.

Newell, A. (1990). *Unified theories of cognition*. Cambridge, MA: Harvard University Press.

Newell, A., and Simon, H. A. (1972). *Human problem solving*. Englewood Cliffs, NJ: Prentice-Hall.

Nickles, T. (Ed.) (1978). *Scientific discovery, logic, and rationality*. Dordrecht, Netherlands: Reidel.

Nordhausen, B., and Langley, P. (1990). An integrated approach to empirical discovery. In J. Shrager and P. Langley (Eds.), *Computational models of scientific discovery and theory formation*, pp. 97–128. San Mateo, CA: Morgan Kaufmann.

Novick, L. R., and Holyoak, K. J. (1991). Mathematical problem solving by analogy. *Journal of Experimental Psychology: Learning, Memory, and Cognition, 17*, pp. 398–415.

Nowak, G., and Thagard, P. (1989). *Copernicus, Newton, and explanatory coherence* (Minnesota Studies in the Philosophy of Science). Minneapolis: University of Minnesota Press.

Omnès, R. (1971). *Introduction to particle physics*. Chichester, England: Wiley Interscience.

Osherson, D. N., and Smith, E. E. (Eds.) (1990). *An invitation to cognitive science: Vol. 3, Thinking*. Cambridge, MA: MIT Press.

Partridge, D., and Wilkes, Y. (Eds.) (1990). *The foundations of AI: A sourcebook*. Cambridge: Cambridge University Press.

Poincaré, H. (1913). *Foundations of science*. G. B. Halstead (Trans.). New York: Science Press.

Popper, K. (1961). *Logic of scientific discovery*. New York: Science Editions.

Qin, Y., and Simon, H. A. (1990). Laboratory replication of scientific discovery processes. *Cognitive Science, 14*, 281–312.

Quine, W.V.O. (1961). *From a logical point of view* (2nd Edition). New York: Harper Torchbooks.

Rajamoney, S. A. (1989). *Explanation-based theory revision: An approach to the problems of incomplete and incorrect theories*. Ph.D. dissertation, University of Illinois, Urbana.

Ranney, M. (1987). Changing naive conception of motion. Ph.D. dissertation, Learning, Research, and Development Center, University of Pittsburgh.

Ranney, M., and Thagard, P. (1988). Explanatory coherence and belief revision in naive physics. *Proceedings of the tenth annual conference of the Cognitive Science Society.* Hillsdale, NJ: Erlbaum.

Read, S. J., and Marcus-Newhall, A. (1993). The role of explanatory coherence in social explanations: A parallel distributed processing account. *Journal of Personality and Social Psychology, 65 (3)*, 429–447.

Ritchie, G. D. and Hanna, F. K. (1984). AM: A case study in AI methodology. *Artificial Intelligence, 23*, 249–268.

Root-Bernstein, R. S. (1989). *Discovering: Inventing and solving problems at the frontiers of scientific knowledge.* Cambridge, MA: Harvard University Press.

Rose, D., and Langley, P. (1986). Chemical discovery as belief revision. *Machine Learning, 1*, 423–451.

Ross, B. H. (1984). Remindings and their effects in learning a cognitive skill. *Cognitive Psychology, 16*, 371–416.

Rychlak, J. F. (1990). *Artificial intelligence and human reason: A teleological critique.* New York: New York University Press.

Schank, P., and Ranney, M. (1991). The psychological fidelity of ECHO: Modeling an experimental study of explanatory coherence. In *Proceedings of the 13th annual conference of the Cognitive Science Society*, pp. 892–897. Hillsdale, NJ: Erlbaum.

Schank, P., and Ranney, M. (1992). Assessing explanatory coherence: A new method for integrating verbal data with models of on-line belief revision. In *Proceedings of the 14th annual conference of the Cognitive Science Society*, pp. 599–604. Hillsdale, NJ: Erlbaum.

Schauble, L. (1990). Belief revision in children: The role of prior knowledge and strategies for generating evidence. *Journal of Experimental Child Psychology, 49*, 31–57.

Shen, W. M. (1990). Functional transformations in AI discovery systems. *Artificial Intelligence, 41*, 257–272.

Sherwood, B. A., and Sherwood, J. N. (1988). *The cT language.* Champaign, IL: Stipes Publishing.

Shrager, J. (1987). Theory change via view application instructionless learning. *Machine Learning, 2*, 247–276.

Shrager, J., and Langley, P. (Eds.). (1990). *Computational models of discovery and theory formation.* San Francisco, CA: Morgan Kaufmann.

Siegler, R. S., and Liebert, R. M. (1975). Acquisition of formal scientific reasoning by 10- and 13-year-olds: Designing a factorial experiment. *Developmental Psychology, 10*, 401–402.

Simon, H. A. (1956). Rational choice and the structure of the environment. *Psychological Review, 63*, 129–138.

Simon, H. A. (1977). What computers mean for man and society. *Science, 195*, 1186–1190.

Simon, H. A. (1979). Information processing models of cognition. *Annual Review of Psychology, 30*, 363–396.

Simon, H. A. (1983). Search and reasoning in problem solving. *Artificial Intelligence, 21*, pp. 7–29.

Simon, H. A. (1990). Invariants of human behavior. *Annual Review of Psychology, 41*, 1–19.

Simon, H. A., and Lea, G. (1974). Problem solving and rule induction: A unified view. In L. Gregg (Ed.), *Knowledge and cognition*. Hillsdale, NJ: Erlbaum.

Sodian, B., Zaitchik, D., and Carey, S. (1991). Young children's differentiation of hypothetical beliefs from evidence. *Child Development, 62*, 753–766.

Soo, V., Kulikowski, C., Garfinkel, D., and Garfinkel, L. (1987). Theory formation in postulating kinetic mechanisms: Reasoning with constraints. Technical Report CBM-TR-150. Department of Computer Science, Rutgers University, New Brunswick, New Jersey.

Soo, V., Kulikowski, C., Garfinkel, D., and Garfinkel, L. (1988). Theory formation in postulating kinetic mechanisms: Reasoning with constraints. *Comput. Biomedical Res., 21*, 381–403.

Sperber, D. and Wilson, D. (1987). Précis of *relevance*: Communication and cognition. *Behavioral and Brain Sciences, 10(4)*, 677–710.

Sternberg, R. J. (Ed.) (1988). *The nature of creativity*. Cambridge: Cambridge University Press.

Sunderam, V. (1990). PVM: A framework for parallel distributed computing. *Concurrency: Practice and experience, 2 (4)*, 315–339.

Thagard, P. (1978). The best explanation: Criteria for the theory of choice. *Journal of Philosophy, 75*, 76–92.

Thagard, P. (1988a). *Computational Philosophy of Science*. Cambridge, MA: MIT Press/Bradford Books.

Thagard, P. (1988b). The dinosaur debate: Application of a connectionist model of theory evaluation. Unpublished manuscript. Princeton University.

Thagard, P. (1989). Explanatory coherence. *Behavioral and Brain Sciences 12*, 435–467.

Thagard, P. (1990). The conceptual structure of the chemical revolution. *Philosophy of Science, 57*, 183–209.

Thagard, P. (1993). Societies of minds: Science as distributed computing. *Studies in History and Philosophy of Science, 24 (1)*, 49–55.

Thagard, P., Holyoak, K., Nelson, G., and Gochfeld, D. (1989). Analogical retrieval by constraint satisfaction. Unpublished manuscript, Princeton University.

Thagard, P. and Nowak, G. (1988). The explanatory coherence of continental drift. In A. Fine and J. Leplin (Eds.), *PSA 1988*, pp. 118–126. Philosophy of Science Association.

Thagard, P., and Nowak, G. (1990). The conceptual structure of the geological revolution. In J. Shrager and P. Langley (Eds.), *Computational models of scientific discovery and theory formation*, pp. 27–72. San Mateo, CA: Morgan Kaufmann.

Torrance, P. E. (1988). The nature of creativity as manifest in its testing. In R. J. Sternberg (Ed.), *The nature of creativity*. Cambridge, MA: Cambridge University Press.

Tschirgi, J. E. (1980). Sensible reasoning: A hypothesis about hypotheses. *Child Development, 51*, 1–10.

Tumblin, A., and Gholson, B. (1981). Hypothesis theory and the development of conceptual learning. *Psychological Bulletin, 90*, 102–124.

Tweney, R. D. (1985). Faraday's discovery of induction: A cognitive approach. In D. Gooding and F. James (Eds.), *Faraday rediscovered*, pp. 187–209. New York: Stockton Press.

Tweney, R. D., Doherty, M. E., and Mynatt, C. R. (Eds.) (1981). *On scientific thinking: A reader in the cognitive psychology of science.* New York: Columbia University Press.

Valdés-Pérez, R. E. (1990). Machine discovery of chemical reaction pathways. Technical Report CMU-CS-90-191. Ph.D. dissertation, School of Computer Science, Carnegie Mellon University, Pittsburgh, PA.

Valdés-Pérez, R. E. (1991). A canonical representation of multistep reactions, *J. Chem. Inf. Comput. Sci., 31 (4),* 554–556.

Valdés-Pérez, R. E. (1992). Algorithm to generate reaction pathways for computer-assisted elucidation. *J. Comput. Chem., 13 (9),* 1079–1088.

Valdés-Pérez, R. E. (1993). Algorithm to test the structural plausibility of a proposed elementary reaction. *J. Comput. Chem., 14 (12),* 1454–1459.

Valdés-Pérez, R. E. (1994a). Algebraic reasoning about reactions: Discovery of conserved properties in particle physics. *Machine Learning, 17 (1),* 47–68.

Valdés-Pérez, R. E. (1994b). Algorithm to infer the structures of molecular formulas within a reaction pathway. *J. Comput. Chem., 15 (11),* 1266–1277.

Valdés-Pérez, R. E. (1994c). Conjecturing hidden entities via simplicity and conservation laws: Machine discovery in chemistry. *Artificial Intelligence, 65 (2),* 247–280.

Valdés-Pérez, R. E. (1994d). Heuristics for systematic elucidation of reaction pathways. *J. Chem. Inf. Comput. Sci., 34 (4),* 976–983.

Valdés-Pérez, R. E. (1994e). Human/computer interactive elucidation of reaction mechanisms: Application to catalyzed hydrogenolysis of ethane. *Catalysis Letters, 28 (1),* 79–87.

Valdés-Pérez, R. E. (1995a). Machine discovery in chemistry: New results. *Artificial Intelligence, 74,* 191–201.

Valdés-Pérez, R. E. (1995b). Generic tasks of scientific discovery. In *Systematic methods of scientific discovery: Papers from the 1995 AAAI [American Association for Artificial Intelligence] symposium.* Technical Report SS-95-03. Menlo Park, CA: AAAI Press.

Valdés-Pérez, R. E. (1995c). Computer-aided elucidation of reaction mechanisms: Application to the partial oxidation of methane. In *Proceedings, 1994 American Chemical Society symposium on methane and alkane conversion chemistry.*

Valdés-Pérez, R. E. (1996a). On the justification of multiple selection rules of conservation in particle physics phenomenology. *Comput. Phys. Commun., 94,* 25–30.

Valdés-Pérez, R. E. (1996b). A new theorem in particle physics enabled by machine discovery. *Artificial Intelligence, 82,* 331–339.

Valdés-Pérez, R. E. (1996c). Computer science research on scientific discovery. *Knowledge Engineering Review, 11 (1),* 57–66.

Valdés-Pérez, R. E. (submitted). Algebraic representation in scientific model building: Discovery of quark structure in physics.

Valdés-Pérez, R. E., and M. Erdmann (1994). Systematic induction and parsimony of phenomenological conservation laws. *Comput. Phys. Commun., 83,* 171–180.

Valdés-Pérez, R. E., Zytkow, J. M., and Simon, H. A. (1993). Scientific model-building as search in matrix spaces. In *Proceedings, American Association for Artificial Intelligence (AAAI)-93,* pp. 472–478. Washington, DC.

Vosniadou, S., and Brewer, W. F. (1992). Mental models of the earth: A study of conceptual change in childhood. *Cognitive Psychology, 24,* 535–585.

Wagman, M. (1988). *Computer psychotherapy systems: Theory and research foundations*. New York: Gordon and Breach.

Wagman, M. (1991a). *Artificial intelligence and human cognition: A theoretical intercomparison of two realms of intellect*. New York: Praeger.

Wagman, M. (1991b). *Cognitive science and concepts of mind: Toward a general theory of human and artificial intelligence*. New York: Praeger.

Wagman, M. (1993). *Cognitive psychology and artificial intelligence: Theory and research in cognitive science*. New York: Praeger.

Wagman, M. (1995). *The sciences of cognition: Theory and research in psychology and artificial intelligence*. New York: Praeger.

Wagman, M. (1996). *Human intellect and cognitive science: Toward a general unified theory of intelligence*. Westport, CT: Praeger.

Wagman, M. (1997a). *The general unified theory of intelligence: Its central conceptions and specific application to domains of cognitive science*. Westport, CT: Praeger.

Wagman, M. (1997b). *Cognitive science and the symbolic operations of human and artificial intelligence: Theory and research into the intellective processes*. Westport, CT: Praeger.

Wagman, M. (1998a). *The ultimate objectives of artificial intelligence: Theoretical and research foundations, philosophical and psychological implications*. Westport, CT: Praeger.

Wagman, M. (1998b). *Cognitive science and the mind-body problem: From philosophy to psychology to artificial intelligence to imaging of the brain*. Westport, CT: Praeger.

Wagman, M. (1998c). *Language and thought in humans and computers: Theory and research in psychology, artificial intelligence, and neural science*. Westport, CT: Praeger.

Wagman, M. (1999). *The human mind according to artificial intelligence: Theory, research, and implications*. Westport, CT: Praeger.

Wason, P. C. (1968a). Reasoning about a rule. *Quarterly Journal of Experimental Psychology, 20*, 273–281.

Wason, P. C. (1968b). On the failure to eliminate hypotheses: A second look. In P. C. Wason and P. N. Johnson-Laird (Eds.), *Thinking and reasoning*. Harmondsworth, England: Penguin.

Whewell, W. (1967). *The philosophy of the inductive sciences*. New York: Johnson Report Corp. (Original work published 1840, London: Parker.).

Wipke, W., Ouchi, G., and Krishnan, S. (1978). Simulation and evaluation of chemical synthesis—SECS: An application of artificial intelligence techniques. *Artificial Intelligence, 11*, 173–193.

Wiser, M. (1989). Does learning science involve theory change? Paper presented at the Biannual Meeting of the Society for Research in Child Development, Kansas City, April 30, 1989.

Wisniewski, E. H., and Medin, D. L. (1991). Harpoons and long sticks: The interaction of theory and similarity in rule induction. In D. H. Fisher, Jr., M. H. Pazzani and P. Langley (Eds.), *Concept formation: Knowledge and experience in unsupervised learning*. San Mateo, CA: Morgan Kaufmann.

Wolfram, S. (1997). *The mathematica book*. Champaign, IL: Wolfram Media.

Zytkow, J. M. (1987). Combining many searches in the FAHRENHEIT discovery system. In *Proceedings, fourth international workshop on machine learning (American Association for Artificial Intelligence)*, pp. 281–287. Irvine, CA: Morgan Kaufmann.

Zytkow, J. M., and Simon, H. A. (1988). Normative systems of discovery and logic of search. *Synthese, 74,* 65–90.

# Author Index

# Subject Index

**About the Author**

MORTON WAGMAN is Professor Emeritus of Psychology at the University of Illinois, Urbana-Champaign.

ISBN 0-275-96654-2

HARDCOVER BAR CODE